Discharging Congress

Government by Commission

COLTON C. CAMPBELL

Westport, Connecticut
London

Library of Congress Cataloging-in-Publication Data

Campbell, Colton C., 1965–
    Discharging Congress : government by commission / Colton C. Campbell.
       p. cm.
    Includes bibliographical references and index.
    ISBN 0–275–97511–8 (alk. paper)
    1. Governmental investigations—United States.   2. Parliamentary practice—United States.
    I. Title.
    JF533 .C36 2002
    328.73′07452—dc21   2001036307

British Library Cataloguing in Publication Data is available.

Library of Congress Catalog Card Number: 2001036307
ISBN: 0–275–97511–8

First published in 2002

Praeger Publishers, 88 Post Road West, Westport, CT 06881
An imprint of Greenwood Publishing Group, Inc.
www.praeger.com

Printed in the United States of America

∞™

The paper used in this book complies with the
Permanent Paper Standard issued by the National
Information Standards Organization (Z39.48–1984).

10 9 8 7 6 5 4 3 2 1

For my grandmothers,
Verna Whitmore Jones
and
Katherine Duensing Campbell

Contents

Tables and Figure

FIGURE

Acknowledgments

The publication of this book would not have been possible without the generous financial support of the Everett McKinley Dirksen Congressional Leadership Research Center, and the Center for Congressional and Presidential Studies at American University under the outstanding direction of James A. Thurber.

I would like to thank all those on Capitol Hill who graciously took time out of their crowded schedules to meet with me. I owe particular gratitude to M. Stephen Weatherford and Bruce Bimber of the University of California, Santa Barbara. Both are incredibly knowledgeable and extremely generous in sharing their expertise. John F. Stack, Jr., and Nicol C. Rae at Florida International University, along with Will Reno at Northwestern University, read early drafts and gave me invaluable support, comments, advice and, above all, patience. I want them to know how much I appreciate and value their detailed and thoughtful reviews; their discerning eyes significantly improved the manuscript. I continue to learn from my colleagues in the congressional scholarly community; there are too many to list here, but I am delighted to thank them all. Finally, there are not enough words to repay my mentors, Roger H. Davidson and Eric R.A.N. Smith of the University of California, Santa Barbara, for reading drafts and (as always) offering encouragement.

As always, I am grateful to my family for their indefatigable love and support: my wife Marilyn; my parents, Budge and Ardis; and my sisters Colby and Kenzie.

Lynn Zelem of the Greenwood Publishing Group shepherded the book through the production process, and I thank her for that.

This book, including any errors or misjudgments in it, is my sole responsibility. I have attempted to present an objective assessment of a particular phenomenon in congressional politics. Perhaps I am guilty of placing too much emphasis on what the practitioners of the lawmaking process say, but the beginning of all insight and wisdom on the subject of Congress is that people who inhabit the institution provide the key to our understanding. Only the reader may judge whether or not I have succeeded.

Introduction

As new discoveries are made . . . institutions must advance also to keep pace with the times.

Thomas Jefferson
Letter to Samuel Kercheval

The creation of temporary, independent bodies that give advice to Congress, develop common-sense recommendations on complex policy issues, and find broadly acceptable solutions to contentious problems, is an important yet under-investigated area of congressional delegation. The term "commission" is a prevalent catch-phrase, but these entities have taken several names. Whether designated as blue-ribbon commissions, committees, councils, boards, or task forces, they consist mostly of nonelected officials, deal with major social crises and policy issues, and perform technical studies. With variations to fit the circumstances, Congress creates commissions to accomplish diverse goals: to cope with increases in the scope and complexity of legislation, forge consensus, draft bills, finesse institutional obstacles, involve non-committee and junior members in issues, coordinate strategy, and promote interparty communication. Commissions deal with issues as disparate as pay raises, obsolete military bases, the budget deficit, Medicare, flue-cured tobacco, wartime relocation and internment of civilians, amateur boxing, telemedicine, government reform, and the regulation of professional baseball.

The origin of the congressional commission may be traced to early times when it was a practice of Congress to refer matters of particular importance to standing and special committees. It was the short legislative session, the lack of technical skill, and the want of leisure on the part of poorly paid lawmakers that largely prompted the creation of the special committee or commission.[1] By the nineteenth century, legislative commissions were usually composed of members of one or both houses of Congress (sometimes supplemented by nonmembers especially qualified for the delegated task) and were commonly employed in investigating some topic that was about to be the subject of legislative action. A notable example was the Industrial Commission created by Congress in 1898, to study and report on questions pertaining to labor, agriculture, and business, and reporting to Congress the results of the investigations and suggestions for legislation upon these particular subjects. Another example was the Armstrong Insurance Commission of New York that Congress created in 1905 to look into the life insurance business of that state. The commission's findings startled the nation by their revelations of neglect of duty on the part of the responsible insurance officials and prompted Congress to institute important reform legislation. Generally, the practical results of such early legislative commissions were limited; no significant legislation, for instance, resulted from the multi-volume report prepared by the Industrial Commission.[2]

Contemporary ad hoc commissions for policy formulation, as opposed to commissions to study specific problems of maladministration, disaster, or wrongdoing, are largely a development of the twentieth century. President Theodore Roosevelt was the first to employ the commission extensively, and he quickly became involved in controversy with Congress over its use, as legislators believed Roosevelt used commissions to expand presidential parameters into policy areas that fell within legislative jurisdiction. Ironically, today's commissions are attaining considerable importance in the arsenal of legislative devices and techniques for policy formulation against an expansive presidency.

But as ad hoc commissions have proliferated and their visibility has increased, critics have charged that Congress is debasing the ad hoc commission by excessive use.[3] Washington is awash in special congressionally mandated commissions, they say. Too many commissions start with the expectation of doing something either that Congress does not want to do or that it does not want to do openly.

Moreover, those who find fault with ad hoc commissions tend to overemphasize avoidance, criticizing them for their lack of direct representation, for their neglect of legislative responsibility, and for their backroom methods of decision making. Cynics treat congressionally created commissions as unconstitutional devices that subvert the democratic process.[4] Accordingly, a potential question of electoral accountability arises because a group of nonelected officials are empowered with what is considered to be a legislative responsibility. Critics say that when Congress sets up an ad hoc commission, it is being unresponsive: lawmakers charged with the duty of representation abdicate their responsibilities by empowering others to perform their legislative tasks.[5] By this sort of delegation, Congress still makes law, just not in the publicly accountable way that the Constitution intends.[6] Consequently, delegation to a commission is a dereliction of legislative duty, typically done to shirk responsibility in order to minimize political losses.[7]

THE PUZZLE OF CONGRESSIONAL DELEGATION

So why and when does Congress formulate policy by commissions rather than by the normal legislative process? Lawmakers have historically delegated authority to others who could accomplish ends they could not. Does this form of congressional delegation thus reflect the particularities of an issue area? Or does it mirror deeper structural reasons such as legislative organization, time, or manageability? In the end, what is the impact on representation versus the effectiveness of delegating discretionary authority to temporary entities composed largely of unelected officials, or are both attainable together?

There is no easy answer to why Congress creates ad hoc commissions, because the circumstances of their creation are quite complex and vary widely. Many variables go into the decision to entrust those bodies to render nonpartisan recommendations: to pacify, to promote incremental decision making, to build support for proposals, or to obtain consensus among different interests. Commissions are often hybrids that result from a multitude of congressional incentives.

While disputes over the desirable or proper extent of delegation are commonplace, our understanding of such congressional action is arguable. The literature contains several variations on the theme that policymaking is sometimes so costly—both in terms of expertise and for political reasons—that it must be delegated to others. A number of political scientists and economists share the assumption that people's motives in the political arena are essentially the same as their motives in the marketplace, resting on rational calculations of self-interest.[8] The problem of delegation is frequently derived from economic models,[9] portraying delegation as an advantageous way for lawmakers to favor constituents,[10] to minimize political losses,[11] or to shift blame.[12] Also considered important are the relationships that are assumed to exist between means and ends, which enable the lawmaker to choose the most rational means to the specified end, as well as the relationships between the costs and benefits involved, in the interest of efficiency.

Others hypothesize that desired outcomes can be achieved only by delegating authority. This perspective outlines the need to delegate as a principal-agent issue.[13] Lawmaking is a complex enterprise that aims at producing a collective good;[14] consequently it presents lawmakers with collective action problems.[15] Overcoming these collective action problems requires delegation to agents such as small, ad hoc commissions.

However, close examination of the creation of these bodies, including personal interviews and exchanges with the architects and others close to ad hoc commissions, reveals a wide range of justifications for delegation.[16] Not every commission begins with the expectation of doing what members want to avoid. Nor do legislators turn to commissions simply because of the complexity of issues. In short, the circumstances that surround the creation of ad hoc commissions are complex and vary widely.

DEVELOPMENT AND ORGANIZATION OF THE BOOK

Fingers are repeatedly pointed at Congress as contributor to or creator of many problems in the policymaking process. A major objective of this study is to sort out situations in which Congress, with sufficient information at hand or with a definite interest in a policy matter, voluntarily delegates to a commission as part of the policymaking process. The use of ad hoc commissions does not always represent a dereliction of legislative duty. Such congressional action often reflects periodic responsibility and curiosity about alternative, different means for Congress to intervene directly and indirectly in policy development and implementation.

In the face of challenging governing circumstances, lawmakers find creative ways to make policy.[17] This has been especially apparent in the period since World War II. In this time period, the trend has been toward tougher governing circumstances, including the rise of divided government, mounting partisanship, increasingly fragmented committees, and a more complex issue agenda. In response to these types of pressures, congressional members seek ways to keep the lawmaking process going.

Chapter 1 provides an account of the use and development of commissions in policymaking. This includes a full description of commissions, including the creation process as well as the duties and powers of these entities. Modern congressional commissions have their antecedents in the independent regulatory commissions. Several of the forces that were at work in their evolution are seen in contemporary ad hoc commissions: politics based on ideas, reasons, and expertise. Congress can be an unlikely environment for such a politics. The institution of Congress is a fragmented body geared to representing and brokering the diverse interests of society instead of encouraging a broad national interest. As such, it can be a dubious vehicle for the collective public good.

Chapters 2 and 3 examine the path and politics of the delegation process, noting specific stages at which motivations become clear. Whatever the time frame, Congress's decision to transfer authority and responsibility to a commission involves two general stages. After the issue is brought to the forefront of the congressional agenda and hence to a decision, a majority of lawmakers determine a course of action. At this second stage issues are discussed and possible solutions are explored. Congress then selects one of three avenues: legislation, obfuscation, and delegation. Each offers a unique set of advantages and disadvantages. The three primary justifications for choosing to delegate to commission include expertise, workload, and avoidance. Which of these three reasons dominates depends in large part on the politics surrounding the issue and the nature of the policy problem. The logic of delegation to each of the three commission types is also different. These categories for delegation are by no means mutually exclusive or pure; on occasion they will overlap. But they do represent the most important justifications, or "ideal" types, for which Congress appropriates ad hoc commissions.

Chapter 4 illustrates how the novelty and complexity of a policy issue can be so daunting that it binds discussion about legislation to generalities instead of specific issues. Although lawmakers have substantial resources including large staffs, considerable uncertainty remains on Capitol Hill. The congressional agenda is often too large and the issues are too complex for any one lawmaker to assess the ramifications of every choice that presents itself. Information deficiency can result from the uncertainty of novel and technical issues, and it leaves members and their staff with insufficient knowledge to legislate intelligently. To tap outside expertise Congress will create a commission of experts to grapple with technically difficult problems. When Congress first coped with AIDS it directed an executive agency to prepare detailed briefs to define what to examine and how to manage the growing health dilemma. But even the agency called on Congress to seek out and establish a commission of experts, because it would have the specialized skills to help understand the epidemic, to provide some strategic planning and direction, and to pool knowledge and expertise to formulate key recommendations for Congress.

Chapter 5 exhibits an occasion when Congress delegated largely to pare down its workload to more manageable dimensions. By all outward signs of activity—such as number of committees and subcommittees, hearings, and votes—members of Congress are battling to keep pace with demands. Nevertheless, information overload, compounded by time constraints, frequently warrants a commission. Lawmakers realize they can manage only a certain amount of public business; the rest they must either neglect or delegate. Various pieces of a legislative problem are delegated to a commission to partition the volume or to handle and manage a problem substantively in a timely manner. The plan for a commission to address the thrift industry's plight during the 1980s was occasioned by the need to assist committee members. Capitol Hill welcomed a single-purpose, independent commission for its capacity to coordinate the varied interests and yield detailed blueprints for the future.

Chapter 6 is a case study of blame avoidance. On occasion, Congress will establish a commission to shift blame for any negative side effects connected with sensitive issues. Because most lawmakers see themselves as agents of their constituents, they are unwilling to sacrifice district prosperity for the collective good. So when members evaluate the costs and benefits of a politically sensitive issue and find that it translates into electoral losses rather than gains, they will create a commission to avoid the unwanted task of making a difficult decision. No fights on Capitol Hill are as contested as the ones over whose districts lose defense dollars. Lobbying for military projects comes naturally to members who are expected to champion local interests. Liberals and conservatives, hawks and doves, Democrats and Republicans all join the fray. The Base Closure Commission enabled lawmakers to turn away from the dilemma of choosing which bases to close, thereby providing a political heat shield. Legislators became advocates for their constituents rather than bearers of bad news, passionately pleading the case for their constituents, thereby doing the job they were elected to do but also confronting a national policy need.

Although it is unlikely that any truly representative cases could be identified, the objective was to select instances that illustrate the predominant justifications for congressional delegation. For each case, the following concepts are described: (1) the policy context; (2) the key events that led to congressional delegation; and (3) the effects of congressional delegation to an ad hoc commission. What is certain is that whether the reasons for inaction or ineffective action are substantive, political, practical, or procedural, there is a legislative response that is applicable in all cases of delegation.

Chapter 7 concludes by offering observations on congressional delegation. Over the years Congress has been a remarkably adaptive institution, finding different means to address and formulate public policy. The ad hoc commission is a tool Congress appropriates to accommodate a variety of goals. In a sense, a commission grows out of the inadequacies in Congress; in some instances, it will develop because of the unusual nature of the policy problem, or because of Congress's determination to protect and expand its own prerogatives in new policy areas and restrain the executive's ambitions in the modern era of the strong, active president.

NOTES

1. Charles A. Beard, "Commissions in American Government," *Cyclopedia of American Government*, vol.1, ed. Andrew C. McLaughlin and Albert Bushnell Hart (Gloucester, Mass: Peter Smith, 1963), 351.

2. Ibid.

3. David Schoenbrod, *Power without Responsibility: How Congress Abuses the People through Delegation* (New Haven, Conn.: Yale University Press, 1993); and R. Kent Weaver, "Is Congress Abdicating Power to Commissions?" *Roll Call*, February 12, 1989, 5 and 25.

4. Schoenbrod, *Power without Responsibility*.
5. Weaver, "Is Congress Abdicating Power to Commissions?"
6. Ibid.
7. The term *shirk* carries multiple meanings. First, an obligation is being evaded. Second, the obligation to deliberate is being avoided. Third, the evasion of responsibility is being concealed. Valerie Sulfaro notes that to claim that lawmakers "shirk" constituents' preferences is to claim that lawmakers deliberately and secretly avoid representing constituent' preferences in order to advance their own hidden agendas. See Valarie Sulfaro, "Does Legislative Shirking Exist? A Perspective from Public Opinion," paper presented at the annual meeting of the Southern Political Science Association, Tampa, Florida, November 1–4, 1995, 3.
8. David R. Mayhew, *Congress: The Electoral Connection* (New Haven, Conn.: Yale University Press, 1974); Dennis Mueller, *Public Choice II* (Cambridge: Cambridge University Press, 1989); Morris P. Fiorina, "Legislator Uncertainty, Legislative Control, and the Delegation of Legislative Authority," in *Regulatory Policy and the Social Sciences*, ed. Roger G. Noll (Berkeley: University of California Press, 1986); R. Douglas Arnold, *The Logic of Congressional Action* (New Haven, Conn.: Yale University Press, 1990); and Daniel Farber and Philip Frickey, *Law and Public Choice: A Critical Introduction* (Chicago: University of Chicago Press, 1991).
9. See Anthony Downs, *An Economic Theory of Democracy* (New York: Harper & Row, 1957).
10. Theodore J. Lowi, "American Business, Public Policy, Case-Studies, and Political Theory," *World Politics* 16 (1964); Grant McConnell, *Private Power and American Democracy* (New York: Vintage Books, 1966); Joseph Stigler, "The Reformation of American Administrative Law," *Harvard Law Review* 88 (1971).
11. Mayhew, *Congress: The Electoral Connection*; Kenneth A. Shepsle, "Institutional Arrangements and Equilibrium in Multidimensional Voting Models," *American Journal of Political Science* 23 (1979): 27–59; Morris P. Fiorina, "Universalism, Reciprocity, and Distributive Policy Making in Majority Rule Institutions," in *Research in Public Policy Analysis and Management*, ed. John Crecine (Greenwich, Conn.: JAI Press Inc., 1981); and Fiorina, "Legislator Uncertainty, Legislative Control, and the Delegation of Legislative Authority"; R. Kent Weaver, "The Politics of Blame Avoidance," *Journal of Public Policy* 6 (1987): 371–98; John W. Kingdon, *Congressmen's Voting Decisions*, 3rd ed. (Ann Arbor: University of Michigan Press, 1989); Arnold, *The Logic of Congressional Action*; Richard L. Hall, *Participation in Congress* (New Haven, Conn.: Yale University Press, 1996).
12. Morris P. Fiorina, "Legislative Choice of Regulator Forms: Legal Process or Administrative Process?" *Public Choice* 39 (1982).
13. Robert Axelrod, *The Evolution of Cooperation* (New York: Basic Books, 1984); Terry M. Moe, "The Economics of Organization," *American Journal of Political Science* 28 (1984); Michael Taylor, *The Possibility of Cooperation* (Cambridge: Cambridge University Press, 1987); Roderick D. Kiewiet and Mathew D. McCubbins, *The Logic of Delegation: Congressional Parties and the Appropriations Process* (Chicago: University of Chicago Press, 1991); Arthur Lupia and Mathew D. McCubbins, "Who Controls? Information and the Structure of Legislative Decision Making," *Legislative Studies Quarterly* 19 (1994).
14. Randall B. Ripley and Grace A. Franklin, *Congress, the Bureaucracy, and Public Policy* (Homewood, Ill: The Dorsey Press, 1984); Lawrence C. Dodd and Richard

L. Schott, *Congress and the Administrative State* (New York: Macmillan Publishing Company, 1986).

15. Mancur Olson, *The Logic of Collective Action* (Cambridge: Harvard University Press, 1965); Kenneth R. Mayer, "Closing Military Bases (Finally): Solving Collective Dilemmas through Delegation," *Legislative Studies Quarterly* 20 (1995).

16. Interviews are most useful for answering these questions, especially when the conversation is frank and spontaneous. As Richard F. Fenno, Jr. (1990, 3), comments: "You watch, you accompany, and you talk with people you are studying. Much of what you see, therefore, is dictated by what they say and do. If something is important to them, it becomes important to you." See Richard Fenno, Jr. *Watching Politicians: Essays on Participant Observation* (Berkeley, Calif.: IGS Press, 1990), 3. See also Richard F. Fenno, Jr., "Observation, Context, and Sequence in the Study of Politics," *American Political Science Review* 38 (1986): 894–917; and Richard F. Fenno, Jr., *Home Style: House Members in Their Districts* (Boston: Little, Brown, 1978). For the benefits of unstructured interviews, see Hall, *Participation in Congress*.

17. David R. Mayhew, *Divided We Govern* (New Haven, Conn.: Yale University Press, 1991).

—Chapter 1—

The Development and Use of Ad Hoc Commissions in Legislative Policymaking

The first question that offers itself is whether the general form and aspect of the government be strictly republican?

James Madison
Federalist No. 39

Sometimes referred to as the "fifth arm of government,"[1] commissions are formal groups established by statute or decree. They have multiple members, with each commissioner sharing equally the responsibility for findings and recommendations. They are sunsetted, limited more or less to a definite time frame to complete work, usually one to two years from the time of creation to the final report to Congress. In some cases, however, Congress may propose a commission to extend over several years. The Commission on a North American Economic Alliance, for example, was designed in 1979 to study the development and utilization of the resources of the United States, Mexico, and Canada, submitting annual reports to Congress until its termination in 1985.

Generally speaking, a commission's mandate includes a termination date more than three years after the date of creation or at a specified date upon submittal of its recommendations or alternatives, which is anywhere from thirty to ninety days after its final report to Congress. Commissions come in various sizes and shapes, with membership ranging anywhere from nine to twenty commissioners, twelve to fifteen being the normal number of members. The final number of commissioners will generally accommodate equal appointments by the majority and minority in both the House and Senate as well as by the president.[2]

With official status recognized by Congress, ad hoc commissions have a policy formulation responsibility limited to an issue or group of related questions (bodies that are set up to investigate wrongdoing, to assign responsibility for disasters, or to make explicit and detailed studies of internal management are not considered a part of this grouping). But because they are largely advisory and rarely have power to implement their findings or recommendations, they are infrequently mandated with administrative authority, except for the powers conferred on them to assist them in collecting and gathering information. Because these entities consist in whole or in part of persons from private life, they can be distinguished from congressional select or special committees, which may be confused with commissions.[3] In most instances advisory commissions hold hearings and request written submissions from interested persons and organizations, secure information from federal departments or agencies, conclude with the publication of a report, and close down. The report may include findings uncovered during testimony, staff studies, background papers, preliminary reports, legal analyses, final reports, and statistical surveys.

Federal commissions are by no means limited to the legislative process. They may be creatures of Congress or the presidency, some created informally by the mutual consent of Congress and the president, others administered by an executive agency. Many federal commissions cover multiple jurisdictions, making it difficult to decide whether a commission is strictly congressional, executive, or judicial. Normally, all three branches of government are willing to support commissions, but the commissions' tasks, purposes, and composition can determine whether they belong to one particular branch or have more diverse origins. "I was a member of the Federal Courts Study Commission, a legislative study group to conduct a study of the jurisdiction of the U.S. courts and report to Congress," recounted one commissioner regarding the inter-branch morphing of his commission. "But it became clear as the commission progressed that the commission was a judicial creature serving the purposes of the judiciary, not Congress, recommending ways for the Court to manage its case workload as opposed to realigning parts of the judiciary."

Until recently there was little standardization of the features, organization, or procedures of commissions. A degree of continuity emerged with the enactment in 1972 of the Federal Advisory Committee Act (FACA), which created requirements for the management and oversight of Federal advisory entities.[4] While the statute concentrated on advisory committees established by mission agencies, its jurisdiction also covered national commissions created by legislative statute and presidential decree. Under Section 3 of the statute, advisory bodies are any committee, board, commission, council, conference, panel, task force, or other similar group, or any sub-committee or other subgroup thereof, which is established

- by statute or reorganization plan;
- by the president by executive order;
- by one or more agencies;
- by law where the Congress specifically directs the president or an agency to establish it;
- by law where the Congress authorizes but does not direct the president or an agency to establish it;
- by an agency under general agency authority in Title 5 of the *U.S. Code* or other general agency-authorizing law.

At the heart of FACA is a series of provisions that maximize the public and broadly representative nature of the panels; the provisions also minimize presidential dominance—at least in the eyes of a Congress resentful of an imperial presidency.[5]

THE CREATION PROCESS

Whether established by a freestanding bill or attached as an amendment (often to expedite consideration), congressional commissions are authorized to use appropriated sums, such as pay and travel expenses for commission members and staff, to carry out their duties.[6] Upon the request of the director or chairperson, commissions may enlist the temporary or intermittent services of experts and consultants as well as any personnel of an executive department or agency, on a reimbursable basis.[7]

There are exceptions, however, as with the absence of congressional funding for the E-Commerce Commission. In 1998, Congress passed the Internet Tax Freedom Act (ITFA), which imposed a three-year moratorium on new Internet taxation. As part of the act, Congress established the Advisory Commission on Electronic Commerce to address the issues related to Internet taxation. The advisory commission conducted a thorough study of federal, state, local, and international taxation and tariff treatment of transactions using the Internet and Internet access, and other comparable intrastate, interstate, or international sales activities. This commission was unique in that Congress did not appropriate any funding but gave the commission "gift authority." As a result, at its first meeting the commission approved a funding strategy that called for initial funding from the state of Virginia and the six corporate members of the commission requested additional funding from Congress for commission activities. On November 29, 1999, President Clinton signed an appropriations bill that included $1.4 million in fiscal year 2000 operating funds for the commission. The initial funding provided by

Virginia and the six corporate members of the commission was fully reimbursed as the commission closed its books.

Although each commission experience is unique and different, commissions generally have a three-tier organizational structure, which consists of the commission members who serve for the life of the commission,[8] the executive director, who is usually chosen by the commission chair and confirmed by the commission, and the research staff. Congress typically selects prominent individuals representing a wide range of opinion for these positions with the hope that such prominent figures will foster bipartisan support when the commission submits its final report to Congress. "Congress is judicious with how it appoints commissions," responded an administrative assistant to the proposed National Commission on Fairness in Military Compensation to review the regular military compensation of members of the Armed Forces and develop recommendations to end the dependence of some members and their families on federal and local assistance programs. "They [lawmakers] look for agreement on what constitutes a reasonable commission and what does not." Generally those individuals who are selected for membership must be specifically qualified by reason of education, training, or experience in the area the commission is designed to study. This broad membership gives the commission better channels to the public. It adds other factors that are not already involved since there might be additional viewpoints. Unlike presidential commissions, many congressional commissions have a bipartisan membership, set up for dialogue between the legislative and executive branches. Specific provisions often concern the number and joint appointment of members by the president, the Speaker of the House of Representatives, and the president pro tempore of the Senate. As one congressional staff aide whose boss recommended the setting up of the Commission on Integration of Workers' Compensation Medical Benefits noted,[9] "Given divided government, you don't see either side solo symbolically without approval from the other."

Table 1.1 shows the institutional balance of commission membership across forty-six different proposed congressional ad hoc commissions. Of the 562 total commissioners appointed between the 103rd (1993–1995) and 105th (1997–1999) Congresses, 27 percent would be appointed by the president, 47 percent would be congressionally appointed, and 26 percent would be appointed by other sources, such as executive department and agency administrators, sub-national governments, and the courts.

A similar logic applies to decisions on staffing. Are the staff aides chiefly lawyers, social scientists, political aides, or, as in some instances, political hacks?[10] These groups will not necessarily share a similar perspective on the tasks, methods, or even goals of the commission, which can produce tension, particularly in the drafting of the final report. From all indications, the 1969 National Advisory Commission on Civil Disorders' initial draft was rejected for inclusion in the final report not only because its conclusions were

Table 1.1
Balance of Commission Membership of Forty-Six Randomly Selected Ad Hoc Commissions

Appointing Body	Total Appointees
President	149
*Speaker	114
*President Pro Tempore	42
House Majority Leader	29
House Minority Leader	3
Senate Majority Leader	60
Senate Minority Leader	18
*Other	147

Institution Appointer	Percentage of Total Appointees
President	27%
Congress	47%
Other	26%

*Unless specified, appointments made by the House Speaker are generally made in consultation with the House minority leader. This is similar to appointments made by the president pro tempore; generally they are based upon the recommendation of the majority leader and the minority leader of the Senate. Other appointments are those not made by Congress or the president: they are made by state and local governments, by executive agencies, by the Supreme Court, or by some other person or organization.

radical but also because documentation for its underlying theory of riot causation was lacking. There was also a problem of communication within the commission, as the social scientists were shocked to find the document that they considered only a draft treated as a final product. Shortly after the draft was rejected, the commission changed its timetable to eliminate its interim report and released most of its staff, about a hundred people.[11] It is often up to the executive director to resolve such differences; however, the commission members make the final decisions on conflicting interpretations and recommendations.

THE COMMISSION'S DUTIES AND RESPONSIBILITIES

Leaders of Congress must determine the mandate of an ad hoc commission, then determine the extent of resources—time, money, and staff—that they are willing to make available for the commission, and select the commission members. Many commissions sanctioned by Congress apply legislative standards to concrete situations, including directives to deal with an issue and the expectation that commissioners orient their research efforts to generate specific recommendations that can be accompanied by executive or legislative authority.[12] The statement of scope guides commissioners and staff as to what they should accomplish, and an extended rationale as to why these recommendations appropriately accompany the commission's recommendations.

No uniform principles apply in the operation of commissions. Each commission functions differently from the next. "You start with no set pattern as to how you conceive a commission," reflected the former chair of the National Commission on Judicial Discipline and Removal.[13] "You know the basics and that you are responsible for making recommendations. But how you do that is sort of touch and feel." In practice, once formed, a commission takes on its own life, with commission members coming together to accomplish what they set out to achieve.

Commissions set up by congressional statute are often given subpoena authority. The first and second Commissions on Organization of the Executive Branch of the Government, both known collectively as the Hoover Commissions (1947–1949; 1953–1955), were authorized to hold hearings, administer oaths, and require by subpoena the attendance and testimony of witnesses and documents. In each case Congress's aim was administrative methods and executive reorganization that would reverse the executive branch's post-1930s expansion. Subpoena powers are rarely used by ad hoc commissions charged with formulating policy proposals, but entities that are set up to investigate alleged wrongdoing, malfeasance, or catastrophe often need such powers to compel key witnesses to attend.

Ordinarily, a commission is tasked to report a final set of recommendations as its end product. Because federal ad hoc commissions vary widely in origin, authority, composition, and purpose, no standard method of submitting reports has emerged. Commissions established by Congress frequently submit their reports directly to Congress or to Congress and the president. The quality of the final report depends in large part upon the competence of the commission staff. The Commission on Obscenity and Pornography (also referred to as the Kerner Commission) released ten volumes of research findings in conjunction with its final report. Table 1.2 outlines the chronological life of the average commission created by Congress based upon interviews and a review of legislation from the 93rd (1973–1975) and 106th (1999–2001) Congresses.

Table 1.3 sets forth what one former U.S. Representative, chair of the Subcommittee on Courts, Civil Liberties, and the Administration of Justice and chair of the National Commission on Judicial Discipline and Removal, stated as the key ingredients that Congress considers when outlining an ad

Table 1.2
Chronology of Ad Hoc Commissions

- Congress enacts statute creating commission.
- Unofficial caucus of commissioners to select chairperson and to chart future direction.
- Commission meeting to select executive director and support staff.
- First round of hearings and working groups on subject matter.
- Site visit(s) to study policy issue.
- Second round of hearings and working groups on subject matter.
- Commission meeting to discuss final report.
- Final report (cumulative recommendations) submitted to Congress.
- Commission ceases to exist.

---

hoc commission. (See also Appendix 2 for creation language.) Ultimately, because ad hoc commissions lack the power to implement their recommendations and cease to exist upon the completion of their study and the rendering of their report, they are influential only insofar as Congress or the president heeds their advice, or to the extent that the commission can energize an interest group or publicize its findings.

Table 1.3
Key Ingredients in the Formation of Ad Hoc Commissions: Advice from a Commission Chair

---

- What is the purpose for which the commission is created?
- How clearly is the purpose of the commission set forth?
- Does the commission produce a report—interim and/or final?
- Can the commission be extended or does it operate within a definite time frame?
- Which branch is the appointing authority?
- How are commission members to be appointed?
- How is the commission funded and what are the limits on its funding?
- Is there boiler-plate language that governs the commission?
- Does the commission have powers to hold hearings, obtain official data, and subpoena?
- Of whom is the staff composed?

ANTECEDENTS OF THE MODERN AD HOC COMMISSION

Modern congressional commissions have antecedents in the early successes of independent regulatory commissions of the Progressive Era.[14] Although regulatory commissions have an entirely different type of authority and task, several of the forces that were at work in their evolution are seen in contemporary ad hoc commissions. The spirit behind the formation of the regulatory commission typified attitudes toward direct democracy that are often seen as contributing to the doctrine behind the ad hoc commission. This includes a belief in the efficiency of changes in the machinery of government, faith in the expert, distrust of the politician, and a habit of viewing government as separate from the rest of society. The independence of regulatory commissions, like ad hoc commissions, kept out the politics and gave them (regulatory commissions) the freedom to make impartial judgments: regulating the economy and society based on an objective public interest as opposed to the narrow interests of business or politicians.

Similar to their regulatory cousin, some ad hoc commissions have extraordinary power, insofar as Congress opts to limit its own discretion on a case by case basis. Recommendations by the Defense Base Closure and Realignment Commission (1991, 1993, and 1995), for example, only went into effect when the secretary of defense approved them and Congress did not reject the recommendations. Moreover, the president could veto a congressional resolution or disapproval.[15]

Independent regulatory commissions developed during the Progressive period in which the political majority effectively demanded reform, but state legislatures failed to translate these popular demands into regulatory policy and administrative operations. The creation and delegation of responsibility to the first regulatory commission, the Interstate Commerce Commission, for instance, were justified on several counts. Early methods of regulation through the legislative and judicial processes proved inadequate at dealing with complex economic matters, and new techniques were needed to satisfy the demand for regulation. The answer was a separate administrative mechanism that could provide more competence and flexibility. Related to the growing issue of complexity, the regulatory commission developed partly in response to the need felt by both citizens and members of Congress for a new type of governmental instrument to handle a new type of problem.[16] The older executive departments were unsuitable for the rapid development of new regulatory techniques, and Congress's deliberative nature could not keep pace. The idea of setting up a regulatory commission seemed more promising than deferring the problem to the executive departments, because the members of commissions could be chosen from among individuals from the business under discussion with background and familiarity. This expertise enabled regulatory commissions to manage difficult regulatory problems, which executive departments, the legislature, or the court could not do.[17]

The idea of regulation without laws reached its heyday during the Progressive period.

The Founders could not conceivably foresee the extent to which the federal government now employs ad hoc commissions, but they did presumably intend Congress to delegate in matters where government must be prepared to respond speedily to bring events under its control.[18] Fashioned gradually, frequently as alternative apparatuses in response to an acknowledgment that the traditional legislative process does not always work, ad hoc commissions are becoming an institutionalized mechanism of Congress reflecting changes in the institution.[19] While disputes over the extent of delegation are commonplace, there is little disagreement with the notion that Congress could not function without at least some degree of delegation. The ways in which Capitol Hill meets its responsibilities have evolved since the founding of the Republic. Congress is historically inventive with process to muster support for its goals or adapt and react to changes in its external environment. When confronted with the stress brought on by outside forces, the institution does not radically transform the characteristics of its work; it pursues alternative strategies.[20] One method is contracting or expanding the organization's effective domain by dividing task responsibilities among a variety of distinct units or adding units according to existing organizational dimensions.[21]

As a representative body, Congress necessarily responds to changes in this context.[22] The institution at the turn of the twentieth century created regulatory commissions to satisfy a restless constituency and to meet demands for effective and flexible ways to grapple with the growing complexity of national politics. The contemporary Congress uses ad hoc commissions in a similar fashion. Commissions are in part an institutional accommodation to citizens' ambivalence (at times suspiciousness) toward politics and politicians. Individual members of Congress get respectable marks, but the institution ranks well below the respondents' own representatives in public esteem.[23] Partly to blame are the size and complexity of the institution as well as the core yet arcane twists and turns of the legislative process such as the contending voices (and messiness), the many committees, and the many decision points.[24] But the public's distrust of the institution and its business go far deeper than unhappiness with specific policies or disgust with scandals, if we are to heed the sobering findings of John R. Hibbing and Elizabeth Theiss-Morse: "People do not wish to see uncertainty, conflicting opinions, long debate, competing interests, confusion, bargaining, and compromised, imperfect solutions. They want government to do its job quietly and efficiently, sans conflict and sans fuss. In short . . . they often seek a patently unrealistic form of democracy."[25] In other words, people today, like people one hundred years ago, despise the very attributes that are the hallmarks of Congress.

The progression toward congressionally created ad hoc commissions offers members of Congress a way to separate politics from policy issues. The carefully crafted "independence" of a commission helps legitimize congressional decisions and make them palatable to an otherwise ambivalent public. Lawmakers and their staffs indicate that many contemporary situations upon which legislative action must be predicated are so complicated that a political body cannot hope to find the real facts. Certain modern-day problems call for analysis by more than one mind with more than one approach by individuals who can access a difficult problem without prejudice and with controlled emotions. A commission set up by Congress, according to one congressional staff aide, "might have the credibility that normal legislative channels such as a committee and that committee's hearings would not have as well as provide credibility to the rest of Congress in dealing with the particular question the commission is handling." Too often, congressional hearings become adversarial proceedings. In the spirit of the regulatory commission a temporary, independent ad hoc commission provides advice from people who are not beholden to public pressure.

THE LEGISLATIVE VALUE OF THE COMMISSION

Congress has historically transferred authority to a host of places: externally to the president, nonelected officials in the federal bureaucracy, the courts, and state and local governments; and internally to committees, legislative support organizations, and party leaders. So why increasingly entrust tasks to ad hoc commissions? What advantages do commissions have compared to the rest of the institutional setting?

In short, the commission fits with the incremental style of policymaking common in the United States, and it infuses a degree of direct democracy with its bottom-up approach to policymaking and its nonpartisan membership. The commission is a flexible device for developing political support on controversial legislation, and for sidestepping legislative gridlock. By delegating to a commission, Congress can resolve intractable problems because lawmakers mitigate the side effects commonly associated with transferring responsibility and authority. At times it may be useful to move out of conventional channels of investigation and communication toward individuals of independent mind and stature—a strategy commonly used to overcome the pathologies of hierarchy and specialization to which the House of Representatives is particularly prone. Whatever its political risks, as a means to counter the expanding influence of unchecked experts, to preserve open discussion of complex issues, and to mobilize elite support for innovations, the independent commission often has no peer.[26]

Piecemeal Policymaking

When faced with policy problems of huge dimensions, rather than looking forward to the ultimate solution, Congress approaches the solution in small discrete steps, building policy and agreement from the bottom up, reflecting the institution's scattered and decentralized structure.[27] Lyndon B. Johnson likened this process to a bottle of bourbon: "If you take a glass at a time, it's fine," he said. "But if you drink the whole bottle in one evening, you have troubles."[28] "Commissions work well for this because they are an incremental step toward a policy end, which often helps in the process by which government adapts to emerging social change," a veteran staff assistant to a Democratic representative explained.

Ad hoc commissions are important aspects of the process of systemic adaptation.[29] They are sometimes legislative instruments of policy incrementalism, for example, with issues that involve difficulties in human adjustment,[30] thereby conforming to an incremental style of public policy, which is common to American policymakers.[31] This process of decision making has been described as the "science of muddling through."[32] Accordingly, the elements of change embodied in public policies are marginal rather than sweeping. Public policy addresses multiple issues concurrently, and offers the opportunity for delay in implementation, appeals and policy reversals, and compromises with the many interests involved. This frequently typifies our political system.[33] Because public policy changes occur in small increments, ad hoc commissions are an integral component of the process by which government adapts to emerging social change.[34]

As participants in an incremental decision making process, ad hoc commissions perform three important functions: they formulate policy recommendations, they garner support for policy proposals, and they offer concessions to appease the policy demands of various political interests.[35] Commissions, therefore, are instruments of policy incrementalism and vehicles for problem solving and conflict management, because they define problems, initiate new responses, and mobilize public opinion.[36] They themselves become part of the governance process, playing an independent role in articulating constituents' concerns to the extent of forcing new issues on to the political agenda, a perspective borne out in the work of the Commission on Civil Rights and the National Commission on Disorders. The reports of the Civil Rights Commission transformed the civil rights debate from a concern about whether a pattern of voting discrimination actually existed to a consideration of the merits of various proposals to halt discriminatory practices. Similarly, the conclusions of the Commission on Disorders (the "Kerner Commission") about white racism shifted the focus of discourse about the causes of black unrest in America. In both instances, these changes in orientation generated new pressures for action and altered the evaluation context of subsequent policy deliberations.[37]

Hybrid System of Democracy

Policymaking has changed over the past several decades with the shifting American political landscape. Public approval of Congress and its members has declined since the 1970s.[38] Public discontent about the legislative branch in the 1990s grew to unprecedented levels.[39] Such dissatisfaction not only reflects a generalized distrust of politicians but also a feeling that government is not working well.[40] The manifest result of this is a growing proportion of new members who lack prior political experience and who echo this same critical sentiment.

With incumbency a seeming curse, politicians often campaign against the government.[41] Congressional leaders heed this populist reaction. They build agreement from the bottom up with the inclusion of practitioners—experts in the field from across the political spectrum who are involved in implementation. In doing so, Congress looks for ways to involve people back home in two-way communication so that constituents can express their reaction to what is going on in Congress. The ad hoc commission has become a device for achieving this goal, allowing individuals who have diverse knowledge and experience to share information and thus reach better results. The Commission on Service Members and Veterans Transition Assistance set up by Congress in 1996 to the review benefits and services available to active duty members and veterans visited over forty military installations around the world during its two-year existence, talking to thousands of service members and family members.[42] "The real beauty of a commission," proclaimed one Senate staff aide whose boss proposed the Commission on Executive Organization,[43] "is the political weight you get from having something put together by 'common people' as opposed to 'politicians.'"

Those on Capitol Hill value commissions for removing from an issue the political dynamics that pervade the institution, such as parochialism and partisan gridlock, as well as for evading the rigidities of institutionalization and the loss of an originally intended purpose that frequently plagues other institutions in government with more restrictive bureaucratic practices. "A commission such as the Federal Workforce Reduction and Realignment Commission[44] is a prevention of too many political interests," noted a congressional aide. Because commissions typically meet for a year or two, they are able to hear from and accommodate many different interests and points of view, and they have the capacity to focus congressional as well as public attention.

Commissions conform to the public's ideal of how decisions should be made by government. Enlisting the help of commissioners with national prominence and competence who are also representative of diverse interests and points of view adds to public support and confidence, something not always given to other institutions in government with their more restrictive bureaucratic practices. This is because Congress limits a commission's operation to a defined purview: commissioners collect and analyze data, arrive at conclusions, submit their recommendations, and terminate shortly thereafter. Commissions keep out the politics, giving them the freedom to make impartial judgments. They help to forge policy and agreement with the inclusion and empowerment of the practitioners who are involved in the day-to-day implementation of policy and who can express their feelings and reactions in two-way communication with lawmakers. "We were very mindful to allow for community involvement," declared a congressional aide in response to the proposed Hudson and Mohawk Rivers National Heritage Corridor Commission.[45] This method of formulating policy differs from the often-criticized backroom methods of normal congressional procedures or the rigidities of institutionalization and the loss of an originally intended purpose exhibited by bureaucratic agencies. In essence, advisory commissions provide an additional check in our separated powers system.

Congressional policymaking is a process driven by the transactional politics needed to sustain coalitions. While it is often a straightforward process to attract a coalition in favor of general statements of principle, forming actual language and detailed policies can divide previously unified interests and splinter coalitions.[46] Commissions can be helpful in overcoming this obstacle. Leadership uses them to cultivate consensus or facilitate a preexisting consensus, to enact or shun policy change, particularly noteworthy when controversial legislation is at stake or when bipartisan deals on major public policy issues are being brokered.[47] Leadership can design commissions to fit issues that do not fall neatly within committees' jurisdictional boundaries. As one staff aide to a Northeastern Democratic senator noted, "There is compelling reason to create a commission on something like national educational readiness when there is an action that Congress needs to take and there clearly is no consensus around how to do that. It may not be perfect, but it's the best we can do under the circumstances."

Cooling Tempers

Life on Capitol Hill has frequently become acrimonious because of escalating partisanship between parties.[48] Increasing polarization in Congress[49] has led to gridlock[50] and stimulated the use of message politics,[51] thereby limiting both the flexibility and the creativity of congressional action through normal legislative channels.

The logic of commissions is that leaders of both parties, or their designated representatives, can meet to negotiate a deal without the media, the public, or interest groups present. When deliberations are private, parties can make offers without being denounced either by their opponents or by affected constituency groups; there is less chance to use an offer from the other side to curry favor with constituents. Agreement to bipartisan commissions and adherence to their logic are consequential because they represent a tacit promise not to attack the opponent. On some issues, for instance, the promise might imply letting the commission pick the solution and relying on party discipline to encourage lawmakers to go along even if their districts are disadvantaged by the solution; on others it might involve nothing more than a bipartisan admission that a commission is the next step Congress should take, without any understanding that all the players are bound ex ante by the commission's resolution.[52] Commissions also mean eschewing partisan attacks and suggest a strong preference for reaching an agreement.[53]

The results of a commission may not be entirely satisfactory to all, but they are usually sufficient to mitigate conflict or to provide a solution on which a majority of rank and file can agree. As a legislative director commented, "A commission is a case builder intended to build up the knowledge base on a particular issue by focusing people on what Congress thinks is an important issue or problem." A former committee staff member agreed: "The commission is a forum for compromise and agreement in policy disputes that inherently involve large numbers of potential winners and losers." Consensus and credibility build around specific problems or issues when Congress creates a bipartisan panel of recognized experts or public luminaries. This, in turn, gives some incentive if a vote for legislative solutions is needed. A senate staff director indicated how a commission serves to promote consensus:

> What we [in Congress] are looking for is a systemic overview, and while a systemic overview can be done by any given player, what happens is people in Congress might question the plan. Any agency, for instance, could do a study, but it would ultimately be viewed as part of that agency's agenda. The agency report does not get you the kind of credibility to move beyond bureaucratic rivalries. This is an important part in the point of using a commission. The commission's report represents a neutral point of view.

One of the best known and most effective ad hoc commissions for accomplishing consensus was the National Commission on Social Security Reform (also referred to as the Greenspan Commission), established in 1981 to deal with a crisis in the funding of Social Security and Medicare. Social Security was on the verge of collapse and the further it went into debt the more people would owe in the future. Members of Congress from both sides of the aisle and senior White House advisors had diverse views on who was to blame and what should be done; a solution required simultaneous tax increases and benefit cuts. In this notable case the commissioners joined in nearly unanimous support of the recommendations, which President Ronald Reagan and House Speaker Thomas P. (Tip) O'Neill, Jr. (D-Mass.), also embraced. With the exception of minor changes, Congress adopted the commission's proposals. The Social Security Commission transformed a very partisan, contentious issue in American politics into a very tractable one.[54]

Over a decade later, under a Republican House, came another commission to propose reforms in the retirement system. "Another commission to study Social Security—it's hard to vote against that," explained Representative Robert T. Matsui (D-Calif.). "Why oppose it? Why make an issue out of it?"[55] "When it comes to Social Security, I believe all of us—in Congress, and yes, the White House too—must rise above partisan politics and put the needs of the nation first," said Representative Bill Archer (R-Texas). "This issue is too important for any one party or branch of government to use as a forum for gaining political advantage."[56]

A main institutional function of commissions, therefore, is to foster collective action. Delegation of authority to a commission to examine an issue helps overcome seemingly unmanageable and intractable problems. Such coordination may be essential in light of the disjointed nature of policymaking in Congress and the fragmentation of institutional power.[57] "A commission such as the National Commission on Health Care Fraud and Abuse[58] facilitated action by others in Congress to find ways to [reduce] health care fraud and abuse," according to a legislative director to a midwestern Democratic representative. "In that sense, the commission built support to encourage action. In the case of entitlements, however, the idea that a commission will produce collective action is wrong. It is an idealistic anticipation to bring people together for something that just will not happen."

Base closing illustrates a problem in which a policy in the collective, common good, but fragmented by the parochial interests of lawmakers, is derived from delegation to a commission. Members knew that the military base structure bordered on the preposterous, and it was equally difficult for anyone to argue that every base was essential to national security, especially when the Pentagon acknowledged nearly a billion dollars in excess base capacity. The lack of coordination stemmed from the discomfort in Congress about closing bases in a fair manner and from fear of retaliation by the administration (and constituents).[59] The 1989 Defense Base Closure and Realignment Commission, with its relatively neutral membership, was an effective policy-forging mechanism. Employing discretion-limiting procedures with carefully defined delegation secured congressional agreement and maintained unity. The commision did this by requiring lawmakers to give up any meaningful power of review over its list of base closures. In this way the commission decided the distribution of costs—an arrangement gaining the prior agreement of a majority of members, with an eye toward the benefit of base closings before individual costs could be tallied.

Similarly a proposed bipartisan measure in the 105th Congress (1997–1999) to establish an independent campaign finance reform commission designed to study the issue and propose reform legislation to Congress was offered to foster consensus. Supporters from both parties argued that the partisan and contentious process of reform was not likely to result in the enactment of new campaign finance laws. They believed that a commission that operated outside of the political arena stood a better chance of suggesting reforms likely to garner significant bipartisan support in both chambers.[60] Moreover, the bill sponsoring the commission offered a way for many Republican lawmakers to cast a vote for reform without supporting the more partisan measure offered by Representatives Christopher H. Shays (R-Conn.) and Martin T. Meehan (D-Mass.). This would allow them to claim to support reform, thus avoiding criticism back home as well as escaping the wrath of their party leaders.[61]

CRITICISMS OF CAPITOL HILL'S USE OF COMMISSIONS

A frequently encountered argument against Congress's use of ad hoc commissions is that this form of delegation perniciously influences American government by breaking up the democratic process, further fragmenting a system in which power is divided among three branches of government and in which Congress is less and less subject to party discipline.[62] Vocal critics charge that commissions represent improper delegation. Representatives and senators charged with a duty of representation abdicate their constitutional responsibility by entrusting others, who make decisions behind closed doors, with their legislative tasks.[63] If commission members had preferences identical to those of legislators, Congress could assure itself of favorable outcomes simply by delegating to commissions with unfettered discretion.

According to the political philosophy of John Locke, as exemplified by the U.S. constitutional system of separate powers, it is thought that a power originally given cannot be delegated away. This *non-delegation* doctrine would appear to limit Congress's authority to transfer power. How much lawmaking authority, then, can Congress delegate to another body and still stay within the realm of public law? One scholar comments that Article I, Section 1, of the U.S. Constitution endows Congress not with "all legislative power," but only with the "legislative powers herein granted."[64] Congress, theoretically, is thus a "legislative body possessing only limited powers—that is, those granted to it by the Constitution."[65]

Congressional delegation is constitutionally acceptable so long as Congress establishes clear directives and limits. These limits include standards in charters and mission statements, specific criteria or formulas for the delegated entity's deliberations, and procedures for mandatory review by the legislative body. If these criteria meet adequate standards given by Congress for conducting general policy and purpose, entities to which responsibilities are delegated may be given the discretion to make judgments from their analyses.[66] As the Supreme Court noted in *Yakus v. United States*, "Congress is not confined to that method of executing its policy which involves the least possible delegation of discretion to administrative officers."[67]

Critics who question the constitutionality of congressional commissions also contend that these entities reduce electoral accountability because they are less representative than Congress, because they reduce congressional discretion, and because they move the decision making process behind closed doors, thereby curtailing civic participation.[68]

One of the great tensions in representative government is the fulfillment of the duty of representation by those elected to public office. How directly should the desires of the lawmakers be reflected in their actions in the assembly? Should members of Congress adhere to constituents' wishes as well as exercise independent judgment in the public interest? This is potentially problematic. An examination of the design of our national institutions reveals a variety of characteristics that suggest that the framers of the Constitution did not intend representation to be a purely local matter: indirect election of senators, widely spaced elections for most offices, and state-level districts for senators illustrate a dilemma sometimes referred to as the mandate-independence controversy.[69] Translated, lawmakers must choose between two different representative roles. The first theory of representation believes legislators are elected solely as representatives of their constituents and must carry out the instructions received from their electors. Plurality elections in distinct, geographically defined constituencies serve to make a delegate an agent of his or her constituents who is bound to pursue the will of those constituents. Under this mandate theory, national interest is the sum of constituency interests rather than the distinct interest of the larger political body.

In sharp contrast to the concept of the legislator as an agent bound by the instructions of his constituents is the Burkean dictum that the legislator is an independent individual who sees political questions as complex and beyond the capacities of ordinary citizens, defining the representative as an "expert." In this case, lawmakers overcome parochial interests and accept a role that is more independent from their constituency, a role in which they are free to act in pursuit of general welfare and national interests, even at the expense of the district.[70] To the independent theorist, the national interest is not the sum of constituent interests but is distinct from them. In the past, strong political parties and centralized congressional leadership pressured legislators to look beyond the district and consider national interests. Increasingly, however, these institutions exert less control over individual legislators and in turn, legislators are being pulled by a geographically defined community with an expectation that the representative should protect the interests of the region he or she represents.[71]

Critics perceive the representative validity of ad hoc commissions as potentially questionable given that there is representation without election for commission members. That is, Congress transfers legislative responsibility to a group of non-elected officials who do not represent constituents' interests. A commission is an unelected body whose members' decisions may not resemble the views of those people they are affecting. Nor are these decision makers held accountable electorally in the way that members of Congress are. According to one observer, delegation to entities such as the ad hoc commission reduces congressional discretion and, thereby, democratic accountability.[72]

Resorting to decisions made by commissions gives the impression that Congress is shirking its responsibility and undermining its traditional role of exercising oversight responsibilities. This is because information may not be fully disseminated and debated by a commission in the same way it would be in Senate or House committee deliberations or floor debates. Instead of being a part of congressional procedures, commissions can negotiate in secret without public records, formal procedures, or input from all interested groups. Moving the decision making process and debate behind "closed doors" may prevent the public from increasing its knowledge and understanding of a given issue. This in turn may keep both the represented and the un-represented from expressing their views to Congress and may exacerbate the traditional difficulties of minority representation.

There is some basis for these arguments against commissions. Congressional leadership may design a commission to allow friendly groups more points of access to members of Congress. For example, special interests could come before the temporary body to plead their case, out of the public view. But as so many on Capitol Hill will say, it is the elected officials who must decide whether to adopt commission recommendations. Legislators accept ultimate responsibility, Congress still determines the basic outlines of national policy, lawmakers remain the paramount representatives of constituents, and the legislative branch is the central agency for legitimizing the decisions of government. In addition, commission recommendations are only advisory. No changes in public policy occur on the authority of a commission. Commissions do not make policy, for their actions do not have the force of law. The implementation of a commission's recommendations is left to the determination of specific authorization by Congress. But as a legislative director to a mid-Atlantic Democratic representative observed, a commission is similar to a jury: "If you don't give them [commissioners] firm marching orders, they may not address the problem you want them to address."

Lawmakers are electorally accountable as well. For example, one aspect of the public nature of commission reports centers on their use by citizens to demand greater public accountability of politicians. One may not necessarily agree with a commission's recommendations, but they provide a basis on which groups can call politicians to task and can inquire about the constructive action that can or should be taken.[73] While lawmakers might wish the time span of the commission's existence would be sufficient to defuse interest, the final report serves to justify the position of those persons who do not believe the issue the commission was created to address has been resolved merely by the passage of time.

Many on Capitol Hill dismiss the charge that the use of commissions amounts to legislative dereliction. "When someone represents over 600,000 different people," a legislative director for a Democratic senator from a northeastern state contended, "it's impossible to find any one person to fully represent." "A commission is representative," added a congressional aide whose boss proposed establishing the National Commission to Support Law Enforcement,[74] "since actors from around the country, or states, or from around the community are involved in the issue, and because Congress is attentive to the different interests involved when they establish commissions."

Lastly, critics focus on congressional motives and suggest that lawmakers rarely use commissions for altruistic reasons. Instead, politicians, pressed to take unpopular action, choose the easy way out. Congress has rewritten President Harry S Truman's old maxim. Even if you cannot stand the heat, you do not have to get out of the kitchen—you appoint a nonpolitical commission.[75] This indirect method of deliberation is convenient at times. Lawmakers do not have to vote for something that could have potentially damaging repercussions. Instead, they wait out a designated period and get something automatically; members can plead their case for something or criticize a commission's final determination, portraying themselves as protectors of local interests. In short, members become advocates rather than bearers of bad news and the hard decisions of national policymaking are left to the commission.

Pervasive politicization remains a fundamental feature of congressional operations. The practice of appointing a commission as an easy way out of making an unpopular decision encourages the cynical view that politicians create commissions solely to avoid unwanted responsibilities.[76] Thus, creating a commission seems a dereliction of legislative duty to some[77] because when Congress delegates it distributes rights without imposing commensurate duties. The process allows members of Congress to manipulate voters' perception of activities, since routine government action is rarely understood and thus eludes the sustained attention of the general public.[78]

This viewpoint is shortsighted. It ignores the fact that so many decisions to create a commission minimize or compensate for most of the more prevalent shortcomings of this process for policy formulation. To be sure, delegation is one method Congress can employ to avoid issues, but a good number of decisions to delegate serve an important function. The proponents of delegation, principally its practitioners, dismiss the critics' claim as a philosophical vision of what Congress should be, not what it is. They acknowledge it would be better if the legislative system could make tough, detailed, politically divisive decisions by up-or-down roll-call votes based on each member's view of the national interest. But at some point political reality and theory clash.

As Congress has had to delegate to deal with the complexity and scope of many contemporary issues, lawmakers must rely on the opinions and actions of persons outside Capitol Hill. Legislation has become much too politically complex to be effectively handled by a representative assembly. Legislators who want to develop effective policies but who lack the skill or time needed to draft such policies often delegate fact-finding and policy development to bureaucrats, presidents, government ministers, party leaders, committees, and others.

CONCLUSION

There are a number of ways in which Congress performs its policymaking functions. Ad hoc commissions are one device at its disposal. Despite criticisms that these entities are inefficient and frequently evade the issues, commissions provide a flexible option, the variation in their composition and organization reflecting the specific mandates that establish them.[79] Commissions can provide expert advice in matters of public policy within a definite time frame. By virtue of their ad hoc status, they can bypass normal bureaucratic channels. Commissions are a public relations device designed to draw attention to certain issues, to elicit public support, and to achieve consensus in a fragmented Congress. Commissions also allow for the direct representation of functional consistencies in the advisory process by seeking the advice of holders of diverse points of view.[80] It is this list of advantages that has encouraged the recent use of commissions and led to their becoming a stable feature of public policies.

The ties between Congress and ad hoc commissions are now complex and symbiotic: elected officials (and their aides) are in a position to construct public policy, in exchange for which commissions can work for members whose roles are comprehensive and highly variable. They also provide the expertise necessary for writing legislation. Of course, some of these relationships are arrangements of blame avoidance. Commissions can allow members of Congress to manipulate voters' perceptions, because routine government action usually eludes the sustained attention of the general public. Consequently, lawmakers use an element of delegation to escape blame for politically sensitive decisions. In practice, most commissions serve more than one purpose. Many provide a basis for informed legislative action and help manage a growing legislative workload; they enable legislators to cope with burgeoning demands—to follow more issues and process more bills.

It is now possible to consider what motivates individual lawmakers to delegate authority to these organizations. One should review the benefits and drawbacks with regard to the use of ad hoc commissions and their applicability to the case at hand. While the disputes over the desirable extent of delegation are numerous, there is no widely accepted explanation of why Congress delegates some of its policymaking authority. In the next chapter a decision tree of legislative decision making will show the conditions that encourage lawmakers to learn from others, to enlist help from others, and to push responsibility onto others.

NOTES

1. The term is derivative of the many federal advisory committees that began with the administrative expansion promoted by the New Deal. They are fifth behind the bureaucratic agencies that are sometimes referred to as the fourth branch of government. Federal advisory committees went unchecked and as their numbers grew and their power increased they collectively became known as a "fifth arm of government."

2. Employing a commission for the purpose of giving partisan representation is based upon the theory that the representatives of the two dominant parties will check and control each other.

3. Select and special committees are temporary study panels that function without legislative authority. Generally these bodies exist for one or two Congresses and are then disbanded. A few, however, will continue over several Congresses. Both the Senate and the House usually set specific boundaries within which each select or special committee must operate. Both select and special committees are authorized by a resolution passed by a majority vote and are provided with operating budgets, staff, and office space. The primary difference between the ad hoc commission and the select and special committee has to do with membership. Where the former is made up of "civilians" the latter is made up of active members of Congress who are assigned by their respective political party organizations. Examples of select and special committees include the House Select Committee to Investigate Covert Arms Transactions with Iran (the Iran-Contra Committee), organized in 1987, and the Senate Select Committee to Study the Senate Committee System (1984).

4. 5 U.S.C. (United States Code) Federal Advisory Committee Act, P.L. (Public Law) 92–463.

5. Hugh Davis Graham, "The Ambiguous Legacy of American Presidential Commissions," *The Public Historian* 7 (1985): 23.

6. This pay is at a rate equal to the daily equivalent of the annual rate of basic pay for a specific government level of the Executive schedule of the United States Code. And in the same manner and under the same franking conditions as other federal departments and agencies, commissions may use the U.S. postal system.

7. The General Services Administration frequently provides resources ranging from office space to advice on staff and the services of trained administrators who manage payrolls. Commissions hold hearings and convene working groups (with occasional site visits), deliver interim reports to the congressional leadership, and hold closing meetings to discuss their final reports and cumulative recommendations.

8. A vacancy usually does not affect the commission's powers, but is filled in the same manner as the original appointment was made.

9. The Commission on Integration of Workers' Compensation Medical Benefits was proposed to study and develop a detailed plan for implementing the transfer of financial responsibility for workers' compensation medical benefits to health

insurance plans and to make a recommendation as to whether such a transfer should be effected.

10. In some cases, federal employees may be detailed to the commission without reimbursement but without interruption or loss of civil service status or privilege.

11. Michael Lipsky and David J. Olson, "Riot Commission Politics," *Transaction* 6 (1969): 8.

12. Ray C. Rist, "Polity, Politics, and Social Research: A Study in the Relationship of Federal Commissions and Social Science," *Social Problems* 21 (1973): 113–28.

13. Established December 1, 1990, by P.L. 101–650, the National Commission on Judicial Discipline and Removal was designed to investigate and study the problems and issues involved in the tenure (including discipline and removal) of an Article III judge; and to evaluate the advisability of proposing alternatives to current arrangements with respect to discipline or removal of judges that would require an amendment to the Constitution.

14. Examples of independent regulatory commissions include the Interstate Commerce Commission (ICC), the Federal Communications Commission (FCC), the Atomic Energy Commission (AEC), the Securities and Exchange Commission (SEC), and the Federal Energy Regulatory Commission (FERC).

15. Established March 26, 1991, under authority of Title 39 of P.L. 1010–510, the Defense Base Closure and Realignment Commission was established to readdress issues from the 1988 Defense Secretary's Commission on Base Realignment and Closure and review recommendations made by the secretary of defense regarding base closures and realignments in 1991, 1993, and 1995.

16. Stephen Skowronek, *Building a New American State* (New York: Cambridge University Press, 1982).

17. Robert E. Cushman, *The Independent Regulatory Commissions* (New York: Octagon Books, 1972).

18. James L. Sundquist, *The Decline and Resurgence of Congress* (Washington, D.C.: Brookings Institution, 1981).

19. The term *institutionalization* refers to the process whereby structures and procedures take shape and become regularized in Congress. An illustrative example is the committee system's division of labor. The committee system was initially intended to be an efficient device to organize the two chambers, shape the measures on which Congress acts, create parliamentary strategy, disentangle complexity, and, most importantly, manage a growing work load. In many instances, committees evolved in connection with historical events and shifting perceptions of public problems. As novel political problems arose, new committees were added.

20. Joseph Cooper, "Organization and Innovation in the House of Representatives," in *The House at Work*, ed. Joseph Cooper and G. Calvin Mackenzie (Austin: University of Texas Press, 1981).

21. Ibid.

22. Burdett A. Loomis, *The Contemporary Congress*, 2nd ed. (New York: St. Martin's Press, 1998), 51.

23. Timothy E. Cook, "Legislature vs. Legislator: A Note on the Paradox of Congressional Support," *Legislative Studies Quarterly* (February 1979): 43–52;

Glenn R. Parker and Roger H. Davidson, "Why Do Americans Love Their Congressmen So Much More than Their Congress?" *Legislative Studies Quarterly* (February 1979): 53–61; Glenn R. Parker, *Characteristics of Congress* (Englewood Cliffs, N.J.: Prentice Hall, 1989); and Richard Born, "The Shared Fortunes of Congress and Congressmen: Members May Run from Congress but They Can't Hide," *Journal of Politics* (November 1990): 1223–41.

24. Roger H. Davidson and Walter J. Oleszek, *Congress and Its Members*, 6th ed. (Washington, D.C.: CQ Press 1998), 409.

25. John R. Hibbing and Elizabeth Theiss-Morse, *Congress as Public Enemy* (New York: Cambridge University Press, 1995), 147.

26. Harold L. Wilensky, quoted in David Flitner, Jr., *The Politics of Presidential Commissions* (New York: Transnational Publishers, Inc., 1986), 24.

27. Davidson and Oleszek, *Congress and Its Members*, 6th ed.

28. Quoted in Donna Cassata, "Swift Progress of 'Contract' Inspires Awe and Concern," *Congressional Quarterly Weekly Report* (April 1995): 909–19.

29. Harold L. Wilensky, *Organizational Intelligence* (New York: Basic Books, 1967).

30. George T. Sulzner, "The Policy Process and the Uses of National Governmental Study Commissions," *Western Political Quarterly* 24 (1971): 438–48.

31. Lawrence J.R. Herson, *The Politics of Ideas: Political Theory and American Public Policy* (Prospect Heights, Ill.: Waveland Press, Inc., 1984).

32. Charles E. Lindblom, "The Science of Muddling Through," *Public Administrative Review* 19 (1959): 79.

33. Herson, *The Politics of Ideas: Political Theory and American Public Policy*.

34. Sulzner, "The Policy Process and the Uses of National Governmental Study Commissions," 438.

35. Ibid.

36. Ibid., 447.

37. Ibid., 443.

38. Everett Carll Ladd, "Public Opinion and the 'Congress Problem,'" *The Public Interest* 100 (1990): 57–67.

39. Hibbing and Theiss-Morse, *Congress as Public Enemy*.

40. Herb Asher and Mike Barr, "Popular Support for Congress and Its Members," in *Congress, the Press and the Public*, ed. Thomas E. Mann and Norman J. Ornstein (Washington, D.C.: American Enterprise Institute/Brookings Institution, 1994).

41. Richard F. Fenno, Jr., *Home Style: House Members in Their Districts* (Boston: Little, Brown, 1978), 168.

42. Linda D. Kozaryn, "Commission Proposes Overhaul of GI Bill, Transition Aid," American Forces Information Service, www.defenselink.mil/news, accessed January 1999.

43. The Commission on Executive Organization was proposed to examine and make recommendations with respect to an effective and practicable organization of the executive branch, and to seek to reduce the total number of federal employees by 5 percent within five years.

44. The Federal Workforce Reduction and Realignment Commission was proposed to develop and submit to the president and Congress recommendations for

reducing the number of federal employees nationwide in non-defense-related agencies by 250,000.

45. The Hudson and Mohawk Rivers National Heritage Corridor Commission was proposed to assist appropriate federal, state, and local authorities and regional planning organizations in the development and implementation of an integrated resource management plan to achieve the goals of the Hudson and Mohawk Rivers National Heritage Corridor Act of 1994.

46. Colton C. Campbell and Roger H. Davidson, "Coalition Building in Congress: The Consequences of Partisan Change, in *The Interest Group Connection: Electioneering, Lobbying, and Policymaking in Washington*, ed. Paul Herrnson, Ronald Shaiko, and Clyde Wilcox (Chatham, N.J.: Chatham House, 1998).

47. John B. Gilmour, "Summits and Stalemates: Bipartisanship Negotiations in the Postreform Era," in *The Postreform Congress*, ed. Roger H. Davidson (New York: St. Martin's Press, 1993).

48. Charles E. Bullock, III, and David W. Brady, "Party, Constituency, and Roll-Call Voting in the U.S. Senate," *Legislative Studies Quarterly* 8 (1983): 29–43; Samuel C. Patterson and Gregory A. Caldeira, "Party Voting in the United States Congress," British Journal of Political Science 18 (1987): 111–31; David W. Rhode, *Parties and Leaders in the Postreform Congress* (Chicago: University of Chicago Press, 1991); Steven S. Smith, "Forces of Change in Senate Party Leadership and Organization," in *Congress Reconsidered*, 5th ed., edited by Lawrence C. Dodd and Bruce I. Oppenheimer (Washington, D.C.: CQ Press, 1993); Sarah A. Binder and Steven S. Smith, *Politics or Principle: Filibustering in the United States Senate* (Washington, D.C.: Brookings Insitution, 1997); Norman J. Ornstein, Robert L. Peabody, and David Rhode, "The U.S. Senate: Toward the 21st Century," in *Congress Reconsidered*, 6th ed., edited by Lawrence C. Dodd and Bruce I. Oppenheimer (Washington, D.C.: CQ Press, 1997); and John B. Badar, "Partisanship in the U.S. Senate, 1969–1996," unpublished manuscript, 1998.

49. Patricia A. Hurley and Rick K. Wilson, "Partisan Voting Patterns in the U.S. Senate, 1877–1986," *Legislative Studies Quarterly* 14, no. 2 (1989): 225–50; and Nicol C. Rae and Colton C. Campbell, "Party Politics and Ideology in the Contemporary Senate," in *The Contentious Senate: Partisanship, Ideology, and the Myth of Cool Judgment*, ed. Colton C. Campbell and Nicol C. Rae (Lanham, Md.: Rowman & Littlefield Publishers, Inc., 2001).

50. Sarah A. Binder, "The Disappearing Political Center," *The Brookings Review* 15 (1996): 36–39.

51. Patrick J. Sellers, "Promoting the Party Message in the U.S. Senate," paper presented at the annual meeting of the Midwest Political Science Association, Chicago, 2000; and C. Lawrence Evans and Walter J. Oleszek, "Message Politics and Senate Procedure," in *The Contentious Senate: Partisanship, Ideology, and the Myth of Cool Judgment*, ed. Colton C. Campbell and Nicol C. Rae (Lanham, Md.: Rowman & Littlefield Publishers, Inc., 2001).

52. Paul Light, *Artful Work: The Politics of Social Security Reform* (New York: Random House, 1985); and Gilmour, "Summits and Stalemates: Bipartisanship Negotiations in the Postreform Era."

53. John B. Gilmour, "Blue Ribbon Commissions," in *The Encyclopedia of the United States Congress*, ed. Donald C. Bacon, Roger H. Davidson, and Morton

Keller (New York: Simon & Schuster, 1995); M. Stephen Weatherford and Thomas B. Mayhew, "Tax Policy and Presidential Leadership: Ideas, Interests, and the Quality of Advice," *Studies in American Political Development* 9 (1995): 287–330.

54. Gilmour, "Summits and Stalemates: Bipartisanship Negotiations in the Postreform Era."

55. Quoted in Juliet Eilperin, "GOP Backs a Social Security Study," *Washington Post*, April 23, 1998, A4.

56. Ibid.

57. Parker, *Characteristics of Congress*, 134.

58. The National Commission on Health Care Fraud and Abuse was proposed to investigate the nature, magnitude, and cost of health care fraud and abuse in the United States, and identify and develop effective methods of preventing, detecting, and prosecuting or litigating such fraud and abuse.

59. If the president (with the guidance of the military) were allowed to pick and choose which bases should be closed or realigned, according to his powers as commander-in-chief, he might use this ability to retaliate against any legislator who had defied him on important legislation.

60. Diana Dwyre and Victoria A. Farrar-Myers, *Legislative Labyrinth: Congress and Campaign Finance Reform* (Washington, D.C.: CQ Press, 2001).

61. Ibid.

62. Susan F. Rasky, "Congress Says: A Commission Made Us," *New York Times*, January 29, 1989, E4.

63. Theodore J. Lowi, *The End of Liberalism: The Second Republic of the United States*, 2nd ed. (New York: W.W. Norton & Company, 1979). Historically, the Supreme Court has given a variety of interpretations to the delegation doctrine. From the time of the debates over the ratification of the Constitution until the late 1920s the Framers and the Supreme Court stated that Congress "might" not delegate its legislative power. Sotirios A. Barber, *The Constitution and the Delegation of Congressional Power* (Chicago: University of Chicago Press, 1975), 42. Cushman (*The Independent Regulatory Commissions*, 429) writes that the Court has adroitly solved the issue of delegation to regulatory commissions by two rather different methods. The first has been by upholding legislative delegations of power as necessary to the administration of government, but without sacrificing the constitutional theory that legislative powers cannot be delegated. The Court has condoned the practice by attaching distinctive names to the powers thus delegated, such as "quasi-legislative" or "sub-delegation," names that avoid constitutional difficulties. That is, while there are clear constitutional prohibitions against delegated legislative powers, there is nothing against the delegation of "quasi-legislative" powers. According to Justice Sutherland in *Humphrey's Executor v. United States*, 295 U.S. 602 (1935), "quasi-legislative" power is what the Federal Trade Commission enjoys. In short, Congress has not invalidly delegated its legislative authority to regulatory commissions, because the power it has delegated is 'quasi-legislative' and not true legislative power. Congressional delegation to various entities has also been rationalized by the Supreme Court through this delegation doctrine, which, historically, has been given a variety of interpretations. For example, congressional delegation to congressional commissions has been

subject to the *non-delegation* doctrine that limits what and how Congress may delegate to other branches. According to Hanlon, referring to *National Federal of Federal Employees v. United States*, 905 F.2d 404, 404 (D.C. Cir. 1990), quoting *Field v. Clark*, 143 U.S. 649, 692 (1892), this *non-delegation* doctrine is rooted in the separation of powers principle, which "protects the 'integrity and maintenance of the system of government ordained by the Constitution' by precluding Congress from delegation." See Natalie Hanlon, "Military Base Closures: A Study of Government by Commission," *Colorado Law Review* 62 (1991): 331–64. In *Panama Refining Co. v. Ryan*, 293 U.S. 388 (1935), and *A.L.A. Schecter Poultry Corp. v. United States*, 295 U.S. 495 (1935), the Court invalidated congressional delegation involving the National Industrial Recovery Act (NIRA). The Court held void delegations of legislative power to the president on the ground that the National Industrial Recovery Act set up no clear standards or criteria to serve as limitations upon the president's uncontrolled discretion. In sum, while the standards limiting delegations of legislative power may be vague and ambiguous, they may not be too vague, and must not be wholly lacking. A standard is too vague when it does not provide guidance seen and followed by those exercising the delegated power (Cushman, *The Independent Regulatory Commissions*, 431–32). That is, the standard must be clear enough to the Court, so that the tribunal can determine whether the officer or agency is following the standard instead of exercising uncontrolled discretion.

64. Laurence H. Tribe, *American Constitutional Law*, 2nd ed. (Mineola, N.Y.: The Foundation Press, 1988), 227.

65. Ibid.

66. *Mistretta v. United States*, 488 U.S. 361, 379 (1989), referring to *Sunshine Coal Co. v. Adkins*, 310 U.S. 381, 398 (1940).

67. *Yakus v. United States*, 321 U.S. 414 (1944).

68. Natalie Hanlon, "Military Base Closures: A Study of Government by Commission," *Colorado Law Review* 62 (1991): 331–64.

69. Hanna Pitkin, *The Concept of Representation* (Berkeley: University of California Press, 1967).

70. Ibid., 145.

71. Ibid., 166.

72. R. Kent Weaver, "Is Congress Abdicating Power to Commissions?" *Roll Call*, February 12, 1989, 5 and 25.

73. Rist, "Polity, Politics, and Social Research: A Study in the Relationship of Federal Commissions and Social Science," 116.

74. The National Commission to Support Law Enforcement was proposed to study and recommend changes regarding law enforcement agencies and law enforcement issues on the federal, state, and local levels.

75. R.W. Apple, Jr., "Keeping Hot Potatoes out of the Political Kitchen," *New York Times*, February 2, 1989, D20.

76. Gilmour, "Blue Ribbon Commissions," 1995.

77. Weaver, "Is Congress Abdicating Power to Commissions?" and David Schoenbrod, *Power without Responsibility: How Congress Abuses the People through Delegation* (New Haven, Conn.: Yale University Press, 1993).

78. Ibid.

79. Stephanie Smith, *Federal Advisory Committees: Their Establishment and Composition*, Congressional Research Service Report, no. 92–89 (Washington, D.C.: 1992).

80. Ibid.

—Chapter 2—

The Path to Delegation

Frankly, I look at each commission on its own.
                              Former U.S. representative and
                              chair of a national commission

THE RATIONAL PERSPECTIVE

Modern theories of legislative behavior begin with David R. Mayhew's book, *Congress: The Electoral Connection*, which suggests that congressional action has a direct electoral connection, in which legislators are single-minded seekers of reelection, motivated primarily by self-interest.[1] Individuals may enter Congress with altruistic intentions, but their behavior in office is best explained by the "electoral connection": the need for reelection. As a consequence lawmakers consider the preferences of their voters, especially on issues of potentially high salience, that is, issues visible to the public.[2] Congress is thus organized to promote the goal of reelection. Members follow conservative strategies to capitalize upon particularized benefits, to respond to organized groups, to claim as much credit as possible, and to mobilize only when they can claim credit.[3] The incentive to delegate, therefore, must have some sort of electoral connection.

Follow Mayhew's line of thought, others have developed what has come to be known as the distributive theory of legislative organization.[4] According to this view, the decision to delegate is a function of the political costs and benefits for which elected officials will be held electorally accountable. Legislative action reflects a desire to maximize net benefits to districts in order to increase the chances for reelection. Delegation enables individual legislators to protect favored constituents[5] or to shift blame for political costs[6] onto other organizations, but makes them unable to claim full credit for any perceived benefits. Delegation is a function of this trade-off. Thus, congressional decisions to delegate occur when the decrease in attributable costs is greater than the decrease in attributable benefits.

R. Douglas Arnold notes that legislators are ever mindful of the direct correlation between their individual performance and the voting booth. According to what he calls the "incumbent performance rule," voters tend to punish legislators for undesirable effects only if there are both identifiable governmental actions and visible individual contributions. Responsibility for unpleasant decisions is therefore frequently delegated to the president, bureaucrats, regulatory commissions, judges, state and local officials, or temporary commissions as a procedural strategy for "masking" legislators' individual contributions.[7] Such delegation is especially prevalent when there is a desire to shed policymaking tasks that are too onerous or when dealing with issues that are likely to provoke disputes with voters. Challengers will take full advantage of reminding citizens about issues as traceable as legislative salaries, for example.

Arnold demonstrates that while the decisions that Congress makes are partially dependent on legislators' own personal policy preferences or their need to trade favors, the quest for reelection is legislators' dominant goal. Thus, members of Congress tend to pursue the preferences of the public on any issue that is salient to the public. Whenever lawmakers must choose among alternative policies they will most likely select the one that will contribute most to their reelection. Legislators' decisions also depend on whether they are dealing with policy effects that are directly traceable to their own individual actions or whether the electoral connection involves only policy positions.[8] Following this logic, delegation to the Quadrennial Pay Raise Commission in 1967 was instituted to distance Congress from a delicate decision—going on record in favor of raising its own pay. The "commission" label provided a shield against public outcry and a way to explain a difficult vote.[9] It also broke the chain of traceability for individual legislators.

R. Kent Weaver contends that most officeholders seek, above all, not to maximize the credit they receive but to minimize blame. Such blame avoidance by lawmakers results from voters' tendency to be more sensitive to their real or potential losses than to their gains. That is, persons who have suffered losses are more inclined to notice loss, to feel aggrieved, and to act on that grievance than those who gain. Weaver suggests four situations that may lead to blame avoidance: when there is a zero-sum conflict among the policymakers' constituents; when all possible alternatives have strong negative consequences for at least some of the policymakers' constituents; when constituency opinion is overwhelmingly on a single side of an issue; or when the personal or policy interests of the policymaker and his or her clientele are opposed.[10] Incentives to avoid blame lead members of Congress to adopt a distinctive set of political strategies, such as "passing the buck" or "defection," that are different from those they would follow if they were primarily interested in pursuing good policy or maximizing credit-claiming opportunities.[11] These strategies lead to important policy effects, such as surrendering discretion even when the policy effect offers important credit-claiming opportunities.

The second theory attributes delegation to a series of principal-agent problems. A legislator's dilemma belongs to a broad class of phenomena known as agency problems.[12] Agency problems involve at least two players: a principal who holds the authority to take certain actions, and an agent to whom the principal has delegated some authority. In the legislative policymaking setting, Congress as a whole acts as a principal that delegates to an expert agent the task of proposing alternatives to an existing policy.

Most forms of congressional delegation, therefore, are seen as rational. By delegating powers, lawmakers can overcome some of the inefficiencies of the legislative process. For example, given some of the structural and procedural flaws of Congress, the benefits of collective action are realized through recourse to smaller organizations.[13] Efficiency gains accrue to both principals and agents if tasks are delegated to those with a comparative advantage in performing them.[14] Often legislators, in seeking to maximize their self-interest, have incentives to take a free ride by acting in ways that do not benefit the institution. Members are uncertain as to which strategies other members will pursue, so coordination may not always be achieved. While uncoordinated groups might overcome collective action problems, the benefits of collective action are most often realized by legislators through organizations to which they have delegated the authority to take action.[15] Therefore, within Congress, devising specific details necessary to implement rules and regulations can be delegated to specialized organizations, taking away from legislators the responsibility of developing the needed expertise while also removing the incentive for individual legislators to shirk this responsibility. Authority is transferred to one or more agents because it is the delegation of authority to a central agent to lead or manage the organization that is the key to overcoming the problems of collective action. Agents performing as leaders or managers must possess the resources they need to discharge their duties effectively.[16]

Delegation from principal to agent can also be vital to the division of labor and development of specialization. Such a division of labor is an analytic expression of the agency relationship, in which one party, the principal, considers entering into a contractual relationship with another, the agent, in the expectation that the agent will subsequently choose actions that produce outcomes desired by the principal.[17] Congressional parties have opted, for instance, to delegate authority to grapple with the complexity of the appropriations process. A party leadership well endowed with powers can foster the passage of legislation that furthers its membership's policy, reelection, and power goals. It can do so by providing basic coordination services, such as legislative scheduling; by facilitating, through side payments or the coordination of logrolling, for example, the passage of legislation various subgroups of its membership want; and by policy leadership, that is, using leadership resources aggressively to influence the congressional agenda and the substance of bills in order to translate broadly shared legislative preferences into law.[18]

Others treat Congress as a firm that makes policy and has the option of internal production through direct legislation or outsourcing to the executive. Accordingly policy is made in the politically most efficient manner, be it through legislation or through delegation. As with actual firms, each alternative has both advantages and disadvantages, so the boundary between legislative and executive policymaking lies where these net benefits "just balance at the margin from legislators' point of view."[19]

In some cases, then, delegation may offer legislators an attractive alternative to making policy themselves. The issue of airline safety is an example. This policy area requires technical expertise but lacks potential political benefits. Lawmakers will gain little credit if things go well and no airline disasters occur, but they will have to withstand intense scrutiny if things go wrong—airline regulation is an issue with only a political downside, and failures tend to be spectacular and well-publicized.[20] The set of individuals receiving benefits, the flying public, is diffuse and ill-organized, while those paying the costs of regulation, the airline companies, are well-organized and politically active. Delegated power is relatively easy to monitor when one keeps in mind the easy observation of deficiencies in the system. Thus, even if legislators had unlimited time and resources, delegation would be the preferred mode of policymaking.[21]

Such delegation, however, can be risky. Agents may use their powers to pursue interests different from those of members of Congress. Thus the degree to which members of Congress are willing to delegate their powers depend on the costs and benefits to members, which in turn depend on the political and institutional environment. When members are ideologically homogeneous and committed to enacting an ambitious legislative program they are most likely to expect their leadership to use its powers and resources expansively and more likely to augment the powers and resources delegated.[22]

ALTERNATIVE THOUGHTS ON DELEGATION

The assumption that members of Congress are constituency-minded is a useful place to start in understanding legislative behavior. But this explanation is often presented as if it alone explains commission creation. In conversation with Hill people, the listener is left with a different perspective. No single theory explains all congressional commissions, and the attachment to the reelection assumption has been a matter of modeling ease or elegance, not theory.[23] Although previous single-cause theories of delegation provide some clues about motivation, and while each may be a useful theoretical building block, neither fully captures every decision to delegate. The previous works are limited because they deal in generalities about delegation, and they fail to provide exact predictions for every commission created by Congress; they only roughly estimate congressional delegation. Moreover, these works do not estimate variations in Congress's decision to delegate over time or across issue areas, and thus they lack a consistent account of which selected policy areas are decided by Congress and which go to commissions. Their arguments are either abstract and nonempirical or focus on post-hoc rationalizations of created commissions.[24] In short, existing theories supply an incomplete picture of the actual conditions under which Congress uses commissions, the nature of the policy problems to which commissions must apply solutions, the transactional politics surrounding delegation, and the variations in motivations for establishing commissions.

One should question the practicality of models of politicians as interested solely in maximizing personal benefits, either electoral or status, within Congress and as acting in ways that further their objectives in as efficient and effective a way as possible. It is not always possible to construct a purely rational decision making process for any but the lowest-level decision. What is politically rational may not be economically rational and vice versa, and politicians very often pursue both political and economic goals. Applying economic concepts of rationality to politics might mislead us, oversimplify the issue, and distract us from the possible variety of motives for delegation. The halls and rooms of Congress echo all the diverse accents of the American public. The institution includes 535 voting members, educationally ranging from those with only high school diplomas to graduate scholar, socially ranging from first-generation immigrants to first-family gentry, with financial standings ranging from paupers to millionaires, increasingly separate and independent with equal voting power. Each member may act for different reasons and may have different motivations, a different understanding of gain, and a different degree of altruism. The immediate goals of members will vary with time and over the course of a congressional career, along with important variations in degree of self-interest exist. A freshman member of the House from a marginal district, facing an uncertain future at the polls, will put more emphasis on helping his or her constituents and getting reelected. A third-term senator who is the ranking member or chair of a key committee will give a higher priority to passing legislation and formulating public policy. Lawmakers are thus motivated by different complexes of goals and drives depending on their reelection possibilities, their seniority, and their committee assignments.[25]

If members are optimizers, little in economic theory says that certain goals and not others determine the expected utility of economically rational actors.[26] Among the many impediments to rationality in the legislative life, for instance, are the impossibility of distinguishing facts from values and of separating ends from means, the impossibility of obtaining agreement among legislators on predominant goals, the ambiguity of many policy goals on Capitol Hill, the pressures of time in which to make a decision, and the inability of lawmakers to handle a vast amount of information at any one time.[27] Other problems include the inability of members of Congress to give their undivided attention to a single problem or decision, the costs of information acquisition, the failure to obtain all possible data because of time constraints, the different levels of expertise, and the inability to predict all consequences of a given choice.

Too often, rational choice theories of lawmaking underestimate the difficulties of passing legislation. Legislating is "hard, pick-and-shovel work," observes Representative John Dingell (D-Mich.), "and it takes a long time to do it."[28] What makes the legislative process so hard to simplify is that there is often an elaborate maze of subtleties to be sorted out. Rational choice theory, with its reduction of congressional decision making to the calculation of optimal means to a clearly defined end, is too blunt an instrument to provide an adequate analysis, and it assumes away much of the political process. The mechanics and poetry of lawmaking often involve networks of personal relationships among people with a range of goals and motives, behind-the-scenes maneuvers and informal arrangements, internal power incentives, and accumulated practice that is seldom present in many rigid rational choice frameworks. Often the best way to start examining Congress and its operations is to recognize former House Speaker Thomas P. (Tip) O'Neill's insight: politics is an art.[29]

Politics suffuses nearly everything Congress does and politicians unquestionably bend the institution toward their own purposes. Legislators are notoriously bad at imposing costs on concentrated groups in order to create diffuse common goods; practice has often demonstrated that they prefer doing the opposite. Still, the repeated judgment that legislators do only what serves their own interest, and that interest is their own reelection, is not altogether accurate. Members may not always see the policymaking process as a means to reelection. When studying the legislative process, it is important to understand goals and contexts. Put simply, all members of Congress pursue a variety of interests and do so in political environments over which they have limited control. Their capacity to achieve this or that policy outcome is determined in large part by the energy and talent they devote to their cause and the challenges they encounter in the process. This outlook directs our attention to the personal characteristics of those who enter the policy fray and the circumstances of their intervention.

The Commission on the Commercial Application of Certain Defense-Related Facilities, Equipment, Processes, and Technologies was proposed in the 103rd Congress (1993–1995) to study the White Sands Missile Range in New Mexico and to provide relevant information on potential dual-use applications of such facilities by the private sector. The Hudson and Mohawk Rivers National Heritage Corridor Commission, also proposed during the 103rd Congress, assisted federal, state, and local authorities and regional planning organizations in developing an integrated resource management plan to put into effect the Hudson and Mohawk Rivers National Heritage Corridor Act of 1994. And in the 104th Congress (1995–1997) the Commission on International Coordination of Financial Regulation identified regulatory bodies and mechanisms supervising international capital markets; appraised cooperation among the various regulatory entities; proposed solutions for improving cooperation among the various agencies; proposed solutions for improving global enforcement of laws and regulations relating to capital markets; analyzed the major clearing and settlement systems and the differences among those systems; proposed solutions for improving coordination among the clearing and settlement systems; identified offshore tax havens; and proposed solutions for minimizing any adverse effects of tax havens. In each case the decision to delegate did not adequately pertain to a policy effect that was directly traceable to a legislator's own individual actions nor did it allow lawmakers to avoid blame. Nor does each commission represent a strategy to capitalize upon particularized benefits or to claim credit. In fact, these commissions suggest that Congress delegates in order to use expertise that is unavailable through institutional resources or prohibitively costly to obtain, or to pare down its workload.

The assumptions of rational choice theory have merit, but an institution such as Congress is too complex and rational choice theories cannot always operationalize matters of the type that I examine. Lawmakers, for example, may act according to "public spirit," the inclination to make an honest effort to achieve good public policy.[30] The public spirit view of Congress thus begins with what some describe as "a startling and—sadly—unconventional assumption: that politicians are neither driven by evil or weak motives, nor are they all, beneath the surface, conniving and dishonest . . . [and therefore] the decisions our policymakers have made have been neither irrational nor irresponsible."[31] Congress is an institution making reasonable and understandable decisions, as its members struggle in good faith to balance legitimate competing views. Elected officials may disagree on which public purposes are worthwhile and which policies are likely to achieve these purposes. But like the commitments themselves, these disagreements are real, not just calculated efforts to enhance political position.[32]

To chart the motives that account for Congress's delegating to commissions we must consider conditions other than just those when action must

Table 2.1
Primary Justifications Suggested for Delegating to Ad Hoc Commissions as
Expressed by Interview Respondents

	Number of Times Mentioned as First Priority	% of All Respondents
Expertise	21	38%
Workload	16	29%
Avoidance	7	13%
Other	11	20%

be taken on highly distasteful legislation or those relating to one broad class of phenomena known as agency problems. The circumstances are complex and vary widely from issue to issue. Each form of delegation has its own set of circumstances.

Table 2.1 provides a breakdown of the primary justifications that explain why Congress delegates to ad hoc commissions, as articulated by the architects of commissions. In the interviews with congressional offices that proposed legislation to establish an ad hoc commission, 38 percent of the respondents noted that expertise was the motive for using a commission, while 29 percent of the respondents cited the need to pare down their workload, 13 percent of the respondents noted avoidance, and 20 percent of the respondents mentioned other motivations.

STRUCTURING LEGISLATIVE CHOICES

Whatever the time frame, the decision to transfer responsibility to an ad hoc commission involves two general stages. The initial stage witnesses a policy problem being identified and put onto the congressional agenda. Once an issue comes to the forefront of the agenda, legislators must decide what action to take. At the second stage issues are discussed, possible solutions are explored, and winning coalitions agree on one of three choices: legislation, obfuscation (intentional inaction), or delegation. Here, a set of benefits encourages Congress to move to delegation. For example, the legislative process inevitably involves both individual representation and institutional lawmaking. The benefits of delegating authority to those with a comparative advantage in performing a given task may exceed the benefits of either legislation or obfuscation. Alternatively, policymaking may be so costly that Congress cannot bear the costs. Tackling the task requires coordinated action by outsiders with the knowledge or time that lawmakers lack. By delegating responsibility to a commission, Congress acquires in a timely fashion information for decision making that may otherwise be subject to uncoordinated or political criteria. Figure 2.1 presents a configuration of the decision tree and the decision making path that leads to the formation of commissions. This includes the characteristic political process associated with each form of commission, the primary concern of the institution, the legislative condition that then prompts delegation, the commission function, and the policy type associated with the commission.

Regardless of how familiar individual lawmakers may be with certain issues, a winning voting bloc of members must learn about an issue. The topics to which legislators and their staff pay serious attention at a given time may come from a reservoir of options generated inside and outside Congress. The president may announce a list of programs in his annual State of the Union address. A cabinet member testifying before a congressional committee may verify the need for legislation. Some problems are heralded by a crisis or other prominent event. The agenda may be set in motion by election results or a turnover in Congress.[33] It may be shaped by proposals that interest groups and other private sector organizations present to a congressional member, to congressional staff, or to a congressional committee.

Agenda setting typically does not change incrementally. Public policy changes in major ways all at once or in a flurry.[34] In addition, several different developments seem to come together at once to produce these changes. People on Capitol Hill focus on certain problems rather than others, and they present policy proposals whether or not they actually solve problems.[35]

Not every topic gets on the congressional agenda. Members and their staffs may know of an issue, for instance, but they may not yet have worked up a solution. These circumstances sometimes lead to symbolic acts: Congress expresses an attitude but prescribes no policy, or Congress prescribes policy but does not act.[36] Severe economic or budgetary constraints, however, may prevent Congress from allocating sufficient funds, even if potential solutions are available. Still, a majority of members may not agree to a solution.

As a collegial, nonhierarchical institution, Congress must construct winning coalitions. Majorities are built in Congress, not elected to it.[37] They are transient and fluctuating; a new majority must be pieced together to deal with each major issue.[38] Congress's decisions reflect this piecing together of majorities, as various leaders (committee chairpersons, party leaders, subject matter experts, and state delegation leaders) negotiate the legislative process to rally enough rank and file members to get a majority, and then maintain these unified blocks at each step of the legislative process to work and vote together in pursuit of legislative goals.[39]

Once a majority of legislators decide what sort of action to take, issues are discussed, possible solutions are sought, and a majority of members must submit to one of three choices: legislation, obfuscation, or delegation.

Figure 2.1
Legislative Path to Commission Formation

	Legislate	Delegate	Obfuscate
STAGE I:		AGENDA SETTING	
STAGE II:		CONGRESSIONAL RESPONSE	
Legislative Decision	**Legislate**	**Delegate**	**Obfuscate**
Institutional Concern	<u>Expertise</u>	<u>Workload</u>	<u>Avoidance</u>
Legislative Condition	Uncertainty, lack of information; lack of technical knowledge	Issues of negligible importance to an office; calendar constraints; legislative scheduling conflicts; multidisciplinary subject matter	Electoral uncertainty
Commission Function	To take advantage of expertise that is unavailable through institutional resources or prohibitively costly to obtain	To pare down workload to more manageable dimensions	To shift blame for unpopular decisions
Policy Type	Distributive	Distributive or Redistributive	Redistributive

When Legislation Is the Preferable Course of Action

Legislation is the most important policymaking device open to Congress. It is the core decision making process of a democratic state.[40] Lawmakers legislate when issues are visible, salient, and solvable; when they feel well-informed about a policy area; when there is substantial agreement on the proper policy; when legislative action will maximize net benefits to their districts and thus help reelection; or when issues are noncontroversial. Until the 104th Congress (1995–1997), for instance, the scope of commemorative legislation gradually broadened, creating federal holidays, recommending special occasions for national observances, funding monuments and memorials, and authorizing the minting of commemorative coins.

In certain policy areas, lawmakers are loath to cede authority. Tax policy, for instance, demands the allocation of considerable congressional resources in order to write detailed legislation. The political advantages of controlling tax policy come not from the duty of setting overall rates, which taxpayers dislike, but from the possibility of granting tax breaks. If outlined correctly, these benefits can target specific clienteles, either through taxes paid into general revenues or through a decrease in revenue sharing stemming from the tax break.[41] Such political benefits are not lightly foregone, not to mention difficult to replicate through a delegation scheme of open-ended mandates.[42] Thus Congress makes tax policy itself, despite the demands that this work entails.

Congress also uses legislation to modify or correct past policy decisions.[43] Review of the effectiveness of statutes through annual appropriations, committee hearings, and other committee investigations often reveals a desire for changes either in basic policy or in administration. New statutes result or old ones change. In this way, legislation provides a means of keeping policy current and responsive to economic and social developments as well as to shifts in public opinion.[44]

Periodically, however, Congress cannot overcome its own shortcomings to craft legislation. The common act of introducing a bill sets off a network of events that may or may not lead to the final passage of a bill. Most bills follow a path in which various steps are fairly predictable but the outcome is usually uncertain.[45] Disparate goals and widely scattered influence on Capitol Hill repeatedly stymie efforts at collective action.

There are limits to what Congress can achieve through the voluntary sacrifices and cooperation that go with legislating. Members are rarely equally concerned about all the issues before Congress. The institution displays the traits and biases of its membership and structure.[46] It is bicameral with different electoral and procedural customs and many competing and in-formed agenda setters. It is representative, especially where geographic interests are concerned. Leaders and committees of both chambers attempt to control the legislative agenda, especially in the absence of unified party control of both the House and the Senate, providing opportunities for

obstruction. Committee leaders who prefer the status quo can use their prerogatives to water down, delay, or even derail a measure. This competition
naturally creates adversarial sources of information for legislators. Even under unified party control, differences in the rules under which lawmakers are
elected may lead them to divide on some issues.[47] Legislative action is divided further by procedure and practice within each chamber of Congress.
Leadership and its committees have the knowledge and incentive to serve
as verifiers of the statements made by competing authorizing committees.[48]
Members of the House minority can use a range of tactics to undermine the
majority's attempts to move legislation. For example, strategically worded
amendments can divide a bill's supporting coalition, and, at least in the short
term, dilatory tactics can slow down legislation. In short, the institution has
become a place where each member is a legislative broker.[49]

Another common hurdle in the contemporary House is that party leaders hesitate to bring major legislation to the floor without a comprehensive
public relations campaign on its behalf. Increasingly, House party leaders lead
by going public.[50] These public relations campaigns require time, money, and
other resources. Additionally, although members typically have well-formed
preferences about the ends they want, considerable uncertainty can exist over
the best means. Proponents of an initiative need to seek out the policy and
political information necessary to draft legislative proposals and persuade
colleagues that such proposals will achieve the desired outcome.[51] The disagreements about policy that characterize even relatively unified partisan
majorities usually require concessions and logrolling if legislation is to move
and party cohesion is to persist. Bringing off these transactions requires time,
effort, and other scarce political resources.[52]

Imperfect information also may hamper legislative action. For a wide variety of issues, information is either unavailable or prohibitively costly to
obtain. Even highly capable members cannot adequately deal with complex
modern problems. No single person can comprehend all of a problem's complexities, collect enough information about a problem, develop a meaningful list of possible choices, or decide which choice maximizes the chances of
the achievement of diverse and often conflicting values.[53] Policymaking may
be so expensive that Congress cannot bear the costs. In such an event, the
legislative branch relies on the expertise of others. Various pieces of a policy
puzzle are given to others for resolution, and the most legislators can do is
lay down the basic outlines of public policy and assemble the recommended
solutions into a final choice.[54]

Imperfect information may arise from considerable technological uncertainty,[55] which makes it difficult for a legislator to know how a policy will
work.[56] Delegating to a panel of experts in specific situations to reduce such
doubt may make sense. For example, the large measure of novelty embodied in the management of the Tsongas National Forest, combined with a
perception of urgency (damage from wildfires), presented a special challenge

to Congress, and proved a major impetus for delegation. Lacking information, time, and technical competence, lawmakers transferred considerable legislative responsibility to the discretion of the National Commission on Natural Resources Disasters (1989). Without the expert advice of the commission, Congress could enact legislation only in vague, general terms, spelling out broad goals rather than providing for the detailed implementation of policy.[57]

Missing information may also be involved when Congress is uncertain about what problems are likely to arise in the future. It would surely be unwise, for example, for a legislature to retain sole authority to give all commands during wartime; the pace of battle is usually far swifter than the pace of legislative decision making.[58] Still another kind of missing information involves political impacts. Even if a legislator has the needed technical information, he or she may be uncertain as to his or her constituents' response to any specific outcome. For the risk-averse lawmaker, the easiest way out of this problem may be to shift responsibility.

When Obfuscation Is the Preferable Course of Action

From time to time Congress will pursue the course of legislating by obfuscating. Forestalling action allows for policy incubation, which entails keeping a proposal alive while it picks up support, while it waits for a better climate, or while consensus begins to form.[59] "There's seven years between the time that a good idea comes along and when it becomes law," a longtime Senate aide commented. Obfuscation enables Congress to forestall hasty action on the issue while the policy matures but also to refine solutions. Both houses fulfill this role, but it is promoted in the Senate because of that body's flexible rules, more varied constituent pressures on senators, and greater media coverage.[60] As one Senate staff assistant to a western Republican representative explained (in reference to the National Commission on Fairness in Military Compensation):[61] "You just don't move 800 pound gorillas through Congress overnight." "If you are hasty in making decisions, you might make the wrong choice," added the legislative assistant to a southwestern Democratic representative. "Waiting may be to your advantage until cooler heads prevail."

The decision to postpone action may also reflect the proximity of the next election. A legislator who wants to preserve his or her political career must not behave so inconsistently toward his or her district that reelection is threatened. If an issue before Congress is sensitive, the closer the date of the next election, the more acutely a lawmaker feels local pressures. Legislators usually need funds for campaigns and do not want to alienate previously supportive interests. Postponing congressional action to a more suitable time may be the safest option. Obfuscation is a legitimate or contrived way to deny responsibility for or to give a plausible defense for an unpopular political action. When local interests collide with larger policy needs in irreconcilable fashion, as in the issue of closing prized military bases, the member might postpone any decision until a nonelection year in order to obscure any causal chain for her decision. Alternatively, lawmakers might want to forge long-term solutions, but as representatives of their constituents they are deterred from acting when most citizens see no difficulty with the immediate situation.[62]

Groups and constituents, however, carry little tolerance for inaction. Doing something is often the only politically feasible option for members, even when no one really knows what to do or when inaction might be just as effective. In such an event Congress looks for what one Senate staff director to a large midwestern state Republican representative calls "an interim or middle measure."

When Delegation Is the Preferable Course of Action

Why does Congress delegate certain policy problems to commissions? Some actions are prompted by the seeming intractable dilemmas endemic to legislative life. Other decisions to delegate are occasioned by imperfect information—legislators who want to develop effective policies, but who lack the expertise needed to draft such policies, often delegate fact-finding and policy development. Still, some delegation happens in the spirit of compromise, as a balanced compromise between legislation and obfuscation. Delegation gives the impression that action is taking place, even when its impact is wholly unknown.

As with most human choices, the motivations for creating commissions are a complex mixture of the obvious and the subtle, the lofty and the crass. In some cases delegation to ad hoc commissions sheds light on the inner workings of Congress. "These things [ad hoc commissions] are a great way for a lot of the politics to be removed from an issue," noted a legislative director whose western Democratic senator proposed the Commission on Executive Organization.[63] "I felt we had to get away from the Congress," remarked a former representative who was responsible for setting up the National Commission on Judicial Discipline and Removal (1989–1990), "because we were making a judgment about ourselves and our own participation."

Party leaders may form commissions to bypass standing committees not only to move legislation more rapidly but also for other substantive reasons such as to circumvent outside committee clienteles or to eschew formal hearings or research reports in favor of informal consultations with colleagues. Many commissions, such as the Commission on the Airplane Crash at Gander, Newfoundland, designed to examine the circumstances surrounding the crash of an Arrow Airlines airplane are a symbolic response to a crisis or are used to satisfy constituencies: "Quite frankly, the commission was kind of a knee-jerk reaction to placate a number of constituents who were trying to get some answers," noted the legislative director whose office repeatedly proposes this commission in each new congress. "A number of television shows air this story over and over and it just pumps people up."

Delegation might test the political waters. As one staff aide to a southwestern senator commented about her boss's then-proposed National Commission on School Finance to Meet the National Education Goals,[64] "We wanted to use a commission as an opportunity for comment and to find out where people stood on a variety of issues." A commission might be used for personal gain, for example, to fend off criticism during political campaigns or to capture personal attention. One staff aide to a midwestern Republican senator declared: "The purpose of this commission [the National Commission on the Future of Disability][65] was to provide some historical context to the senator's record on these issues. Our intent was to draw attention to his [the senator's] record on these issues by creating historical parallels, that is, he introduced this commission back in the 1970s. The rediscovery of this commission really sort of stunned the Clinton [President Bill Clinton] people."

Congressional delegation to a commission might be designed to investigate social crises; to gain public or political consensus; to bring exposure and prestige to new policies and problems and arouse and focus public concern for them; to reformulate a federal program or commitment or to develop a new approach to a problem; to respond to national crises; to foster a winning coalition; to convey a message to executive agencies; to respond to initiatives from presidents who either desire support from Congress or want to fund commissions through the regular appropriations process; to satisfy constituents or interest groups from the member's district or state; because of precedent; for congressional involvement into or oversight of presidential business; or as an option of last resort when Congress has no institutional precedent for dealing with a novel problem.

Table 2.2 summarizes the many justifications members of Congress have used in seeking to create commissions, according to those who were interviewed.

CONCLUSION

Commissions have become a crucial part of legislative life, yet the relevant literature is sparse and unsatisfying. To understand the nuances of lawmaking, it is important to transcend the common focus on the reelection motive and examine the needs, considerations, and motivations for legislative behavior. Every lawmaker is a complex product of the pulling and pushing of a myriad individual, economic, social, and political pressures. As one congressional observer indicates, members scarcely have any other common denominator among themselves other than their equal pay and the

Table 2.2
General Categories of "Problems" Ad Hoc Commissions Are Created to Address as Expressed by Hill People

- to investigate social crises;
- to help formulate innovative domestic policies and facilitate their adoption;
- to attract media attention;
- to educate;
- to gain public or political consensus;
- to legitimize, conceptualize, and bring exposure and prestige to new policies and problems, and arouse and focus public concern for them;
- to reformulate a federal program or commitment, or conceive a new approach to a problem;
- in response to national crises or to bring attention to some volatile social issue;
- to serve as a symbolic response to a crisis;
- to forestall precipitate action;
- to provide a holding action in order to keep an issue alive until Congress is ready to expend direct resources;
- to facilitate a winning coalition;
- to fend off criticism during political campaigns;
- to avoid blame for unpopular decisions;
- to set legislative agendas;
- to convey a message to executive agencies;
- in response to initiatives from presidents who either desire political support from Congress or want to fund commissions through the regular appropriations process;
- to satisfy individual constituents or interest groups from the member's district or state;
- to provide technical support and expertise to grapple with the complexity of modern-day policy problems;
- to manage a growing workload;
- for congressional involvement in or oversight of presidential business;
- because of precedent; and
- as an option of last resort when Congress cannot think of anything else to do.

responsibility of representing a similar number of people.[66] They are as different as the districts and states from which they have come, as different as a California vineyard and a New York City borough.

Yet out of this conglomerate assembly of often conflicting and contradictory elements come collective decisions to create advisory commissions. What different policy issues are given to commissions to manage? As we will see in the next chapter, members of Congress justify their decisions to delegate for a host of reasons, which are not always congruent with the academic literature.

NOTES

1. David R. Mayhew, *Congress: The Electoral Connection* (New Haven, Conn.: Yale University Press, 1974).

2. John W. Kingdon, *Congressmen's Voting Decisions*, 3rd ed. (Ann Arbor: University of Michigan Press, 1989); and R. Douglas Arnold, *The Logic of Congressional Action* (New Haven, Conn.: Yale University Press, 1990).

3. David R. Mayhew, *Congress: The Electoral Connection* (New Haven, Conn.: Yale University Press, 1974).

4. Kenneth A. Shepsle, "Institutional Arrangements and Equilibrium in Multidimensional Voting Models," *American Journal of Political Science* 23 (1979); Morris P. Fiorina, "Universalism, Reciprocity, and Distributive Policy Making in Majority Rule Institutions," in *Research in Public Policy Analysis and Management*, ed. John Crecine (Greenwich, Conn.: Jai Press, Inc., 1981); Barry R. Weingast and William Marshall, "The Industrial Organization of Congress," *Journal of Political Economy* 91 (1988): 775–800.

5. Theodore J. Lowi, "American Business, Public Policy, Case-Studies, and Political Theory," *World Politics* 16 (1964): 677–715; Grant McConnell, *Private Power and American Democracy* (New York: Vintage Books, 1966); Joseph Stigler, "The Reformation of American Administrative Law," *Harvard Law Review* 88 (1971).

6. Morris P. Fiorina, "Legislative Choice of Regulator Forms: Legal Process or Administrative Process?" *Public Choice* 39 (1982): 33–71.

7. Arnold, 1990 *The Logic of Congressional Action*, 101.

8. Ibid., 71.

9. Roger H. Davidson, "The Politics of Executive, Legislative, and Judicial Compensation," in *The Rewards of Public Service*, ed. Robert W. Hartman and Arnold R. Weber (Washington, D.C.: Brookings Institution, 1980); Louis Fisher, *Congressional Abdication on War and Spending* (College Station: Texas A&M University Press, 2000).

10. R. Kent Weaver, *Automatic Government: The Politics of Indexation* (Washington, DC: Brookings Institution, 1988).

11. Ibid., 371.

12. Arthur Lupia and Matthew D. McCubbins, "Who Controls? Information and the Structure of Legislative Decision Making," *Legislative Studies Quarterly* 19 (1994): 361–84.

13. Mancur Olson, *The Logic of Collective Action* (Cambridge: Harvard University Press, 1965); Kenneth R. Mayer, "Closing Military Bases (Finally): Solving Collective Dilemmas Through Delegation," *Legislative Studies Quarterly* 20 (1995): 393–413. Delegation can prevent free riding and enforce discipline in lieu of strong parties. This gives Congress the capacity to discipline members as in parliamentary systems. Thus, delegation to an organization like a commission fulfills

a function that in other systems of government is performed by strong parties.

14. Randall B. Ripley and Grace A. Franklin, *Congress, the Bureaucracy, and Public Policy* (Homewood, Ill.: Dorsey Press, 1984); Lawrence C. Dodd and Richard L. Schott, *Congress and the Administrative State* (New York: MacMillan Publishing Company, 1986); and D. Roderick Kiewiet and Matthew D. McCubbins, *The Logic of Delegation: Congressional Parties and the Appropriations Process* (Chicago: University of Chicago Press, 1991).

15. Robert Axelrod, *The Evolution of Cooperation* (New York: Basic Books, 1984); and Michael Taylor *The Possibility of Cooperation* (Cambridge: Cambridge University Press, 1987).

16. Kiewiet and McCubbins, *The Logic of Delegation*, 28.

17. Terry Moe, "The New Economics of Organization," *American Journal of Political Science* 28 (1984): 756.

18. Barbara Sinclair, "Partisan Imperatives and Institutional Constraints: Republican Party Leadership in the House and Senate, in *New Majority or Old Minority? The Impact of the Republicans on Congress*, ed. Nicol C. Rae and Colton C. Campbell (Lanham, Md.: Rowman and Littlefield Publishers, Inc., 1999).

19. David Epstein and Sharyn O'Halloran, *Delegating Powers: A Transaction Cost Politics Approach to Policy Making under Separate Powers* (New York: Cambridge University Press, 1999), 12.

20. Ibid., 6.

21. Ibid.

22. Sinclair "Partisan Imperatives," 5.

23. Richard L. Hall, *Participation in Congress* (New Haven, Conn.: Yale University Press, 1996), 66.

24. Similar criticisms of other areas are made by Donald P. Green and Ian Shapiro. They argue that the rational choice approach should be fundamentally rethought. Many of the methodological failings of applied rational choice scholarship, for instance, are traceable to a style of theorizing that stresses the development of post hoc accounts of known facts. Donald P. Green and Ian Shapiro, *Pathologies of Rational Choice Theory* (New Haven, Conn.: Yale University Press, 1994), 33–46.

25. Rochelle Jones and Peter Woll, *The Private World of Congress* (New York: Free Press, 1979), 10.

26. Hall, *Participation in Congress*, 66.

27. George J. Gordon and Michael E. Milakovich, *Public Administration in America*, 5th ed. (New York: St. Martin's Press, 1995).

28. Quoted in Margaret Kriz, "Still Changing," *National Journal*, December 6, 1997, 2461.

29. Thomas P. O'Neill, with William Novak, *Man of the House* (New York: St. Martin's Press, 1987).

30. Steven Kelman, *Making Public Policy* (New York: Basic Books, 1987), 250.

31. Norman J. Ornstein, "The Deficit: A Look at the Bright Side," *New York Times Book Review*, June 3, 1990. Ornstein is reviewing Joseph White and Aaron Wildavsky, *The Deficit and the Public Interest* (Berkeley: University of California/Russell Sage Foundation, 1989).

32. Mark Carl Rom, *Public Spirit in the Thrift Tragedy* (Pittsburgh: University of Pittsburgh Press, 1996), 15.

33. John W. Kingdon, *Agendas, Alternatives and Public Policies* (Boston: Little Brown, 1984).

34. Ibid.

35. John W. Kingdon, "Agendas," in Donald C. Bacon, Roger H. Davidson, and Morton Keller, eds., *The Encyclopedia of the United States Congress* vol. 1 (New York: Simon & Schuster 1995): 183–184.

36. Mayhew, *Congress: The Electoral Connection*, 1974, 132. Mayhew asserts that the reason why a legislative body arranged like Congress can be expected to engage in symbolic action is that in a large class of legislative undertakings the electoral payment is for positions rather than for effects.

37. John Manley, "The Conservative Coalition in Congress," *American Behavioral Scientist* 7 (1973): 224.

38. Norman C. Thomas and Karl A. Lamb, *Congress: Politics and Practice* (New York: Random House, 1964).

39. John Bibby and Roger H. Davidson, *On Capitol Hill: Studies in the Legislative Process* (New York: Holt, Rinehart and Winston, Inc., 1967), 15.

40. Charles O. Jones, "A Way of Life and Law: Presidential Address, American Political Science Association, 1994," *American Political Science Review* 89 (March 1995): 1–9.

41. Epstein and O'Halloran, *Delegating Powers*, 1997.

42. Ibid.

43. Thomas and Lamb, *Congress: Politics and Practice*, Roger H. Davidson and Walter J. Oleszek, *Congress and Its Members*, 4th ed. (Washington, D.C.: CQ Press, 1994).

44. Davidson and Oleszek, *Congress and Its Members*, 4th ed.

45. Walter J. Oleszek, *Congressional Procedures and the Policy Process*, 3rd ed. (Washington, D.C.: CQ Press, 1989); and James A. Robinson, *The House Rules Committee* (Indianapolis: Bobbs-Merrill, 1963).

46. Davidson and Oleszek, *Congress and Its Members*, 4th ed.

47. Ibid., 391.

48. Weingast and Marshall, "The Industrial Organization of Congress"; Kiewiet and McCubbins, *The Logic of Delegation*; Gary W. Cox and Mathew D. McCubbins, *Legislative Leviathan: Party Government in the House* (Berkeley: University of California Press, 1993).

49. Paul Light, *Artful Work: The Politics of Social Security Reform* (New York: Random House, 1985).

50. Barbara Sinclair, *Legislators, Leaders, and Lawmaking: The U.S. House of Representatives in the Postreform Era* (Baltimore: Johns Hopkins University Presss, 1995).

51. C. Lawrence Evans and Walter J. Oleszek, "Procedural Features of House Republican Rule," in Nicol C. Rae and Colton C. Campbell, ed., *New Majority or Old Minority? The Impact of the Republicans on Congress* (Lanham, Md.: Rowman and Littlefield Publishers, Inc., 1999).

52. Ibid., 9.

53. Amihai Glazer and Thomas H. Hammond, "A Review Essay on Theories of Delegation," paper presented at the annual meeting of the American Political Science Association, Chicago, 1995; Christine DeGregorio, "Assets and Access: Linking Lobbyists and Lawmakers in Congress," in *The Interest Group Connection:*

Electioneering, Lobbying, and Policymaking in Washington, ed. Paul S. Herrnson, Ronald G. Shaiko, and Clyde Wilcox (Chatham, N.J.: Chatham House, 1998).

54. Thomas and Lamb, *Congress: Politics and Practice*, 22.

55. James E. Katz, "Science, Technology, and Congress," *Science* 30 (1993): 41–50.

56. Elizabeth M. Martin, "The Impact of Costly Decision Making on Congressional Delegation," paper presented at the annual meeting of the American Political Science Association, Chicago, 1995.

57. U.S. Congress, House, Committee on Agriculture, "Establishment of the National Commission on Natural Resources Disasters," 100th Cong., 1st sess., Serial 101-4, March 15, 1989.

58. Glazer and Hammond, "Review Essay," 4.

59. Nelson W. Polsby, "Policy Analysis and Congress," *Public Policy* 18 (1969): 61–93.

60. Oleszek, *Congressional Procedures*, 3rd ed. 25.

61. The National Commission on Fairness in Military Compensation was designed to (1) determine the extent to which military personnel or their dependents rely on food stamps, the special supplemental food program under the Child Nutrition Act of 1966, and other federal or local assistance programs as necessary supplements to their regular military compensation, and the circumstances that lead to such reliance; and (2) submit to the president and Congress a report on its findings and its recommendations on possible changes in the military pay structure so that military personnel would receive adequate compensation and no longer rely on such other forms of assistance.

62. Davidson and Oleszek, *Congress and Its Members*, 4th ed., 386.

63. The Commission on Executive Organization was proposed to examine and make recommendations with respect to an effective and practicable organization of the executive branch of the federal government.

64. The National Commission on School Finance to Meet the National Education Goals was proposed in order to study what has been learned from the research on innovations in practice that furthers an understanding of what is necessary and what the cost implications are for achieving the national education goals.

65. The National Commission on the Future of Disability was proposed to study and report to the president and Congress on the adequacy of federal programs serving persons with disabilities, especially programs authorized under the Social Security Act.

66. Neil MacNeil, *Forge of Democracy: The House of Representatives* (New York: David McKay Company Inc., 1963), 116.

—————Chapter 3—————

The Politics of Congressional Delegation

Table 3.1 samples the different policy issues that are managed by the three dominant commission types, according to interview respondents. As noted in the introduction, these categories are not mutually exclusive or empirically pure types. They occasionally compete and overlap with other policy questions. However, they do represent the primary justifications which Capitol Hill appropriates in setting up ad hoc commissions. A search of the workload for the 93rd (1973–1975) through 105th (1997–1999) Congresses suggests that an average of 71 of the 10,000 or so bills introduced in each Congress propose establishing bipartisan congressional commissions (see Appendix 3). It is not feasible to track systematically the creation of all congressional commissions, due to their possible creation as part of large, omnibus measures. Of the 856 measures introduced between 1973 and 1999 the preponderance of these bills appear to have been tabled in committee.

DELEGATING TO ACQUIRE EXPERTISE

Congress appoints an ad hoc commission to untangle especially difficult policy problems where members (and their staffs) do not have sufficient knowledge, background, or expertise to make a well-informed decision. Many policy problems recur in slightly altered form, leaving few issues on which an individual member of Congress (especially an incumbent who finds that the same issues arise year after year) must undertake more comprehensive

Table 3.1
Sample of Subjects for Which Commissions Have Been Proposed

Workload	Expertise	Blame Avoidance
Academia	Air/Highway Safety	Entitlements
Business Development	Biomedical Research	Congressional Ethics
Child Support	Behavior Research	Closures & Realignment
Commemorative Events	Fire Protection	Federal Election Laws
Educational Readiness	Geothermal Energy	Federal Pay
Federal Holidays	Infant Mortality	Gun Control
Productivity & Work Quality	Telemedicine	Tax Reform
Federal Court Studies	Telecommunications	Welfare Reform
Sports/Recreation	Sleeping Disorders	Campaign Reform
Freight Rates	Wildlife Disasters	Federal Aid Reform
More Effective Government	Electronic Fund Transfers	Presidential Nominations
Supplies and Shortages	Organ Procurement and Transplant Reimbursement	Deficit Reduction
Obesity	Genetic Research & Engineering	Federal Retirement Reform
Export Development & Promotion	Emission of Ozone-Depleting Chlorofluorocarbons & Halons	Fiscal Priorities
Records of Congress	Methanol	Economic Reform
Federal Paperwork	Superconductivity	Medicare Reform
Hostel System	Sciences Review	Campaign Practices
Libraries	Terrorism	Presidential Debate
Youth Employment	Medical Policy	Fair Elections
U.S. Rep. Bicentennial	Year 2000 Computer Problem	Census Data

analysis.[1] Still, there are instances that occur when Congress faces an issue that is new for most. It is expensive for lawmakers to become experts, in terms of time, which equates to political capital. Therefore, lawmakers are likely to remain novices on many issues. When the legislative branch lacks knowledge in matters of technical expertise, it looks for ways to enlist help.[2] A veteran legislative director to a western Democratic representative highlighted this point in connection with the proposed creation of the Commission on Integration of Workers' Compensation Medical Benefits:[3] "There are times when it's more beneficial to the public to get a group of people who are trained in the specific area Congress is looking at and who don't have a political bent one way or the other to help with a complex problem."

Whereas in the past many lawmakers did their own research and drafting, they now delegate these tasks to personal staff assistants, committee aides, experts from the legislature's three analytic agencies—the Congressional Research Service (CRS), the Congressional Budget Office (CBO), the General Accounting Office (GAO)—or outside experts. Today, the vast majority of lawmakers, especially in the Senate, are generalists, not specialists.[4] Members vary in their familiarity with policy issues. Many lack professional or specialized backgrounds and acquire substantive knowledge through service,[5] but they are not elected on the basis of professional qualifications. Today's members are more dependent on staff than were their colleagues of a few decades ago, in part because the issues are more complex and because more informed constituents look to Capitol Hill for assistance and information.[6]

Table 3.2 lists prior occupations of members of Congress from the 83rd (1953–1955) through 105th (1997–1999) Congresses. While lawyers, business executives, and bankers continue to dominate both chambers, the number of scientists and engineers is relatively small. "We have a nonscientific Senate confronting a world of scientific challenges and opportunities that dwarf those available to previous generations," wrote Republican Senator Pete Domenici of New Mexico.[7] "Yet only a couple of members of the United States Senate might be able to run a proper test-tube experiment." Although the overall educational level in Congress has increased in proportion to earlier times, the number of day-one representatives and senators ready to disentangle technically complicated problems remains small; thus, they constitute a group ready to seek expertise.

Additionally, most personal aides in the House and Senate are well educated but young and transient, and few are likely to be Capitol Hill lifers.[8] In their words, they are fresh from college, "learned in undergraduate level material" but lacking the advanced schooling required to master "extremely complicated issues," such as the technical nature of telemedicine, fire protection, air and highway safety, geothermal energy, sleeping disorders, and narcotics, or areas like the military's grand strategy or other problems that

Table 3.2
Prior Occupations of Representatives, 83rd–105th Congresses, 1953–1997

Occupation	83rd	84th	86th	89th	90th	91st	92nd	93rd	94th	95th
Acting/ entertainer	—	—	—	—	—	—	—	—	—	—
Aeronautics	—	—	—	—	—	—	—	—	—	—
Agriculture	53	51	45	44	39	34	36	38	31	16
Business or banking	131	127	130	156	161	159	145	155	140	118
Clergy	—	—	—	3	3	2	2	4	5	6
Congressional aide	—	—	—	—	—	—	—	—	—	5
Education	46	47	41	68	57	59	61	59	64	70
Engineering	5	5	3	9	6	6	3	2	3	2
Journalism	36	33	35	43	39	39	30	23	24	27
Labor leader	—	—	—	3	2	3	3	3	3	6
Law	247	245	242	247	246	242	236	221	221	222
Law enforcement	—	—	—	—	—	2	1	2	2	7
Medicine	6	5	4	3	3	5	6	5	5	2
Military	—	—	—	—	—	—	—	—	—	—
Professional sports	—	—	—	—	—	—	—	—	—	—
Public service/ politics	—	—	—	—	—	—	—	—	—	—
Veteran	246	261	261	310	320	320	316	317	307	—

Note: Dashes indicate years and occupations for which data were not compiled.
Source: Norman J. Ornstein, Thomas E. Mann, and Michael J. Malbin, *Vital Statistics on Congress, 1997–1998* (Washington, D.C.: American Enterprise Institute, 1998). Reprinted with the permission of The American Enterprise Institute for Public Policy Research, Washington, D.C.

might take years to understand. Many staff assistants also note that they are exceptionally busy "learning the ropes" of congressional work. The bulk of personal staffers explain that their positions are rarely defined by professional qualifications; they are hired within a political context and their stay on Capitol Hill often lasts only two or three years. Members hire them young, burn them out, and send them on.[9] In a 1998 survey of 234 House and Senate staffers, a majority of aides on both sides of the aisle said it was no longer "rewarding and fun to work in Congress." And they expect to be gone within three years after starting their jobs.[10]

Generally these bright and ambitious people draft bills, write speeches and briefing materials, suggest policy initiatives, analyze pending legislation, prepare position papers on assigned legislative issues, and act as liaisons with other House and Senate staff, government agencies, and outside groups.[11]

96th	97th	98th	99th	100th	101st	102nd	103rd	104th	105th
—	—	—	—	1	2	2	1	1	1
—	—	3	4	3	3	1	2	1	1
19	28	26	29	20	19	20	19	20	22
127	134	138	147	142	138	157	131	162	181
6	3	2	2	2	2	2	2	2	1
10	11	16	16	—	—	—	—	—	—
57	59	43	37	38	42	57	66	75	74
2	5	5	6	4	4	7	5	6	8
11	21	22	20	20	17	25	24	15	12
4	5	2	2	2	2	3	2	2	1
205	194	200	190	184	184	183	181	171	172
5	5	5	8	7	8	5	10	11	10
6	6	6	5	3	4	5	6	10	12
—	—	1	1	0	0	1	0	0	1
—	—	3	3	5	4	3	1	2	3
—	—	—	—	94	94	61	87	102	100
—	—	—	—	—	—	—	—	—	—

In a typical interview, the legislative director for Democratic senator from a small northeastern state described how his staff's limited knowledge in a technical area was the genesis of the Commission on Retirement Income Policy:[12]

> This is an area where you have a network of systems, some may work together, some may work at cross-purposes. My staff aides are not proficient with the skills, the background, or the information needed to comprehend and bring together all these complexities. To build a staff that had the ability in this alone would take more than the limited resources of this office. What we [the senate office] are trying to do with the commission is to build our capability of dealing with each of these issues.

Another legislative director described how his staff's limited knowledge in a technical area prompted the proposal of the Commission on the Dual-Use Application of Facilities and Resources at White Sands Missile Range:[13]

"If you go around Congress, there really isn't a certain profile or background in a staffer, especially on a member's staff. No one in this office, for instance, has been trained, specifically, to investigate this type of thing." No institution in the United States is the focus of a greater volume of studies and analysis exploring public problems and recommending solutions. The flow of information through the office of even the most junior legislator can be overwhelming. Analysis of policy problems arrives in a river of books, papers, articles, memoranda, reports, videotapes, and electronic mail messages. It is presented in hearings, in private meetings, through the electronic "Net," at fund-raisers, in phone conversations, and over meals in Washington's restaurants.[14]

Congressional government may or may not be committee government, as Woodrow Wilson held.[15] But much of Congress's fact-finding takes place in committee and subcommittee rooms. These work groups are critical to deliberation. They are gatherers of information, sifters of alternatives, drafters and refiners of legislation.[16] Committees create cadres of experts. As policy experts, committee members provide direction for those unfamiliar with a particular policy area. For the non-committee member, reliance upon the judgments of experts is an efficient and rational way to make decisions in policy matters beyond one's area of specialization.[17] Thus when these traditional channels of lawmaking are stymied the quality of legislation suffers.[18]

A legislative environment in which issues are too difficult for committees to manage and which is so fast-paced that even executive agencies are ill-equipped to do adequate analysis, is the usual situation that interview respondents said compels them to seek advice from a commission of experts. Once Congress conceded the seriousness of the AIDS problem, for instance, the unprecedented nature of the disease was too daunting for Congress and its committees. As we will see in the next chapter, when Congress tried to direct an executive agency to prepare detailed briefs defining what to examine, even the agency called on Congress to establish a commission of experts. Scientists from the Institute of Medicine and National Academy of Sciences requested that a commission should be created outside the federal administrative structure. An independent commission, according to the Institute of Medicine, would have the specialized skills to help understand the epidemic, to provide some strategic planning and direction, and to pool knowledge and expertise in order to formulate key recommendations for Congress.[19]

By delegating some of its policymaking authority to "expertise commissions," Congress creates institutions that reduce uncertainty. Tremendous gains accrue as a result of delegating tasks to other organizations with a comparative advantage in performing them. Commissions are especially adaptable devices for addressing problems that do not fall neatly within committees' jurisdictional boundaries. They can complement and supplement the regular committees. In the 1990s, it became apparent that committees were ailing—beset by mounting workloads, duplication and jurisdictional battles, and conflicts between program and funding panels. But relevant expertise can be mobilized by a commission that brings specialized information to its tasks, especially if commission members and staff are selected on the basis of education, their training, and their experience in the area which cross-cut the responsibilities of several standing committees.

The presence and politics of the sorts of problems that are given to expertise commissions are not always discernible to the public. The policy issue will likely deliver plentiful group and geographic benefits, which makes many interests better off and a few obviously worse off. Constructing a comprehensive public health policy to fight a novel disease like AIDS, for instance, did not impose any direct harmful effects on constituents. To the contrary, government actions that provide for medical research are popular with legislators and their constituents because they appear beneficial and do not encounter opposition on the basis of distributional issues. Distributive impulses are irresistible when they convey tangible benefits and make many interests together—whether directly affected or not—better off, and they are natural in Congress, which as a nonhierarchical institution must build coalitions in order to function.[20] The broadly distributive nature of AIDS placated the more vocal opponents of delegation to the National Commission on AIDS. The complexity of AIDS reduced the level of conflict on Capitol Hill, and thus removed the need for techniques to disguise the allocation of resources or to make them more palatable. Although controversial aspects were present in the formation of the commission, the distributive character of fighting a deadly hazard that embodied such an immense measure of novelty did not separate liberals and conservatives.

The arena that develops around distributive policies is one where there is no real basis for discriminating between those who should and those who should not benefit.[21] In the congressional deliberation over the creation of the Commission on AIDS, lawmakers were responsive to considerations of equality, impartiality, and moderation to the extent that they saw the AIDS epidemic as a public health crisis.

Unlike more visible public issues, technical areas generally do not display patterns in which the decentralized character of Congress comes into play when local interests collide with larger policy needs. The purpose of delegating tasks to expert commissions is not to protect legislators from the wrath of their constituents. Such distributive politics reflects national policy that is a mosaic of local interests.

DELEGATING TO REDUCE WORKLOAD

Issues of negligible importance, legislative problems that overload normal congressional channels, calendar constraints (due to the logjam of bills near the end of Congress or the end of a session necessitating long, hectic sessions which impair efficiency and tempers of lawmakers), shortness of legislative time, and legislative schedule conflicts lead to workload commissions. Though sometimes hard to measure and subject to manipulation and packaging, the workload commission is an important determinant of Congress's structure, its patterns of activity, and its policy outputs. Despite the amount of effort Congress expends, the workload is still overwhelming. Time spent constructing legislative proposals, holding hearings and investigations, writing reports, striking deals, and building coalitions requires the expenditure of valuable resources and involves the use of legislative and staff resources that could go to more pressing matters. Some tasks are too cumbersome to manage through normal channels. Where lawmaking was once a part-time occupation, Congress's workload has today grown to huge proportions and complexity.[22] As John F. Kennedy was fond of remarking, the Clays, Calhouns, and Websters of the nineteenth century could afford to devote a whole generation or more to deliberating the great controversies at hand. Representative and Speaker Jospeh W. Martin (R-Mass.), who entered the House in 1925, described the unhurried atmosphere of earlier days and the workload changes during his service:

> The issues themselves were fundamentally simpler than those that surge in upon us today in such a torrent that the individual member cannot analyze all of them adequately before he is compelled to vote. In my years in Congress the main issues were few enough so that almost any conscientious member could with application make himself a quasi-expert at least. In the complexity and volume of today's legislation, however, most members have to trust somebody else's word or the recommendation of a committee. Now days bills, which thirty years ago would have been thrashed out for hours or days, go through in ten minutes.[23]

In recent decades, legislative business has kept the House and Senate almost continuously in session.[24] The average two-year Congress sees the Senate in session nearly 300 eight-hour days, with the more efficient House close behind.[25] And while their number of days in session has dropped considerably in the past ten years, the number of trips the average member takes to vote on the House floor has more than quadrupled, going from 240 in the 87th Congress (1961–1963) to 1,122 in the 103rd Congress (1993–1995)—roughly three votes a day while the House is in session.[26] In the first session of the 105th Congress (1997–1999) the House was presented with 3,430 bills and resolutions.[27] If it had remained in session every minute for the full first year of its term, the House could have given roughly fifty minutes to each measure. In short, most proposals that go into the "hopper" are never expected to pass.

Contemporary lawmakers are stretched too thin, pulled between allocating their legislative resources to constituency concerns, opportunities, and policy formulation. The congressional career is so time-consuming and so mentally and physically absorbing that lawmakers rarely have energy left to give to anyone or anything else.[28] In 1997, at the beginning of the 105th Congress, House members claimed nearly five committee—including sub-committee—assignments and senators averaged almost ten. Multiple assignments mean inevitable scheduling conflicts and "committee hopping" when two or more panels are meeting at once. In resolving this strain, members seldom have sufficient time, information, or foresight to consider the range of viable activities, weigh their relative costs and benefits, and rank them. "Everything happens at once," said Representative Walter B. Jones, Jr. (R-N.C.), "so the challenge is to use time efficiently."[29] "Time and practicality require that some issues go out of the mainstream of the legislative body," said one senate staff aide who was interviewed.

Members of Congress realize they can manage only a certain amount of public business; the rest they must either neglect or delegate. Various pieces of a legislative problem are delegated to others for resolution, and the most Congress may be able to do is assemble the recommended solutions. The Reciprocal Trade Agreements Act (RTAA) of 1934 provides an early example of Congress's use of delegation to partition its workload. Congress yielded to the president its authority over an area that had engrossed its energies for more than a hundred years. Tariffs became a duty too time-consuming and too intricate for a large legislative body, and by their nature all but impossible for a legislator to approach from the standpoint of national rather than constituency interest.[30] The problems of the Great Depression were too overwhelming for Congress, and the extended time required to adjust thousands of individual tariff schedules too demanding.

The century-long trend toward institutionalization of Congress slows down the processing of legislation. While structure and routine enable Congress to cope with a certain amount of contemporary change, they can also lead to organizational rigidity. This can frustrate policymaking, especially in times of rapid social or political change.[31] Complex structures can create multiple points of entanglement, producing delays and confusion. Such obstacles frustrate even altruistic intentions; necessary information is costly to obtain; bicameralism and supermajority requirements inhibit speedy action; and legislative bargaining (logrolling)[32] can inflate the costs of even the simplest policy initiatives.[33]

The growth of government and the changing role of the individual legislator have added work for Congress as well. The institution's workload—in terms of both legislation and constituency service—has expanded in scope. Capitol Hill today confronts a variety of demands unmatched in all but the most turbulent years of its earlier history.[34] The overall number of measures introduced and enacted in Congress, votes, hours in session, meetings, and hearings have seen several pronounced increases or decreases, from an average of about 10,000 bills per Congress in the 1940s and early 1950s to nearly

20,000 in the 89th Congress (1965–1967), although the number dropped steadily in the 1970s to 15,587 in the 95th Congress (1977–1979). But the overall trend reflects a larger workload that affects output and job difficulty.[35] The introduction of measures in both the House and Senate follows a pattern of long-term growth followed by gradual downturns. This reflects not so much slackened activity as an altered agenda: for example, the tendency to enact lengthy "megabills"—to which many commissions are attached—for matters that cannot be easily resolved, thus enabling Congress to devote more time to executive oversight.[36] Table 3.3, focusing on congressional productivity shows the number of public and private bills enacted into law and the number of pages contained in enacted bills. The number of bills enacted has fluctuated, but broader patterns are evident. An average of 900 or so bills per Congress in the 1950s fell to 700 or so bills in the 1960s and 600 or so in the 1970s and 1980s.[37] From the 1950s through the mid-1960s, the average number of pages per statute was approximately 2.5, jumping to approximately 5 pages in the mid-1970s, and reaching 7 pages in the 1980s. The slow decline in the number of private bills (such as claims for damages or immigration matters) enacted indicates efforts to reduce the workload.

Time is a most precious commodity on Capitol Hill.[38] As a former staff aide who spent several years working on the House Armed Services Committee contended, "It's very difficult with all the issues before Congress to spend months studying one issue." Commissions that ease workload pressures develop around such concerns. The pressure of time constraints proved to be the overriding reason for creating the National Commission on Judicial Discipline and Removal:

> Congress didn't believe, with three [judicial] impeachments, that it had time to try all these cases individually before the House and then in the Senate. The impeachments could go on for weeks. That was clearly a point of view that was widely shared. Generally, you don't use a commission unless the problem is large and long-term, multidisciplinary, or difficult for a committee to handle. You could hold hearings and still not have a grasp of the picture. The problem gets to be more than a committee can handle.

A survey of legislative staffers in members' personal offices provides similar accounts: "Legislatively, there are maybe six or so areas we really end up getting involved in, and all these other things are just blips that show up on the screen and disappear. There just isn't time."[39]

The average lawmaker's daily schedule, both at home and in the nation's capital, is long on demand and short on time (see Tables 3.4 and 3.5). Less time goes to serious study of legislation. Legislators spend only about a third of their time in the House or Senate chamber or in committee or subcommittee meetings.[40] Casework has become a significant part of a legislator's activities. The average number of days the House member spent at home in the district increased from about 25 per congress in the early 1960s to more than 250 per congress in the early 1980s.[41] Congressional offices engage in more constituency casework, now generating from five to ten times as much mail as they did three decades ago,[42] and this does not include electronic mail. More than 44 percent of the personal staffs of representatives and 31 percent of those of senators now work in district or state offices, marking a dramatic increase since the early 1970s.[43]

Most casework requests involve questions on the status of applications, requests for services or preferments, explanations of bureaucratic decisions, or complaints.[44] While this work can become complicated, the necessary response often involves contacting the appropriate agency and asking for a reply. The request does not require the legislator's staff to do intensive investigation or to make questionable judgments. But it does take time away from the more labor intensive writing of a bill or the job of original research and data analysis.

Committees may also act as hurdles in the long obstacle course that any bill must successfully complete to become law. Legislative concerns require days of hearings, hours of sitting, and pages of testimony, not to mention the thousands of measures delegated to committees, of which only a small percentage are considered or prioritized by leadership. Committee leaders are also obliged to review an administration's agenda. Committee work is not limited to bills and resolutions. Among committees' other tasks is the oversight of agencies. An increasing number of hearings and reports are devoted to this function. One study found that oversight has become more a part of routine work and not just the work of specialized units.[45] Looking at congressional committee hearing and meeting activity for the first six months (January 1 to July 4) of each odd-numbered year from 1961 to 1983, the study concludes that the overall level of hearing and meeting activity did not vary much from 1961 to 1971. The mean for this period was 1,888 days. In 1973, however, the total number of days of activity jumped by 450 days. By 1975, the total number of oversight days averaged 477, more than three times the 1961–1965 average.[46] Table 3.6 indicates the increasing work added by congressional oversight. The workload commission alleviates certain committee workload pressures.

Besides oversight, the Senate holds time-consuming hearings to give advice on and consent to presidential nominations of judges and other appointees—hearings that may require much effort by the senators involved.[47] Staff, both personal and committee, observe that time constraints—a consequence of recent staff cuts,[48] increased constituent casework, and expanded committee activities, additional legislative proposals, and scheduling conflicts—keep personal offices and committees from devoting to every issue the kind of attention needed. "There are not enough hours in the day, or days in the

Table 3.3
Congressional Workload, 80th–104th Congresses, 1947–1996

Congress		Public Bills			Private Bills		
		No. of bills enacted	Total pages of statutes	Average pages per statute	No. of bills enacted	Total pages of statutes	Average pages per statute
80th	(1947–49)	906	2,236	2.5	458	182	0.40
81st	(1949–51)	921	2,314	2.5	1,103	417	0.38
82nd	(1951–53)	594	1,585	2.7	1,023	360	0.35
83rd	(1953–55)	781	1,899	2.4	1,002	365	0.36
84th	(1955–57)	1,028	1,848	1.8	893	364	0.41
85th	(1957–59)	936	2,435	2.6	784	349	0.45
86th	(1959–61)	800	1,774	2.2	492	201	0.41
87th	(1961–63)	885	2,078	2.3	684	255	0.37
88th	(1963–65)	666	1,975	3.0	360	144	0.40
89th	(1965–67)	810	2,912	3.6	473	188	0.40
90th	(1967–69)	640	2,304	3.6	362	128	0.35
91st	(1969–71)	695	2,927	4.2	246	104	0.42

92nd	(1971–73)	607	2,330	3.8	161	67	0.42
93rd	(1973–75)	649	3,443	5.3	123	48	0.39
94th	(1975–77)	588	4,121	7.0	141	75	0.53
95th	(1977–79)	633	5,403	8.5	170	60	0.35
96th	(1979–81)	613	4,947	8.1	123	63	0.51
97th	(1981–83)	473	4,343	9.2	56	25	0.45
98th	(1983–85)	623	4,893	7.8	54	26	0.48
99th	(1985–87)	664	7,198	10.8	24	13	0.54
100th	(1987–89)	713	4,839	6.8	48	29	0.60
101st	(1989–91)	650	5,767	8.9	16	9	0.56
102nd	(1991–93)	590	7,544	12.8	20	11	0.55
103rd	(1993–95)	465	7,542	16.2	8	9	1.10
104th	(1995–97)	333	6,369	19.1	4	4	1.00

Source: Norman J. Ornstein, Thomas E. Mann, and Michael J. Malbin, *Vital Statistics on Congress, 1997–1998* (Washington, D.C.: American Enterprise Institute, 1998). Reprinted with the permission of the American Enterprise Institute for Public Policy Research, Washington, D.C.

Table 3.4
Washington Schedule for Senator Bob Graham, Tuesday, June 17, 1999

8:00 A.M.	Breakfast with staff in Senate Dining Room
9:00 A.M.	Priorities Office
FYI 9:30 A.M.	Environment and Public Works Committee Hearing re: Solid Waste
9:30–9:55 A.M.	Phone calls Office
10:00–11:00 A.M.	Finance Committee Hearing re: Nomination of Larry Summers 215 Dirksen
FYI 10:00 A.M.–2:00 P.M.	CARE Event to assemble packages to be sent to Honduran families left homeless in the wake of Hurricane Mitch HC-5 Capitol
11:00–11:50 A.M.	Legislative Time Office
12:00–1:00 P.M.	Lunch with former Senator David Pryor Senate Dining Room **Also in the Dining Room will be Sen. Torricelli and NFL Commissioner Paul Tabliabue
1:00–1:40 P.M.	DPC Lunch (Lunch begins at 12:30 P.M.) Guest speaker: Secretary of Education, Dick Riley S-211, the Capitol
1:40–1:50 P.M.	Photo with the students of the F. K. Sweet Elementary School in Ft. Pierce Senate Steps
2:00–2:25 P.M.	Aging Committee Hearing re: Graham Pension Bill 106 Dirksen
FYI 2:00 P.M.	Finance Committee Hearing re: Medicaid and School-Based Services 215 Dirksen
2:30–2:50 P.M.	Pensacola Chamber of Commerce Fly-In You will be making brief remarks to the group 385 Russell
3:00–3:50 P.M.	Closed Intelligence Hearing re: former Sen. Warren Rudman will be testifying on DOE reorganization 219 Hart
4:00–4:30 P.M.	Meeting on Medicare and Prescription Drugs Office
4:30–5:00 P.M.	Phone calls Office
5:00–5:20 P.M.	Jefferson Awards Presentation You will be presenting awards to three Floridians in honor of their commitment to volunteer work Russell Caucus Room
5:30–6:00 P.M.	Meeting with Congressmen Alcee Hastings, Bill Dalahunt, and John Conyers re: Haiti Office

Table 3.4 (continued)

FYI	6:00–8:00 P.M.	National Wetlands Awards Reception SC-5, the Capitol
FYI	6:30–8:30 P.M.	Campaign Reception for Mel Carnahan Phoenix Park Hotel, Powerscourt Restaurant 520 North Capitol Street, NW
FYI	7:00–9:00 P.M.	Informal Dinner of the Inter-American Dialogue Honoring: Rubens Antonio Barbosa, Ambassador of Brazil 1211 Connecticut Avenue, NW

session, to secure the number of co-sponsors needed to warrant a hearing or a mark up for the bill, or to provide staff with enough time to adequately investigate," declared a tired administrative assistant to a western Republican representative. "So you introduce a commission to highlight the issue and to move it forward," she added.

Skilled committee chairs can use hearings to affect the chances of proposed legislation as well as sermonize. Scheduling of committee activities is complicated by the large number of committees and subcommittees, and is sometimes haphazard. Schedules overlap and hearings are not always well attended. The average senator holds ten committee and subcommittee seats and the average representative seven seats. Committee quorums are not guaranteed, and members are hard-pressed to cope with their crowded schedules.

Committees select a small percentage of bills for consideration. Many staff observe that time constraints prevent committees from devoting the necessary attention to every issue, especially large comprehensive packages. Additional committee business outside traditional legislative procedures also occupies a large amount of committee attention. Some is routine and requires no legislative action, but other items mandate reports or recommendations to be provided to Congress on major questions. These require detailed review by the committee staff or even hearings and full committee participation. While the numbers of executive communications transmitted to the House decreased in the 1980s, the overall trend of the last fifty years has been one of dramatic growth.[49] For instance, the number of executive department messages rose from a low of 504 in the 73rd Congress (1933–1935) to a high of 4,164 in the 98th Congress (1983–1985).

Frustration with the slow pace is plentiful on Capitol Hill. Despite reform efforts to decentralize the formal authority of the committee system, participation in decision making is still relatively selective, often closed to junior

Table 3.5
Travel Schedule for Senator Bob Graham, Friday, December 11, 1998

Press Call **Request** **for Today:**	PLEASE CALL AT SOME POINT TODAY BEFORE 5:00 P.M.: Political Editor, *St. Petersburg Times* Topic: **End of political career article on Governor Lawton Chiles and review of the Askew-Chiles-Graham influence on Florida politics.**
6:35 A.M.	Depart Washington townhouse for Ronald Reagan Washington National Airport. Drive Time: **20 minutes**
6:55 A.M.	Arrive Ronald Reagan Washington National Airport. Proceed to American Airlines Flight 1763 to Miami International Airport.
7:25 A.M.	Depart Ronald Reagan Washington National Airport. Travel Time: **2 hours and 25 minutes**
10:00 A.M.	Arrive Miami International Airport. **PROCEED TO V.I.P. PARKING LOT AREA WHERE CAR WILL MEET YOU.**
10:10 A.M.	Depart Miami International Airport for Mellon United National Bank Building. Drive Time: **20 minutes**
10:30 A.M.	Arrive Mellon United National Bank Building. **PROCEED TO THE FOURTH FLOOR EXECUTIVE OFFICES FOR YOUR MEETING.**
10:35 A.M.	Meeting, President of Mellon United National Bank.
11:30 A.M.	Meeting concludes.
11:35 A.M.	Depart Mellon United National Bank Building for Miami office. Drive Time: **15 minutes**
11:50 A.M.	Arrive Miami office.

VERY IMPORTANT: THE ATTORNEY GENERAL WILL CALL THE MIAMI OFFICE PROMPTLY AT 12:00 P.M.

12:00 P.M.	Telephone call with Attorney General Janet Reno begins.
12:20 P.M.	Telephone call with Attorney General Janet Reno concludes.
12:30 P.M.	Fall 1998 Miami intern holiday luncheon begins.
1:30 P.M.	Fall 1998 Miami intern holiday luncheon concludes.
1:35 P.M.	Phone time begins. **NOTE: CITY COMMISIONER WILL MEET WITH YOU IN MIAMI OFFICE AT THIS TIME FOR 25 MINUTES SHOULD HIS SCHEDULE BECOME AVAILABLE.**
2:00 P.M.	Depart Miami office for **Camillus House**. Drive Time: **10 minutes**
2:10 P.M.	Arrive Camillus House.

Table 3.5 (continued)

2:15 P.M.	Courtesy meeting with Brother Raphael Mieszala begins (including tour of new facility).
2:55 P.M.	Courtesy meeting with Brother Raphael Miezala concludes.
3:00 P.M.	Depart Camillus House for **Esserman International Acura**. Drive Time: **25 minutes**
3:25 P.M.	Arrive Esserman International Acura. **PROCEED TO THE SHOWROOM RECEPTION DESK.**
3:30 P.M.	Meeting with Ron Esserman begins.
3:50 P.M.	Meeting with Ron Esserman concludes.
3:55 P.M.	Depart Esserman International Acura for **Miami International Airport**. Drive Time: **15 minutes**
4:10 P.M.	Arrive Miami International Airport.
4:15 P.M.	Depart Miami International Airport for **Miami Lakes Townhouse**. Drive Time: 35 minutes
4:50 P.M.	Arrive Miami Lakes townhouse. **END OF SCHEDULE FOR FRIDAY, DECEMBER 11**

members. Members in committee simply have too much to do and too little energy for work. They cannot take on every issue; they must choose.

Commissions circumvent this problem by managing those issues that are not considered, not addressed, or otherwise would not receive further committee action. Members and staffers acknowledge the commission process as an alternative apparatus for responding to frustration. The effective control of congressional committees over the legislative workload is threatened, especially when controversial or complicated legislation is at stake.[50] A commission is a politically expedient way of getting Congress to act on something it otherwise would not act on. A (then) minority legal counsel to the Senate Committee on Governmental Affairs said: "If Congress creates a commission, Congress is basically saying that it wants an end result that we on Capitol Hill are unable to achieve ourselves without outside assistance." "Generally, I would advocate a commission for something that I could not resolve in a hearing myself," added a former representative.

When legislators delegate some of their policymaking authority to a workload commission, they create an extra-committee body outside formal institutional channels designed to handle certain tasks, to gather informa-

Table 3.6
Hearings and Meetings of Congressional Committees, January 1–July 4,
1961–1983[a]

Year	Total days[b]	Oversight days[c]	Oversight as percentage of total
1961	1,789	146	8.2
1963	1,820	159	8.7
1965	2,055	141	6.9
1967	1,797	171	9.5
1969	1,804	217	12.0
1971	2,063	87	9.1
1973	2,513	290	11.5
1975	2,552	459	18.0
1977	3,053	537	17.6
1981	2,222	434	19.5
1983	2,331	587	25.2
Percent change			
1961–71	15.3	28.1	11.0
1961–77	70.7	267.8	114.6
1961–83	30.3	302.1	07.3

Note:
a. Hearings and meetings held by Appropriations, Rules, Administration, and Joint Committees are excluded.
b. Total days means the total number of days that committees met for any purpose during the time covered.
c. Oversight days means days committees devoted to primary-purpose oversight. "Day" is shorthand for a hearing or meeting.
Source: Joel D. Aberbach, *Keeping a Watchful Eye* (Washington, D.C.: Brookings Institution, 1990).

tion, to cut through the mounds of irrelevant information to obtain that which is pertinent, to develop a meaningful list of possible options, and to make the choices which maximize a set of values. Congress lays down the basic outlines of public policy, establishing objectives and providing guidelines for action, but it leaves many of the details of policy to the commission. "Congress's purpose is not to deal with the nitty-gritty but to debate large, chunky things," remarked a personal aide to a midwestern Democratic representative who sponsored legislation to create the Commission to Eliminate Welfare.[51] In this way a commission functions to manage burgeoning personal and institutional demands, complementing or supplementing committees. It augments Congress's efforts, serving as an integrative framework for multi-interest consideration of problems, and creates a "future for further legislative action." Additionally, a commission provides continuity by keeping attention on an issue between legislative sessions. Members and their staff are able to follow more issues and process more legislation. "Commissions are a form of subcontracting for particular and immediate needs" (in reference to the National Commission on Educational Readiness),[52] noted one staff aide to a northeastern Democratic senator. "They provide free labor and data so that members and committees can look at other things that may be more pressing," added another legislative aide, in reference to the National Commission to Support Law Enforcement. "We need to move some things off 'campus.'" Such a concern is particularly pressing for congressional offices that are limited in staff. In 1997 House offices were entitled by House rules to hire no more than eighteen full-time and four part-time employees. The average Senate staff consists of thirty-five full-time employees, but according to Senate rules senators are allocated staff allowances based on the population of their state. A senator from California (seventy-one) or New York will have more staff members than a senator from Nevada or Rhode Island (thirteen).

The problems that go to workload commissions are generally visible to the public. The decision to delegate can be a rough calculation on an issue-by-issue basis of either minor or noncontroversial concerns. Problems that are of negligible or "trivial" importance can sensibly be delegated. Doing this permits such matters to be given thoughtful consideration without the formality of a vote. A policy issue given to a workload commission also may deal with broad issues. Time constraints caused by annual recesses, adjournments, or structuring the legislative schedule to minimize conflicts between activities in Washington and at home may occasion a need to transfer responsibility to a commission. According to interview respondents, federal holidays, commemorative issues,[53] and recreation and sports are examples of the policy issues Congress has seen as being trivial and has created commissions to manage.

Workload commissions often deal with distributive problems (although some can involve self-regulation and/or redistributive issues), and for this reason the line between the two types of commissions is sometimes fuzzy. But where technically complicated issues present a special challenges Congress can undertake cases of workload management. Indeed, in many cases there is documented historical involvement. Yet the policy issues may be such that they take a great deal of time and resources or they are perceived as being trivial. During the February 1990 congressional hearings on a proposed advisory commission on national commemorative events, for instance, many lawmakers argued that a commission would save Congress time and money and might ensure a more rational commemorative process.[54] The limited information before a commission itself improves decision making. An administrative assistant to a Democratic representative from a large midwestern state says: "By focusing on one issue and one goal, commissioners dodge information 'overload' and take on more directed analysis than do most committees in Congress."

DELEGATING TO AVOID BLAME

The third major reason for Congress to delegate to a commission is the strategy of distancing itself from a politically risky decision. These instances generally occur when Congress faces redistributive policy problems, such as Social Security, military base closures, Medicare, and welfare. Such problems are the most difficult because legislators must take a clear policy position on something that has greater costs to their districts than benefits, or that shifts resources visibly from one group to another. Institutionally, Congress has to make national policy that has a collective benefit, but the self-interest of lawmakers often gets in the way. Members realize that their individual interests, based on constituents' demands, may be at odds with the national interest, and this can lead to possible electoral repercussions.[55] Even when pursuing policies that are in the interests of the country as a whole, legislators do not want to be blamed for causing losses to their constituents. In such an event, the split characteristics of the institution come into direct conflict.

Many on Capitol Hill endorse a commission for effectively resolving a policy problem rather than the other machinery available to Congress. A commission finds remedies when the normal decision making process has stalled. A long-time Senate staff director said of the proposed Second National Blue Ribbon Commission to Eliminate Waste in Government: "At their most effective, these panels allow Congress to realize purposes most members cannot find the confidence to do unless otherwise done behind the words of the commission."[56]

When an issue imposes concentrated costs on individual districts yet provides dispersed benefits to the nation, Congress responds by masking legislators' individual contributions and delegates responsibility to a commission for making unpleasant decisions.[57] Members avoid blame and promote good policy by saying something is out of their hands. This method allows legislators—especially those aiming for reelection—to vote for the general benefit of something without ever having to support a plan that directly imposes large and traceable geographic costs on their constituents. The avoidance or share-the-blame route was much of the way Congress and the president finally dealt with the problem of financially shoring up Social Security in the late 1980s. One senior staff assistant to a western Republican representative observed that the creation of the Social Security Commission was largely for avoidance: "There are sacred cows and then there is Social Security. Neither party or any politician wants to cut this. Regardless of what you say or do about it, in the end, you defer. Everyone backs away from this." Similarly, a legislative director to a southern Democratic representative summarized: "So many people are getting older and when you take a look at who turns out, who registers, people over sixty-five have the highest turnout and they vote like clockwork."

The Commission on Executive, Legislative, and Judicial Salaries, later referred to as the Quadrennial Commission (1967), is another example. Lawmakers delegated to a commission the power to set pay for themselves and other top federal officials, whose pay they linked to their own, to help them avoid blame. Increasing their own pay is a decision few politicians willingly endorse. Because the proposal made by the commission would take effect unless Congress voted to oppose it, the use of the commission helped insulate legislators from political hazards.[58] That is, because it was the commission that granted pay raises, legislators could tell their constituents that they would have voted against the increase if given the chance. Members could get the pay raise and also the credit for opposing it.

Redistribution is the most visible public policy type because it involves the most conspicuous, long run allocations of values and resources. Most divisive socioeconomic issues—affirmative action, medical care for the aged, aid to depressed geographic areas, public housing, and the elimination of identifiable governmental actions—involve debates over equality or inequality and degrees of redistribution. These are "political hot potatoes, in which a commission is a good means of putting a fire wall between you [the lawmaker] and that hot potato," the chief of staff to a midwestern Democratic representative acknowledged. Base closing took on a redistributive character as federal expenditures outpaced revenues. It was marked not only by extreme conflict but also by techniques to mask or sugarcoat the redistributions or make them more palatable. The Base Closure Commission (1991) was created with an important provision that allowed for silent congressional approval of its recommendations. Congress required the commission to submit its reports of proposed closures to the secretary of defense. The president had fifteen days to approve or disapprove the list in its entirety. If approved, the list of recommended base closures became final unless both houses of Congress adopted a joint resolution of disapproval within forty-five days. Congress had to consider and vote on the recommendations en bloc rather than one by one, thereby giving the appearance of spreading the misery equally to affected clienteles. A former staff aide for the Senate Armed Services Committee who was active in the creation of the Base Closure Commission contended, "There was simply no political will by Congress. The then-secretary of defense started the process [base closing] with an in-house commission [within the Defense Department]. Eventually, however, Congress used the commission idea as a 'scheme' for a way out of a 'box.'"

CONCLUSION

Many congressional scholars attribute delegation principally to electoral considerations.[59] For example, in the delegation of legislative authority to standing committees, legislators, keen on maximizing their reelection prospects, request assignments to committees whose jurisdictions coincide with the interests of key groups in their districts. Delegation of legislative functions to the president, to nonelected officials in the federal bureaucracy, or to ad hoc commissions also grows out of electoral motives. Here, delegation fosters the avoidance of blame.[60] Mindful that most policies entail both costs and benefits, and apprehensive that those suffering the costs will hold them responsible, members of Congress often find that the most attractive option is to let someone else make the tough choices.

Others see congressional delegation as unavoidable (and even desirable) in light of basic structural flaws in the design of Congress.[61] They argue that Congress is incapable of crafting policies that address the full complexity of modern-day problems.[62] Another charge is that congressional action can be stymied at several junctures in the legislative policymaking process. Congress is decentralized, having few mechanisms for integrating or coordinating its policy decisions; it is an institution of bargaining, consensus-seeking, and compromise. The logic of delegation is broad: to fashion solutions to tough problems, to broker disputes, to build consensus, and to keep fragile coalitions together. The commission co-opts the most publicly ideological and privately pragmatic, the liberal left and the conservative right. Leaders of both parties or their designated representatives can negotiate a deal without the media, the public, or interest groups present. When deliberations are private, parties can make offers without being denounced either by their opponents or by affected groups. Removing external contact reduces the opportunity to use an offer from the other side to curry favor with constituents.

Ad hoc commissions are helpful when action must be taken on highly distasteful legislation. But they are equally valuable when members and their staff do not have sufficient knowledge to make a decision on difficult problems; when action must be taken on problems that are of negligible importance to legislators who, therefore, delegate authority; when action must be taken on broad issues that affect a wide range of multidisciplinary matters; and when time is of the essence and the deliberative nature of Congress inhibits legislative action. Another justification is the requirement that Congress must have access to good information if it is to legislate intelligently.

As the activities of the national government become more complex, congressional commissions assume increasing importance. Commissions search for information that can guide legislators and spur Congress to enact new or corrective legislation. Congress uses commissions to inform the public of conditions in such a way that members judge that they can address them either for electoral advantage or at least to minimize political damage. Through these entities, Congress influences the development of public opinion that will support or at least tolerate particular policies.

NOTES

1. Edward V. Schneier and Bertram Gross, *Legislative Strategy: Shaping Public Policy* (New York: St. Martin's Press, 1993), 76.

2. Robert L. Chartrand, Jane Bortnick, and James R. Price, *Legislator as User of Information* (Washington, D.C.: Congressional Research Service, 1987).

3. The Commission on Integration of Workers' Compensation Medical Benefits was designed to study and develop a detailed plan for implementing the transfer of financial responsibility for workers' compensation medical benefits to health insurance plans, and recommend whether such a transfer should be effected.

4. Walter J. Oleszek, 1989. *Congressional Procedures and the Policy Process*, 3rd ed. (Washington, D.C.: CQ Press, 1989), 26; and Ross K. Baker, *House and Senate*, 2nd ed. (New York: W.W. Norton & Company, 1995).

5. Legislators often select a topic of specialization because of its effect on their district or because of their own interest or ideological commitment. While members hope to get committee assignments that will enable them to develop the area of expertise they prefer, as Malcolm Jewel and Samuel Patterson note, "in some cases, service on a committee leads them into unanticipated areas of specialization." Malcolm E. Jewell and Samuel C. Patterson, *The Legislative Process in the United States*, 4th ed. (New York: Random House, 1986), 219.

6. Oleszek, *Congressional Procedures*, 27.

7. Pete V. Domenici, "Science and the U.S. Senate," in *Science Technology: Advice to the President, Congress, and Judiciary*, ed. William T. Golden (New York: Pergamon Press, 1988).

8. Studies of congressional staff by Harrison W. Fox and Susan W. Hammond show that nearly half of the personal staff professionals in the Senate are under thirty-five and a sizable majority of them in the House are under thirty. Typically, committee professional staff are older—16 percent under thirty and 40 percent under forty. Harrison W. Fox, Jr., and Susan W. Hammond, *Congressional Staffs* (New York: Free Press, 1977).

9. Michael J. Malbin, *Unelected Representatives: Congressional Staff and the Future of Representative Government* (New York: Basic Books, 1980), 20. See also Thomas J. Klouda et al., *1996 House Staff Employment: Salary, Tenure, Demographics, and Benefits* (Washington, D.C.: Congressional Management Foundation, 1996), 2–3.

10. Mark Murrary, "Top Aides Agree the House Is a Mess," *National Journal*, June 27, 1998, 1510–11.

11. Susan W. Hammond, "Legislative Staffs," *Legislative Studies Quarterly* 9 (1984): 271–317.

12. The Commission on Retirement Income Policy was designed to study and

report to the president and Congress on (1) trends in retirement savings in the United States; (2) existing federal incentives and programs to encourage and protect such savings; (3) new federal incentives and programs needed for such purposes; and (4) issues to be addressed and measures addressing specified needs of future retirees.

13. The Commission on the Dual-Use Application of Facilities and Resources at White Sands Missile Range was designed to study and report to the congressional defense committees on the manner in which the defense-related equipment, facilities, processes, and technologies at White Sands Missile Range in New Mexico might be utilized by the private sector.

14. Bruce Bimber, *The Politics of Expertise in Congress* (Albany: State University of New York Press, 1996).

15. Woodrow Wilson, *Congressional Government: A Study in American Politics* (New York: Meridian Books, 1956 [1885]).

16. Roger H. Davidson, "Leaders and Committees in the Republican Congress," in *New Majority or Old Minority? The Impact of the Republicans on Congress,* ed. Nicol C. Rae and Colton C. Campbell (Lanham, Md.: Rowman and Littlefield Publishers, Inc., 1999).

17. Glenn R. Parker, *Characteristics of Congress* (Englewood Cliffs, N.J.: Prentice Hall, 1989), 140.

18. Steven S. Smith indicates that today, when committees act, they are often bound by external forces or are likely to be second-guessed by members when their legislation reaches the floor. See Steven S. Smith, *The American Congress* (Boston: Houghton-Mifflin Company, 1995).

19. 100th Cong., 1st sess., *Congressional Record,* August 4, 1987, H22248.

20. Roger H. Davidson and Walter J. Oleszek, *Congress and Its Members,* 6th ed. (Washington, D.C.: CQ Press, 1998), 354.

21. Theodore J. Lowi, "American Business, Public Policy, Case-Studies, and Political Theory," *World Politics* 16 (1964): 693.

22. Allen Schick, "Complex Policymaking in the United States Senate," in *Policy Analysis on Major Issues, Senate Commission on Operation of the Senate, Senators: Offices, Ethics, and Pressure* (94th Cong., 2nd sess., Committee Print, 1977); Thomas J. O'Donnell, "Controlling Legislative Time," in *The House at Work,* ed. Joseph Cooper and G. Calvin Mackenzie (Austin: University of Texas Press, 1981); Roger H. Davidson and Carol Hardy, *Indicators of House of Representatives Workload and Activity* (Washington, D.C.: Congressional Research Service, 1987); and Christopher S. Yates, "A House of Our Own or a House We've Outgrown? An Argument for Increasing the Size of the House of Representatives," *Columbia Journal of Law and Social Problems* 25 (1992): 157–96.

23. Joseph W. Martin, *My First Fifty Years in Politics* (New York: McGraw-Hill, 1960).

24. Raymond Bauer, Ithiel de Sola Pool, and Lewis Anthony Dexter, *American Business and Public Policy* (New York: Atherton Press, 1963); and Roger H. Davidson and Walter J. Oleszek, *Congress and Its Members,* 5th ed. (Washington, D.C.: CQ Press, 1996).

25. Robert Moon and Carol Hardy Vincent, *Workload and Activity Report: United States Senate* (Washington, D.C.: Congressional Research Service, 1993).

26. Richard L. Hall, *Participation in Congress* (New Haven, Conn.: Yale University Press, 1996), 22.

27. Data are found in *Congressional Record* (105th Cong., 2nd sess.), December 15, 1997, D1281.

28. Rochelle Jones and Peter Woll, *The Private World of Congress* (New York: Free Press, 1979).

29. Quoted in Nicol C. Rae, *Conservative Reformers: The Freshmen Republicans and the Lessons of the 104th Congress* (Armonk, N.Y.: M.E. Sharpe, Inc., 1998), 83.

30. Judith Goldstein and Stefanie Ann Lenway, "Interests of Institutions: An Inquiry into Congressional—ITC Relations," *International Studies Quarterly* 33 (1989): 303–27.

31. Davidson and Oleszek, *Congress and Its Members*, 5th ed.

32. Bargaining is a ubiquitous feature of the legislative process that describes the various symmetrical manipulations that occur among lawmakers. Glenn R. Parker rightly observes that one cannot accomplish anything in Congress without striking a bargain or two. "Congressmen are unable to get pet bills passed without striking bargains, perhaps 'rolling a log' or two [trading favors] in the process, and party leaders frequently barter with members for their votes. . . . Bargaining occurs whenever one congressman, preoccupied with his own distinctive agenda, seeks to bring another member around to his position, though this other member is preoccupied with his own particular agenda. The result is normally a sequence of moves and countermoves of a highly interdependent nature and recognized as such by those involved." See Parker, *Characteristics of Congress*, 117.

33. David Epstein and Sharyn O'Halloran, *Delegating Powers: A Transaction Cost Politics Approach to Policy Making under Separate Powers* (New York: Cambridge University Press, 1999).

34. Roger H. Davidson, "The Legislative Workload of Congress," paper presented at the annual meeting of the American Political Science Association, Washington, D.C., 1986.

35. Norman J. Ornstein, Thomas E. Mann, and Michael J. Malbin, *Vital Statistics on Congress, 1997–1998* (Washington, D.C.: American Enterprise Institute, 1998).

36. Davidson and Oleszek, *Congress and Its Members*, 5th ed., 29.

37. Ornstein, Mann, and Malbin, *Vital Statistics on Congress, 1997–1998*, 157.

38. Charles L. Clapp, *The Congressman: His Work as He Sees It* (Washington, D.C.: Brookings Institution, 1963).

39. Hall, *Participation in Congress*, 24.

40. U.S. Congress, Commission on Administrative Review, House, *Final Report*, 2 vols., 95th Cong., 1st sess. (Washington, D.C.: Government Printing Office, 1977).

41. Parker, *Characteristics of Congress*, 30.

42. Norman J. Ornstein, Thomas E. Mann, Michael J. Malbin, Allen Shick, and John F. Bibby, *Vital Statistics on Congress: 1984–1989 Edition* (Washington, D.C.: American Enterprise Institute, 1990), 164.

43. Ornstein, Mann, and Malbin, *Vital Statistics on Congress, 1997–1998*, 129.

44. John R. Johannes, *To Serve the People: Congress and Constituency Service* (Lincoln: University of Nebraska Press, 1984).

45. Joel D. Aberbach, *Keeping a Watchful Eye: The Politics of Congressional Oversight* (Washington, D.C.: Brookings Institution, 1990).

46. Ibid.

47. The bulk of these are executive-branch officers such as cabinet secretaries and sub-cabinet officials, bureau chiefs, key officers of independent agencies, and ambassadors. Other nominations include military and Coast Guard officers, officers in the Foreign Service, and officials in the legislative branch (e.g., the comptroller general and the librarian of Congress).

48. The procedural reforms of the 104th Congress (1995–1997) significantly reduced congressional staffing. Section 101 of H. Res. 6 required House committee staff to be reduced by at least one-third. Furthermore, committee chairs were granted control over the hiring of subcommittee staff with subcommittee chairmen and ranking minority members losing the authority to hire one staff aide each.

49. Davidson, "The Legislative Workload of Congress."

50. Davidson, "Leaders and Committees in the Republican Congress," 4.

51. The Commission to Eliminate Welfare was proposed to design a plan for transition from certain welfare, job training, and child care programs to new programs providing temporary financial aid and assistance in locating permanent employees.

52. The National Commission on Educational Readiness was proposed to (1) recommend to Congress a national policy to prepare children for formal learning; (2) recommend specific changes in federal laws and policies to effectuate the federal role; (3) encourage state and local initiatives and monitor progress toward school readiness; (4) run a national clearinghouse for information and materials on readiness to learn; and (5) arrange for provision of consultation and technical assistance to state or community entities for integrated comprehensive health or child development services or educational services to pregnant women, infants, toddlers, and preschool children.

53. Stephen W. Stathis indicates that before 1900, commemoratives rarely comprised more than 1 percent of all legislation enacted by a particular Congress and never exceeded 5 percent until the 85th Congress (1957–1959). Over the next two decades commemoratives accounted for 5 to nearly 10 percent of all legislation. By the 96th Congress (1979–1981) commemorative legislation increased by more than 70 percent. By the 98th Congress (1983–1985) commemoratives constituted more than one-third of all bills signed into law by the president. See Stephen W. Stathis, "Commemorative Legislation," in *The Encyclopedia of the United States Congress*, ed. Donald C. Bacon, Roger H. Davidson, and Morton Keller (New York: Simon & Schuster, 1995).

54. U.S. Representatives, *Advisory Commission on Commemorative Events*, 101st U.S. Cong., 2nd sess., Serial No. 101–42, 1990.

55. Arnold emphasizes the importance of this perception of constituency desires and of how legislators anticipate and respond to citizen policy preferences in conjunction with electoral needs. When voting, a legislator can vote as he or she chooses, possibly even for good policy, when there is little traceability. When the issue is controversial, however, the legislator must attempt to gauge the po-

tential preference of the electorate and vote with it. See R. Douglas Arnold, *The Logic of Congressional Action* (New Haven, Conn.: Yale University Press, 1990).

56. The Second National Blue Ribbon Commission to Eliminate Waste in Government was proposed to conduct a study and make recommendations to eliminate waste in government.

57. R. Kent Weaver, "The Politics of Blame Avoidance," *Journal of Public Policy* 6 (1987): 371–98; and Arnold, *The Logic of Congressional Action*.

58. Davidson, "The Legislative Workload of Congress"; R. Kent Weaver, *Automatic Government: The Politics of Indexation* (Washington, D.C.: Brookings Institution, 1988); and Arnold, *The Logic of Congressional Action*.

59. David R. Mayhew, *Congress: The Electoral Connection* (New Haven, Conn.: Yale University Press, 1974).

60. Weaver, "The Politics of Blame Avoidance."

61. D. Roderick Kiewiet and Mathew D. McCubbins, *The Logic of Delegation: Congressional Parties and the Appropriations Process* (Chicago: University of Chicago Press, 1991).

62. James L. Sundquist, *Politics and Policy: The Eisenhower, Kennedy, and Johnson Years* (Washington, D.C.: Brookings Institution, 1968); and Samuel P. Huntington, *The Common Defense* (New York: Columbia University Press, 1961).

—————Chapter 4—————

A Case of Expertise: The National Commission on AIDS

Congress cannot do it all. Congress does not have all the expertise within its own branch. Maybe they [legislators] need to reach out and appoint others who can ferret out the information in a more efficient manner and to bring in experts.

Chief of staff to a
Democratic House member

Congress, on occasion, will establish ad hoc commissions and fill them with experts to grapple with technically difficult problems. Legislators specialize in policymaking and policy evaluation but lack the training and knowledge necessary for the comprehension of many modern-day problems. Many lawmakers have professional backgrounds and they gain specific specialized knowledge through service.[1] And for the individuals who want to have an impact upon policymaking, the decision to specialize is virtually imperative.[2] But lawmakers are not elected on the basis of their professional qualifications.

There are marked differences between the executive branch and Congress in the ways in which scientific and technical advice enters the respective systems and is utilized.[3] The president can have a scientific advisor as a channel for studies and information, and this advisor in turn has a staff and an advisory body composed of distinguished scientists, engineers, or other experts. Additionally, within the executive branch, there is a large body of competent experts in such organizations as the National Institutes of Health and the National Scientific Foundation. The technical resources that Congress has must serve 435 representatives and 100 senators. A complicating factor is that each lawmaker has a special constituency, and the interests and concerns of the constituents differ. Therefore, when the legislative branch lacks the necessary knowledge or skills in matters of technical detail, it often looks for alternative ways to enlist help.[4] As one long-time congressional aide to a Republican representative of a large western state puts it: "There are times when it's more beneficial to the public to get a group of people who are trained in the specific area Congress is looking at and who don't have a political bent one way or the other, to help with a complex problem." And as another aide to a southern Democratic senator notes, "Politicians are not focused on technical matters like the experts on a commission; they are with political issues, however."

The identification and description of the acquired immune deficiency syndrome (AIDS) yielded newfound political and practical difficulties, stretching, as Christopher H. Foreman says, "across each phase of policy response."[5] The novelty of the disease, combined with a perception of urgency, presented a special challenge. Acquiring expertise was expensive for a winning coalition of legislators to become authorities on the subject matter. Thus, lawmakers would likely remain novices on the issue. The dilemma was not so much a lack of congressional action with respect to the disease as it was a lack of direction for comprehending an elusive issue. By the late 1980s people started looking to Washington for solutions. Capitol Hill felt the need for an impartial and expert panel to study the epidemic; to review the nation's research and medical systems and assess their adequacy for addressing the epidemic; to examine the implications of various policies and their alternatives; and to make recommendations for effective policy action.[6]

THE COMPLICATED AND NOVEL DYNAMICS THAT GENERATED AN EXPERTISE COMMISSION

Typhoid, typhus, smallpox, measles, cholera, and influenza scourged the world, but their spread was slowed by distance. These early diseases inched across distances with plodding caravans, with soldiers and sailors returning home from faraway places, or with other carriers such as rats and insects. Time and space have now become more conditioned by human technology. In our age, in the words of one observer, "space is compressed and time speeds up, enabling deadly epidemics to appear unexpectedly and spread rapidly."[7] And because the costs of governmental inaction are immediate, Capitol Hill is expected to respond to such policy problems expeditiously without obfuscating.

Congress has built itself an extensive system of experts, establishing new internal agencies and occasionally turning to external experts—think tanks, lobbying organizations, universities, and agencies of the executive branch.[8]

Committees and subcommittees still provide the information-gathering stage for policymaking; they may conduct open investigations or staff studies.[9] In recent years committee staff have become increasingly specialized, with some aides assigned to specific policy issues, and this shift has allowed many congressional leaders to develop expertise and political intelligence, and to participate in a broader range of issue areas.[10] AIDS was, and is, not so narrow in scope that it could be handled by just one committee. The disease was a special challenge when it arrived on Capitol Hill as a policy concern, its uniqueness highlighting Congress's lack of the resources and experience necessary to make an informed judgment on the matter. As one Senate staff aide recalled, "Even when I worked on committee, there were issues that none of my colleagues or I had any knowledge about so we went to experts."

Describing AIDS and the HIV virus and their effect on the human body is not a simple task. Research has become so advanced that even those in closely adjacent fields find difficulty communicating with one another. Essentially, the basic structure of HIV resembles a tiny ball—its diameter is about 100 nanometers. This measurement is so unfamiliar to the scientific and medical communities, that as one scientist said, "If we made a square box one thousand HIV diameters on each side, and crammed a billion viruses into it, we might just be able to see it as a dot about a quarter of the size of the period at the end of this sentence."[11] Prospects for a cure or for an effective vaccine or remedy are distant. There is only palliative treatment. The general understanding of AIDS has improved, but finding a panacea continues to baffle experts, not to speak of policymakers.

Although the AIDS epidemic had been a leading concern of the nation's medical community for several years, Congress moved relatively slowly to address the problem. Congress pumped increasing funds into AIDS research, but until the 100th Congress (1987–1989), it shunned policy decisions.[12]

Congress Faces up to AIDS

President Ronald Reagan initially addressed concerns about the growing problems of AIDS by convening two special commissions: the Presidential Commission on the Human Immunodeficiency Virus Epidemic (chaired by retired Admiral James D. Watkins) and the National Commission on AIDS (chaired by June Osborne). The commissions were charged with providing the executive branch with recommendations regarding certain aspects of AIDS policy. Leaders of the AIDS community expressed outrage at how unqualified and biased most of the Reagan commissions' appointees were, almost all of them favoring mandatory testing for the AIDS virus, a measure overwhelmingly opposed by public officials and the National Academy of Sciences Panel on AIDS as raising serious ethical and practical problems. Charged Jeffry Levi, then the executive director of the National Gay and Lesbian Task Force, "They don't have the expertise. . . . [T]he commission should be addressing the policies the government can implement to deal with the epidemic."[13] The presidential commissions were regarded by many in the gay and scientific communities as lethargic.

In any event, the president refused to endorse his commissions' final reports, declining to comment. Instead, he directed his drug-abuse advisor, Dr. Donald Ian Macdonald, to review, report, and make recommendations for policy implementation. Macdonald stressed that more than 40 percent of the commissions' 340 recommendations pertaining to the federal government were already being implemented, with another 30 percent to be included in the administration's fiscal 1990 budget request.[14]

The Reagan plan directed the Food and Drug Administration to take steps to protect the nation's blood supply and instructed the secretary of health and human services to conduct a study of the current system of health care financing and to find ways to promote out-of-hospital care for AIDS patients. The plan also ordered all federal agencies to adopt AIDS policies based on guidelines to be issued by the Office of Personnel Management (OPM). Those guidelines directed federal managers to treat employees with AIDS the same as workers with any other serious illness, and allowed managers to discipline workers who refused to work with those with AIDS. But Reagan did not issue an executive order to implement the OPM guidelines. Instead, the administration announced that individual directives to each agency would have the same force of law.

This announcement was met with ridicule and cynicism from many people throughout the country. Upset by the lack of leadership from the White House, gay rights organizations and health care activists—following E.E. Schattschneider's dictum—expanded the scope of conflict by turning to the congressional arena.[15]

Congress Creates a Commission

Congress approached the enormity of the AIDS problem in a way not much different than the general public's struggle to understand the illness. Members were wary of public opinion on AIDS issues, leaving it to sympathetic advocates to take the lead. In this early period, lawmakers did not see AIDS as a pressing issue. In the second stage, members began to recognize the deadly nature of the virus and the broad array of problems that it produced. Eventually, a majority in Congress conceded the seriousness of the problems but also recognized that there would be no quick fixes, given the immense technical complexity of the disease.[16] According to Representative Barney Frank (D-Mass.), once the dimensions of the AIDS epidemic became known, many representatives "started voting pro-gay because they saw that life-and-death issues were at stake. They had to do the right thing, even though they thought it might hurt them politically."[17]

Because most initial cases of AIDS in this country were concentrated in the gay community and among intravenous drug abusers and the early public image of the virus was linked to homosexual men, the disease was known popularly as "GRID" or "gay-related immune deficiency."[18] Gays as a group were often perceived as politically irrelevant, largely because they were not seen as a voting constituency capable of swinging many districts. Indeed, many lawmakers sensed political liabilities in the issue and viewed avoidance or denial as the safest course. This accounted in part for the early lack of frank discussion about the epidemic as well as the timid support for action in Congress.[19] Lawmakers spent more time debating whether AIDS was an appropriate topic for the political arena than they did discussing how to deal with the epidemic.[20] Representative Sander M. Levin (D-Mich.) speculated that some of his colleagues were apprehensive about politically distasteful and delicate issues such as sex, illegal drug use, and death, all of which are part of the AIDS epidemic: "I think there's an understandable human tendency to push this aside, to hope it doesn't affect us."[21]

The characterization of AIDS as being gay-related was weakened, however, as it became clearer that there was no inherent or necessary connection between AIDS and homosexuality, and that other groups were and are equally at risk.[22] (Scientists discovered this when people with hemophilia began getting AIDS, indicating that HIV was caused by a blood-borne infection agent.) This proved an impetus for "de-gaying" the issue, gradually converting Congress's dithering into a more proactive concern. Senator Edward M. Kennedy (D-Mass.), who chaired the Senate Committee on Labor and Human Resources, described this broadened interest: "Recognizing that AIDS and the HIV epidemic have now reached every one of the fifty states and into the territories and possessions of the U.S., the Committee believes that a new and concerted national effort is required to mobilize the resources of this nation to overcome the menace that AIDS poses to the American people and to all future generations."[23]

Although the AIDS epidemic had been an urgent public health concern of the nation's medical community for several years, Congress found itself ill-equipped to address the problem. First, few if any members of Congress or their staff aides were knowledgeable about the AIDS virus and the problems associated with it. The vast number of people working on Capitol Hill are generalists, not specialists. Noting that only one member in the House had any medical background (Representative Roy Rowland [D-Ga.]), Representative James Scheuer (D-N.Y.) asserted that a void in expertise and technical certainty about AIDS was impeding legislative action.[24] Conservative Representative Dan Burton (R-Ind.) admitted as much during a House floor debate: "You know, we have 435 Members of this body and 100 Members of the other body. I will tell you from personal conversations with many of them, they are not very conversant with the problems we are facing with AIDS."[25]

This uncertainty confined early discussion to generalities. In 1987, lacking the information and the technical competence to deal legislatively with the scientific aspects of AIDS and hampered by its jurisdiction and procedures, the House approved a fifteen-member commission to study and make policy recommendations regarding all aspects of the AIDS epidemic. The measure, HR 2881, which had eighty-four co-sponsors (many of whom were avowed conservatives such as Dan Burton, Robert Dornan of California, and Newt Gingrich of Georgia) and which passed 355–68, was viewed as an alternative technique to satisfy the demand for public policy on this rapidly spreading disease. Mindful that most policies entail both costs and benefits and apprehensive that the people bearing the costs will hold them responsible, members of Congress often find that the most attractive option is to let someone else make the difficult choices. This allows legislators, especially those aiming for reelection, to vote for the general benefit of something without ever having to support a plan that directly imposes large and traceable costs on their constituents. Thus the AIDS Commission became a device to provide Congress with needed expertise as well as to legitimize congressional action on a distasteful subject.

The idea of setting up the National Commission on AIDS also originated in response to the need felt by gay rights organizations, scientists, and member of Congress for a better governmental device to handle the unprecedented problem.[26] Assigning responsibility to a commission of experts seemed more promising than delegating the problem to the executive departments (who by their own admission were incapable of mounting a rapid response to the epidemic) or to Congress's deliberative and political processes. Research scientists from the Institute of Medicine and National Academy of Sciences, for example, requested a commission not created within the administrative structure of the federal executive branch. An independent commission, according to the Institute of Medicine, would have the skills to help understand the epidemic, to provide some strategic planning, and to pool knowledge in order to formulate recommendations.[27]

For Congress the commission would provide an understanding of the uniquely complex problems linked with AIDS and its relationship to the human immunodeficiency virus (HIV) without expending an inordinate amount of legislative resources. Representative G.V. (Sonny) Montgomery (D-Miss.), chair of the House Committee on Veterans' Affairs, summarized the merits of the broad-based, knowledgeable, and impartial panel:

> While it is inevitable that the ultimate decision whether or not to implement some of the Commission's recommendations may be biased on political factors not considered by the Commission, the Committee believes that the Commission should not conduct itself as a political body. Its analysis and conclusions should be guided by the highest ideals and concern for the persons who are affected by AIDS; its recommendations should not be tempered by a fear of a backlash of public opinion regarding its recommendations.[28]

In a floor debate, Representative Rowland (R-Ga.) stated: "It is so important for us to bring together people who are experts in their areas and who have some knowledge about AIDS in medicine, in science, in ethics, and in legal matters to advise Congress and its members."[29] "This commission will have the best opportunity to pool knowledge and expertise to formulate key recommendations for Congress and the Nation in addressing the challenge presented by AIDS" added Representative Waxman.[30] "The National Commission proposed by this legislation will rely on the expertise rather than the political or philosophical ideology of its members to address the AIDS crisis. . . . Congress will have the opportunity to bring together the most qualified experts in the field." Democratic Representative Nancy Pelosi of California neatly summarized the need for expert direction: "This bill would call upon our most qualified scientific and medical professionals to assist the Congress in setting the national agenda for responding to the medical and psychological crisis of AIDS. The Commission created by this legislation would include a minimum of eight scientific and medical experts. This is exactly the expertise that is needed in this time of crisis."[31]

Consensus among lawmakers on the best approach to treatment, research, education, and prevention was too difficult to achieve through normal legislative channels. The commission process was a step toward accommodating this assignment. "It is the hope of the Committee that the Commission serve as a forum for the development of coordinating and consolidating a national consensus for a comprehensive national policy, mapping citizens' preferences and potential choices for the various policy proposals put forth in Congress," the Senate Labor and Human Resources Committee declared subsequently.[32]

The National Commission on AIDS had critics though they were vastly outnumbered by the commision's supporters. Cynics noted that Congress already had access to extensive expertise. "We already have a commission in existence to deal with communicable diseases in America," charged Representative William E. Dannemeyer (R-Calif.).[33] "It is called the Public Health Services." The critics believed that Congress's motive was an attempt to counter the administration. "Nobody has a monopoly on this. Nobody is omnipotent," answered Representative Burton.[34] "You know, when we talk about fighting AIDS and looking for a scientific solution to this, we do not ask just one scientific body to do research. We try to get as many well-qualified scientists as we can possibly find to research this virus. Policy debate between various commissions may be very healthy and good for coming up with a solution to the policy problem." To bring to light what he considered a deliberate attempt to politically outmaneuver the presidency, Senator Orrin Hatch (R-Utah) argued, "The establishment of the National Commission on AIDS would be the third standing commission on the subject and thus a duplication of effort."[35] "The left hand does not know what the right hand is doing."

Another problem during the debate came when a few members objected that the bill had no legislative history and was being rushed through the House, bypassing subcommittees and full committees. "Would the members believe that the subcommittee of jurisdiction did not even consider this legislation at any time?" charged Representative Dannemeyer.[36] "If I did not know any better, I would suspect that we were attempting to just railroad this piece of legislation through the House." Other opponents heaped scorn on the fast-tracking. Representative Howard C. Nielson (R-Utah) claimed that the Subcommittee on Health and the Environment had been bypassed by the full Committee on Energy and Commerce and no hearings had been held.[37] "There have been hearings on this legislation. . . . during which our Members discussed extensively the need for this legislation," countered Representative Montgomery.[38] "The Committee on Energy and Commerce, to which the bill was jointly referred, has also reported the bill, so it has had appropriate committee scrutiny," added Representative Gerald B.H. Solomon (R-N.Y.).[39]

HR 2881 was sent to the Senate, and then to its Committee on Labor and Human Resources. Eventually, it was attached as an amendment to the Senate's own AIDS bill.

Framing the Issue

A second obstacle to early congressional action was the deep schism—at times highly partisan—among members over the best way to slow the march of the disease, which was transmitted primarily through sexual contact and intravenous drug use. Beneath the political concerns about AIDS was an issue of political framing: between those who saw the disease as a public health disaster that required a nonjudgmental response and those who viewed it as a product of moral turpitude, to be addressed though behavioral change.[40] The winning coalition around the Commission, thus, was co-optation rather than conflict, and delegation to a commission was one step in defining AIDS as a health issue against arguments that it was a personal behavior issue.

One side was led by public health experts and their congressional allies, Representative Henry A. Waxman (D-Calif.), chairman of the House Energy and Commerce Subcommittee on Health and the Environment, and Senators Kennedy and Lowell P. Weicker, Jr. (D-Conn.). Buttressed by the American Medical Association and the federal public health agencies, they urged stepped-up public education efforts and increased access to blood testing and counseling. They pushed for confidential test results and an assurance that those infected with the virus would not suffer discrimination. "If —on the one hand—we create a program of testing that is punitive, that exposes people to loss of employment or housing," Senator Kennedy argued, "those most likely to be infected will do all in their power to evade the test. We must not treat the victims of illness as villains. AIDS is spreading like wild-fire and ideology can't stop it." [41]

The opposing faction was a small but vocal group of conservatives led by Representative Dannemeyer and Senator Jesse Helms (R-N.C.). They urged mandatory, routine testing of large groups within the AIDS population, with names of infected individuals reported to public-health officials.[42] They also wanted to require that the sexual contacts of all those testing positive be contacted and warned of their risk.[43] Helms and his allies feared that educational efforts aimed at homosexual men and at users of illicit intravenous drugs would have the effect of promoting homosexuality and drug abuse. Dannemeyer, fixated on the sexual aspect of the problem, distributed to his colleagues publications produced by the New York City-based Gay Men's Health group, which he argued had used federal funds to promote homosexual activity. He also placed explicit materials about homosexual practices in the *Congressional Record.*

During the Senate debate, Helms insisted that the AIDS crisis was being exaggerated by a powerful AIDS lobby that was requesting funds that were needed to combat diseases that afflicted far larger numbers of people. "I think one of the saddest things is that the taxpayers' money is being proposed to be used to proselytize a dangerous lifestyle," Helms said.[44] "In the meantime, millions of other Americans, gravely ill with Alzheimer's or cancer or diabetes are being cast aside, along with common sense, in the headlong rush to feed the appetite of a movement which will not be satisfied until the social fabric of the nation is irreparably changed."

The Senate took the lead on AIDS research and treatment issues, leaving the more controversial testing and confidentiality issues to the House.[45] Members of the Senate Labor and Human Resources Committee in 1987 approved an AIDS bill (S 1220, initially sponsored by Senator Kennedy) that authorized close to $600 million for fiscal 1988 for AIDS education and treatment and unspecified amounts for research.

Throughout the debate, tempers often became frayed. At one point when Majority Leader Robert C. Byrd (D-W.Va.) attempted to interrupt consideration of S 1220 to get a time agreement on two veterans' bills, Senator Weicker exploded, "I find it strange that we can pass veterans' legislation so speedily and so cleanly, but somehow we cannot address the greatest threat that has been posed to this nation since World War II."[46]

Arresting the spread of the HIV epidemic could not, in the words of the Senate Committee on Labor and Human Resources, "occur as a result of legislative fiat or the adoption of punitive approaches imposed upon individuals."[47] As the debate over AIDS intensified, the committee advocated an inclusive policy that would include coordinated action by persons other than Congress.[48] "I think that it's important that we remember, as we carry on debate and carry out policy related to AIDS, that AIDS represents the ordinary workings of biology—that it's not an irrational or diabolical plague," commented Senator Tom Harkin (D-Iowa). "This is a very, very serious problem. But let's make sure that we approach it rationally and that we base our judgments on facts—not on pernicious mythologies, misperceptions, ignorance or irrational fears."[49]

On other occasions the AIDS fight transcended traditional Democratic-Republican or liberal-conservative lines. In defending an amendment directing that education programs stress the public health benefits of single, monogamous relationships (without stipulating that such a relationship should be heterosexual), Senator Hatch pleaded, "This bill is to help people who need help, and this includes homosexuals." Finding this unacceptable, Senator Helms shot back: "The point is, we should not allow the homosexual crowd to use the AIDS issue to promote and legitimize their lifestyle in American society."[50] A large majority of lawmakers responded positively to the former interpretation, with its elements of equality, impartiality, and moderation. Conservatives, however, were able to craft amendments to S 1220 that members found politically impossible to vote against.

On October 13, 1988, lawmakers in both chambers passed by voice vote a watered-down version of S 1220, the Health Omnibus Act (P.L. 100-607). The measure, which the House passed, 355 to 68, with 10 members not voting, and the Senate passed 87 to 4, contained the first significant federal policy outlines for dealing with the AIDS epidemic: it authorized increased research, education, and prevention activities and the establishment of a temporary advisory commission. The AIDS portion of the measure authorized a minimum of $270 million over three years for AIDS education and a total of $400 million over two years for anonymous blood testing and counseling and for home community-based health services for AIDS patients.[51] It also authorized $2 million for operating costs for a new congressional AIDS commission. The bill expedited federal AIDS research activities, ordering the hiring of 780 new workers for the Public Health Service, and formally authorized several elements of the federal government's effort against AIDS that had already been launched. Several more controversial elements contained in another AIDS bill (HR 5142) passed overwhelmingly in the House but failed to make it into law when conservative senators threatened to filibuster the entire package. Excluded were the provisions authorizing $1.2 billion for voluntary blood testing and counseling, with guaranteed confidentiality of test results.

WORK BY THE AIDS COMMISSION

The National Commission on AIDS was a bipartisan panel designed to be broad-based, knowledgeable, and impartial. The Commission was composed of fifteen voting members, including five appointed by the president, five by the Speaker of the House of Representatives, and five by the president pro tempore of the Senate. Congressional appointments were made upon the joint agreement of the majority and minority leaders. At least eight of the members had to be specifically qualified by reason of education, training, or experience in the areas of medicine, science, law, or ethics. Jurisdictional committees in both chambers believed that because of the urgency of the AIDS hazard, commission members should have a basic understanding of some aspect of the relevant issues. While members recognized that the ultimate decision on whether to implement some of the commission's recommendations might be based on political factors not considered by the commission, they did feel that the commission should not conduct itself as a political body.

The commission would provide continuing expert advice and leadership to help Congress make "sound, objective, cost-effective decisions" concerning the effort toward AIDS.[52] Charged first with monitoring the implementation of the recommendations of the presidential commission, it would also be responsible for evaluating the financing of health care and research needs related to AIDS, studying and recommending national policy and priorities with respect to health care financing, education and prevention, testing, confidentiality of test results, discrimination, resource allocation, and research regarding treatment of AIDS. It would also consider appropriate roles for federal, state, and local governments concerning the protection of the public from infectious diseases, including laws relating to immigration, liability, and discrimination, and problems in employment, housing, insurance, and education encountered by people with the virus. Although many topics for which Congress sought recommendations were already receiving increased attention, no consensus emerged. Such topics included ways to improve coordination among various agencies involved in treating persons with the virus; sharing of resources such as laboratory facilities to accommodate testing of at-risk people; identification of particularly promising areas of research; legislation regulating the manner in which the cost of needed medical care would be allocated among various payers; and legislation regarding the confidentiality of AIDS-related personal records.[53]

A large majority in Congress were mindful that the congressional commission was intended neither to duplicate nor to conflict with the existing functions of state and federal agencies. Nor did they intend for the Commission to overlap or replicate the efforts of the scientific and medical communities. However, the executive branch did not necessarily share information with the legislative branch. At times, it used or released reports for its own or the administration's purposes.[54] Representative John D. Dingell (D-Mich.) commented: "The President has a Commission—made up in part of lay individual—to provide the executive branch with recommendations regarding certain aspects of AIDS policy."[55] "There is an equal need for an impartial and expert Commission to study the scientific, economic and social aspects of this epidemic to provide the Congress with recommendations for effective policy action. The need for this Commission grows daily." Representative Montgomery added that the commission should provide Congress with "an opportunity to become involved in setting a national AIDS agenda."[56] Members of the Senate Committee on Labor and Human Resources stated in their background report: "There is an ongoing need for a forum in which to develop further recommendations and monitor implementation of the recommendations of the Presidential Commission. The National Commission proposed in this bill is designed to fulfill that role for the next two years."[57]

The overall sense on Capitol Hill was that the presidential commissions would make positive contributions but could not provide the full coordination and expertise called for in a report issued by the Institute of Medicine (IOM). "A proper examination of effective policy would dictate serious study of the reasons for these startling numbers as well as practical steps that could be taken to slow the spread of AIDS and to care for those already affected by it," declared Representative Dingell.[58] The very organizations that opponents mentioned as advisors asked Congress to set up the AIDS Commission.

Work by the AIDS Commission did not begin until after the termination of the presidential commission, which submitted its final report on June 24, 1988. The congressionally created commission was charged with submitting to Congress and the president an interim report on its activities (thirteen such interim reports were produced) including any recommendations for legislation and administration action, at the end of its first year's work. A final report was submitted two years after the date of constitution, and the commission terminated thirty days later.

The AIDS Commission concluded with two recommendations. The first was its foremost recommendation since its inception: leaders at all levels must speak about AIDS to their constituencies. The commission commented that the lack of frank discussion contributed to a serious underestimation of the problem. Second, the commission recommended a national strategic plan.

Several findings of the Commission on AIDS worked their way into later congressional action, the data helping to define funding levels, for instance. In 1990, following the Commission on AIDS' report that 5 percent of the nation's hospitals were treating half the nation's AIDS patients, the Senate Labor and Human Resources Committee unanimously authorized a total of $1.2 billion to help combat the AIDS epidemic. Upon the recommendation of the commission, money was earmarked for emergency grants to the metropolitan areas hardest hit by the epidemic as well as grants to states to develop and operate cost-effective programs to provide comprehensive care for AIDS patients.[59]

THE POLITICS OF DISTRIBUTION

The complexities of AIDS were not discernible to most of the general public. The AIDS policy did, however, offer distributive goods, imposing only general costs on society while delivering potentially plentiful group and geographic benefits, which make many interests better off and few, if any, worse off.

As discussed in chapter 2, devising a broad public health policy to combat AIDS did not produce any truly harmful effects on constituents. To the contrary, government actions that supply medical research are favored by legislators and their constituents because they are perceived as being beneficial and do not take away from anyone. Distributive impulses are irresistible when they convey tangible benefits and make many interests—whether directly affected by the virus or not—better off. The distributive nature of AIDS policy added to the appeasement of the more vocal opponents of delegation to the National Commission on AIDS. The complex dimensions of AIDS reduced conflict on Capitol Hill and removed the need for techniques to avoid moral debates on the provision of resources or to make this policy decision more palatable. Although debatable aspects were present in the formation of the AIDS Commission, the distributive character of combating a deadly disease that embodied such a large measure of un-chartered information did not divide liberals and conservatives by upsetting relationships between social and economic classes. Neither Democrats nor Republicans saw any electoral advantage from such debates. As with the abortion issue, AIDS presented members with potential electoral divisions since AIDS could energize a vocal minority in the Republican party, which, were it to be successful in articulating positions, would alienate swing voters.

The legislative arena around distributive policies provides no real basis for discriminating between those who should and those who should not benefit.[60] Generally speaking, lawmakers were responsive to considerations of equality, impartiality, and moderation once the AIDS epidemic was perceived as a public health crisis. The basis of coalition around the commission was co-optation rather than conflict, and delegation to a commission was one step in defining AIDS as a health issue against the arguments that it was a personal behavior issue.

Issues that are highly emotional, cultural, or moral divide the electorate but elicit intense feelings from relatively few people. AIDS did not exhibit a pattern in which the decentralized character of Congress came into play when local interests collided with larger policy needs. Delegating the task was not to break the traceability chain and protect legislators from the wrath of their constituents, because members' individual interests were not at odds with the national interest. Instead, distributive politics of this kind are emblematic of national policy that is a mosaic of local interests.

CONCLUSION

Creating a comprehensive national policy toward AIDS involved a unique blend of technical, political, and institutional challenges. The technical aspect alone made AIDS a challenging problem. The circumstances surrounding commissions vary because of the different political dynamics, and in this instance, these dynamics involved the complicated and anomalous nature of the issue, which was so vast that no one had adequate knowledge of it. Even for highly capable members and staff, problems are often too complicated. The legislative process cannot always comprehend all of a problem's complexities. This shortage in expertise and information leaves Congress at a loss. For information, analyses, research, and policy options and recommendations, commissions of expertise become more and more important, especially with the downsizing trend in Congress regarding staff and committees. As a staff aide for a western Democratic representative said, "We knew clearly that the issue was too complicated to come right in and say 'this is something we understand.'" Staffed with specialized experts, commissions provide Congress with analytical talent matching the talent found in legislative support agencies, executive agencies, or universities.

Many lawmakers were uncomfortable—personally and politically—dealing with a sensitive subject and were cautious about whether AIDS was an appropriate topic for the political arena. As the debate progressed, however, legislators became interested. But the complexity and uncertainty of the AIDS epidemic limited understanding and thereby congressional anticipation and response to citizens' policy preferences. A direct correlation existed between congressional unpreparedness and information deficiency about the virus and its broader implications for public health policy. Delegation to the National Commission on AIDS was occasioned by this imperfect information. Tremendous gains were accrued by delegating tasks to an impartial and expert panel. The AIDS Commission was an organization that could reduce uncertainty so that Congress could know something before acting. It also brought specialized information with its members and staff who were selected on the basis of their education, their training, and their experience. Finally, collective action was effectively coordinated and a winning coalition formed, because the Commission on AIDS was a compromising method used to solicit support instead of exacerbating scores of potential fissures.

Other political dynamics necessitate yet a different type of commission. When Congress is overloaded with business, for instance, it delegates to ease its workload to more manageable dimensions. Delegation under these conditions is a way of subcontracting, necessitated by the limits imposed by time and rising demands. The circumstances under which this type of delegation works are characterized by the scope, complexity, and volume of today's legislative environment. It is this type of commission which I now address.

NOTES

1. John R. Hibbing contends that as members of Congress gain in seniority they become more knowledgeable, efficient, and valuable legislators. "Senior members are the heart and soul of the legislative side of congressional service," Hibbing observes. Over the course of their careers, members of Congress typically become more active in legislation as well as more specialized and more efficient. John R. Hibbing, *Congressional Careers* (Chapel Hill, N.C.: The University of North Carolina Press, 1991), 126.

2. Roger H. Davidson, "Leaders and Committees in the Republican Congress," in *New Majority or Old Minority? The Impact of the Republicans on Congress*, ed. Nicol C. Rae and Colton C. Campbell (Lanham, M.D.: Rowman and Littlefield Publishers, Inc., 1998), 2.

3. Philip H. Abelson, "Scientific Advice in Congress," in *Science and Technology Advice to the President, Congress, and Judiciary*, ed. William T. Golden (New York: Pergamon Press, 1988).

4. Robert L. Chartrand, Jane Bortnick, and James R. Price, *Legislator as User of Information*, Congressional Research Service Report (Washington, D.C.: 1987); and Bruce Bimber, *The Politics of Expertise in Congress* (Albany: State University of New York Press, 1996).

5. Christopher H. Foreman, Jr., *Plagues, Products and Politics: Emergent Public Health Hazards and National Policymaking* (Washington, D.C.: Brookings Institution, 1994), 11.

6. U.S. Congress, Senate, Committee on Labor and Human Resources, *AIDS Research*, 100th Cong., 1st sess., May 15, 1987.

7. Peter Gould, *The Slow Plague: A Geography of the AIDS Pandemic* (Cambridge: Blackwell Publishers, 1993).

8. Bimber, *The Politics of Expertise in Congress*.

9. Roger H. Davidson, "Subcommittee Government: New Channels for Policy Making," in *The New Congress*, ed. Thomas E. Mann and Norman J. Ornstein (Washington, D.C.: American Enterprise Institute, 1981); Christopher J. Deering, "Subcommittee Government in the U.S. House: An Analysis of Bill Management," *Legislative Studies Quarterly* 7 (1982): 533–46; Lawrence Evans and Richard L. Hall, "The Power of Subcommittees," *Journal of Politics* 52 (1990): 335–55; and Christopher J. Deering and Steven S. Smith, *Committees in Congress*, 3rd ed. (Washington, D.C.: CQ Press, 1997).

10. Michael Malbin, "Delegation, Deliberation, and the New Role of Congressional Staff," in *The New Congress*, ed. Thomas E. Mann and Norman J. Ornstein (Washington, D.C.: American Enterprise Institute, 1981); C. Lawrence Evans, "Participation and Policy Making in Senate Committees," *Political Science Quarterly* 106 (1991): 479–98.

11. Peter Gould, *The Slow Plague: A Geography of the AIDS Pandemic*.

12. Congressional Quarterly, *Almanac*, vol. 44 (Washington, D.C.: Congressional Quarterly Inc., 1988), 300.

13. Quoted in Charles Marwick, "AIDS Commission's Next Report Focuses on Four Critical Issues," *Journal of the American Medical Association* 259 (1988): 169.

14. Congressional Quarterly, *Almanac*, vol. 44 (Washington, D.C.: Congressional Quarterly Inc., 1988), 301.

15. E.E. Schattschneider, *Semisovereign People: A Realist's View of Democracy in America* (Hinsdale, Ill.: Dryden Press, 1975).

16. Julie Rovner, "Congress Stalemated over AIDS Epidemic," *Congressional Quarterly Weekly Report* 5 (December 1987).

17. Jeffrey Schmalz, "Gay Politics Goes Mainstream," *New York Times*, October 11, 1992, sec. 6.

18. Dennis Altman, "The Politics of AIDS," in *AIDS: Public Policy Dimensions*, ed. John Griggs (New York: United Hospital Fund of New York, 1987).

19. Edmund F. Dejowski, "Federal Restrictions on AIDS Prevention Efforts for Gay Men," *St. Louis University Public Law Review* 8 (1989): 275–98.

20. Rovner, "Congress Stalemated over AIDS Epidemic," 2986.

21. Quoted in ibid., 2986.

22. Dennis Altman, *AIDS in the Mind of America* (Garden City, N.Y.: Doubleday, 1986); and Simon Watney, *Policing Desire* (London: Comedia, 1987). Ryan White, a hemophiliac, was a useful symbol of the pervasiveness of the AIDS threat.

23. Senate Committee on Labor and Human Resources, *AIDS Research*, 3.

24. 100th Cong., 1st sess., *Congressional Record* August 4, 1987, H22244.

25. 100th Cong., 1st sess., *Congressional Record* August 4, 1987, H22247.

26. U.S. Congress, House, Committee on Veterans' Affairs, *National Commission on Acquired Immune Deficiency Syndrome Act*, 100th Cong., 1st sess., May 15, H. Rept. 100–245, 1989.

27. 100th Cong., 1st sess., *Congressional Record* August 4, 1987, H22248.

28. House Committee on Veterans' Affairs, *National Commission on Acquired Immune Deficiency Syndrome Act*, 9.

29. 100th Cong., 1st sess., *Congressional Record* August 4, 1987, H22244.

30. 100th Cong., 1st. sess., *Congressional Record* August 4, 1987, H22247.

31. 100th Cong., 1st. sess., *Congressional Record* August 4, 1987, H22248.

32. Senate Committee on Labor and Human Resources, *AIDS Research*, 4.

33. 100th Cong., 1st sess., *Congressional Record* August 4, 1987, H22243.

34. 100th Cong., 1st sess., *Congressional Record* August 4, 1987, H22246.

35. Senate Committee on Labor and Human Resources, *AIDS Research*, 4.

36. 100th Cong., 1st sess., *Congressional Record* August 4, 1987, H22242.

37. 100th Cong., 1st sess., *Congressional Record* August 4, 1987, H22244.

38. 100th Cong., 1st sess., *Congressional Record* August 4 1987, H22245.

39. 100th Cong., 1st sess., *Congressional Record* August 4, 1987, H22248.

40. Congressional Quarterly, *Almanac*, vol. 44 (Washington, D.C.: Congressional Quarterly Inc., 1988), 302.

41. Ibid., 5.

42. Rovner, "Congress Stalemated over AIDS Epidemic," 2986.

43. Congressional Quarterly, *Almanac*, vol. 46 (Washington, D.C.: Congressional Quarterly Inc., 1987), 516.

44. Quoted in Congressional Quarterly, *Almanac*, vol. 45 (Washington, D.C.: Congressional Quarterly, Inc., 1990), 583.

45. Congressional Quarterly, *Almanac*, vol. 44 (Washington, D.C.: Congressional Quarterly, Inc., 1988).

46. Quoted in Congressional Quarterly, *Almanac*, vol. 44 (Washington, D.C.: Congressional Quarterly, Inc., 1988), 302.

47. Senate Committee on Labor and Human Resources, *AIDS Research*, 3.

48. Ibid., 5.

49. Ibid., 9.

50. 100th Cong., 2nd sess., *Congressional Record*, April 28, 1988, S9312.

51. Congressional Quarterly, *Almanac*, vol. 44 (Washington, D.C.: Congressional Quarterly, Inc., 1988), 296.

52. U.S. Congress, Senate Committee on Labor and Human Resources, *National Commission on Acquired Immune Deficiency Syndrome Act*, 100th Cong., 2nd sess., H. Rept. 100–400, 1989, p. 3.

53. House Committee on Veterans' Affairs, *National Commission on Acquired Immune Deficiency Syndrome Act*, 8.

54. James Everett Katz, "Congress Needs Informal Science Advisors: A Proposal for a New Advisory Mechanism," in *Science and Technology Advice to the President, Congress, and Judiciary*, ed. William T. Golden (New York: Pergamon Press, 1988).

55. 100th Cong., 1st sess., *Congressional Record* August 4, 1987, H22243.

56. 100th Cong., 1st sess., *Congressional Record*, August 4, 1987, H22240.

57. Senate Committee on Labor and Human Resources, *National Commission on Acquired Immune Deficiency Syndrome Act*, 100th Cong., 2nd sess., 2.

58. 100th Cong., 1st sess., *Congressional Record* August 4, 1987, H22243.

59. Congressional Quarterly, *Almanac*, vol. 55 (Washington, D.C.: Congressional Quarterly Inc., 1990). 583.

60. Theodore J. Lowi, "American Business, Public Policy, Case-Studies, and Political Theory," *World Politics* 16 (1964): 693.

Chapter 5

A Case of Workload Management: The National Commission on the Thrift Industry

> In a perfect world with the time and with the staff, and with the ability to hire people with the expertise to make the appropriate judgments, you would have a Congress available to grapple with every issue.
>
> Staff aide to the House Armed
> Services Committee

Despite the effort Congress expends, issues still hamper the legislative process. Situations arise when it is impractical or inappropriate to commit proposals requiring congressional attention to normal legislative channels. Some tasks are substantively or procedurally cumbersome. Congress is limited by the size of its chambers. Members are stretched too thinly. Committees do not always have the time to examine every measure referred to them. These limitations shape opportunities for delegation. Congress gives various pieces of a legislative problem to others for resolution, and the most it may be able to do is assemble the recommended solutions into a final choice. As one aide to a southwestern senator asserted: "Time and practicality require that some issues go out of the mainstream of the legislative body."

The plight of the thrift institutions was one of both magnitude and complexity. The Savings and Loan (S & L) industry began to collapse in the early 1980s as more than a thousand S & L institutions bankrupted the insurance fund that protected thrift depositors, and another six hundred were became penniless but remained open for business, necessitating a wholesale salvage operation.[1] As the financial bases of the thrift failure have become better understood, attention has increasingly turned to the political causes: dishonest, blundering politics.[2] Several key lawmakers such as "The Keating Five,"[3] along with other key members of the banking committees and the congressional leadership, did receive lavish campaign contributions from the thrift industry.[4] But the downfall of the thrift industry contained all the elements of tragedy.[5] The thrift system was created for honorable purposes, to protect savings and to provide homes. The system was, however, vulnerable to economic forces that neither regulators nor members of Congress could control.[6] Once these forces struck, the demise of the thrift business was "inevitable no matter what the officials did."[7]

Rescuing the Savings and Loan industry was by no means a minor or trivial concern. Policy choices were rarely easy. In general, lawmakers deliberated cautiously when no consensus existed and decided quickly when one did; they deliberated when the solutions were not clear and acted when they were.[8] The dilemma became unmanageable, especially for jurisdictional committees, before the sine die adjournment of the 100th Congress (1987–1989). The issue was too important to be deferred to a later date.[9] If Congress did not solve this problem, it was not for lack of trying.[10] To be sure, congressional forbearance was an important component of the thrift debacle. Lawmakers were pressured by the S & L lobby into writing forbearance into law, encouraging industry excesses and delaying final resolution.[11] A useful parallel can be drawn between the Alaskan oil spill of 1989 and the collapse of S & Ls; in each case, initial damage from the "spill" was severely compounded by delaying and mishandling the clean up that was required.[12] Numerous congressional hearings addressed the S & L crisis directly, suggesting policy solutions ranging from corrective legislative statutes to regulatory reform. The proposal to temporarily delegate certain workload responsibilities to an ad hoc commission, a proposal that emerged out of committee oversight, served as a legislative crutch to support the numerous oversight committees' activities (Congress's own specialists and workload managers who proved ill-prepared)[13] of both chambers until the next Congress convened to take remedial action.

THE ENCUMBERING DYNAMICS THAT GENERATED THE WORK COMMISSION

The regulation of financial enterprises has long been a closely monitored activity (see Table 5.1). Congress exercised its authority to regulate financial institutions through its generous interpretations of Article I of the Constitution. Additionally, the "commerce clause" empowers Congress to regulate commerce. The role of the Supreme Court and its broad translations of these clauses have, over time, established the supremacy of Congress in finance and the national economy and justified the passage of thousands of laws that, collectively, govern the thrift industries. The Thrift Commission was not the first commission to help with national banking problems. At the turn of the twentieth century, Congress established the National Monetary Commission in its effort to improve the nation's fragile financial system. As part of its report to Congress the Monetary Commission recommended the creation of a central banking system, which Congress established five years later under the Federal Reserve Act. The act provided for a thoroughgoing revision of the nation's banking situation.

Initially designed to finance the purchase and construction of homes for middle-income families, the thrift industry diversified through considerable change, which helped contribute to many insolvencies in the early 1980s. Three types of financial intermediaries make up thrift institutions: Savings and Loan associations, mutual savings banks, and credit unions. Traditionally, thrifts earned their profits from the "spread" between the amounts of money they received as interest payments from borrowers and the amounts they were obliged to pay in interest. By the early 1980s, thrift institutions were engaging in numerous enterprises other than financing: home improvement loans, commercial real estate loans, consumer loans, investment in securities, educational loans, service corporations, credit cards, trust services, and others.[14] These changes transformed the Savings and Loan industry from a temporary undertaking to one characterized by permanence.

Change for the S & L industry began in the years 1966–1979 with record-setting inflation, large increases in money supply, market interest rate fluctuation, legal and regulatory changes, competition within the housing-related industries, public pressure, and technological change.[15] Computer technology, for instance, enabled the creation of money market funds and other financial instruments whose higher yields lured depositors away from thrifts.[16] S & Ls held millions of fixed-rate mortgages that were worth less than their face value. Thrifts faced competition from commercial banks that began issuing consumer deposits, and from governmental agencies that offered more attractive securities. Savings banks thus had a hard time offering depositors competitive rates of return, which eventually led many firms to insolvency. As the rates paid on such alternative investments of money market funds increased, Regulation Q, a federal rule limiting the maximum rate of interest that could be paid on savings and other demand deposits, made it virtually impossible for Savings and Loan institutions to attract funds.[17]

Not surprisingly, banking interests wished to remove the restrictive Regulation Q from thrift activities. By the late 1970s and early 1980s, a deregulation movement began to unfold on Capitol Hill. Premised on the notion that regulation and excessive costs resulted in inefficiency, deregulation found bipartisan support in Congress and the executive. These regulatory reforms had their deepest consequences in the nation's banking and financial sectors. In the Savings and Loan industry, deregulation left an indelible mark that contributed to a public policy problem of mammoth proportions. Congress

Table 5.1
Evolution of Banking Legislation

1789—Congress establishes the U.S. Department of the Treasury.

1791—Congress passes legislation incorporating the First United States Bank.

1816—President James Madison signs into law an act incorporating the Second Bank of the United States.

1832—President Andrew Jackson vetoes a re-chartering bill dissolving the First United States Bank.

1863—Congress passes the National Banking Act to set up a national banking system. The act contained provisions for national Incorporation of banks and for the issuing of bond-secured bank currency. Specific requirements regarding services held against deposit liabilities were to be regulated. The Office of the Comptroller of the Currency was established.

1908—Congress creates the National Monetary Commission to recommend changes in the banking and currency laws.

1911—Congress enacts the Aldrich-Freeland Act enabling the government to issue emergency currency, ultimately leading to the creation of the Federal Reserve System.

1913—The Federal Reserve Act is established based on the recommendations of the National Monetary Commission. The act provides for a thoroughgoing revision of the banking system.

1931—President Herbert Hoover initiates a plan to relieve the banking situation.

1932—Congress enacts the Federal Home Loan Bank Act establishing Federal Home Loan Bank Board.

1933—Congress enacts the Federal Reserve Act, establishing the Federal Deposit Insurance Corporation (FDIC) to provide and preserve public confidence in banks.

1934—Congress enacts the National Housing Act creating the Federal Savings and Loan Insurance Corporation (FSLIC) to insure the safety of savings in thrift and home-financing institutions.

1950—Congress passes the Federal Deposit Insurance Act.

1966—Congress passes the Bank Merger Act requiring FDIC approval for bank mergers involving an FDIC-insured bank and an uninsured nonmember bank.

1968—Congress enacts the Bank Protection Act authorizing federal financial institution supervisory agencies to issue rules establishing minimum security measures.

1977—Legislation is passed expanding the powers of federal credit unions in lending and saving areas.

1978—Congress passes the International Banking Act allowing U.S. branches of foreign banks to be eligible to obtain federal deposit insurance.

1980—Congress enacts the Depository Institutions Deregulation and Monetary Control Act to restore the competitive position of thrifts and banks.

Table 5.1   (continued)

1982—Congress passes the Garn-St.Germain Depository Institutions Act creating new competitive opportunities for chartered thrifts by increasing their ability to make commercial and consumer loans.

1983—Congress enacts the Domestic Housing and International Recovery and Financial Stability Act establishing the supervision and regulation of international lending by the FDIC and other federal bank regulatory agencies.

1987—Congress passes the Competitive Equality Banking Act establishing the Financing Corporation to undertake a special financing program to recapitalize the FSLIC.

Source: Adapted from "Savings and Loan Controversy," *Congressional Digest*, 68 (June–July 1989).

responded in order to boost thrifts and make their deposits more profitable with the passage of the 1980 Depository Institutions Deregulation and Monetary Control Act. The act was a Carter administration initiative aimed at eliminating many of the distinctions among different types of depository institutions and ultimately removing interest rate ceilings on deposit accounts. A major provision of the law permitted the Federal Home Loan Bank Board to reduce mandatory net worth requirements on Savings and Loans. The Bank Board responded swiftly, making it easier for thrifts to grow rapidly, since they could attract depositors with high interest rates, as the act phased out interest rate ceilings for both bank and thrift accounts. The new law also increased the level of deposit-insurance coverage and allowed thrifts to diversify into areas previously reserved for commercial banks, by abolishing geographic restrictions on investment activities of S & Ls, thereby bringing a national market within the purview of individual institutions that had operated locally for decades.

These legislative measures did not suffice, however, to restore the thrift industry to profitability. Although the move retarded the movement of thrift deposits into money market funds, it increased the liability of the insurance fund.[18] While thrifts could now retain deposits by paying higher interest rates than Regulation Q had permitted, payment of higher rates, coupled with increasing reliance by many thrifts on market-rate advances from the Federal Home Loan Banks, significantly increased the industry's costs.[19] Many S & Ls also compounded their problems by involving themselves in questionable investment schemes.[20] Without ties to deposits generated in their immediate communities, unregulated savings could give account and credit privileges and other banking services nationwide by offering through brokers the high rates of interest made available by deregulation itself.[21]

The Savings and Loan issue moved to the top of the legislative agenda when thrifts began suffering large net losses. When Congress gave federal thrifts additional powers, some states followed the deregulation model adopted earlier in Texas (which was then booming with the rise in the price of oil). These states extended the powers of their state-chartered institutions to enhance their profitability and to discourage them from changing to federal charters. California, for example, enacted a law providing for a very liberal set of powers.

It is easy to make mistakes when exercising new powers. Some institutions entered the market too late, acquired only projects that the experts avoided, or were deceived or even defrauded. In other instances, thrifts that were approaching insolvency used the new powers that promised high returns to gamble toward recovery. But high returns involved high risk and many that risked and failed left the Federal Savings and Loan Insurance Corporation with the bill.[22] As the consequence of these imprudent and fraudulent investments came home to roost, the industry's rate of decay accelerated. By early 1982, as a result of paying too much interest and receiving too little, of bad loans, and of industry-wide clamity, thrift institutions started to disappear at a rate of one per day.[23] Table 5.2 outlines the losses

Table 5.2
Losses and Insolvencies in the S & L Industry, 1979–1982

	1979	1980	1981	1982
Net income (billions)	$0.781	($4.631)	($4.142)	$1.945
Number of unprofitable as percentage of all S & Ls	7%	36%	85%	68%
Assets in unprofitable as percentage of total S & L assets	4%	33%	91%	61%
Number of insolvent* S & Ls	34	43	112	415
As percentage of all S & Ls	1%	%	3%	13%
Assets in insolvent S & Ls (billions)	—	—	$29	$220
As percentage of total S & L assets	—	—	5%	32%
Tangible net worth as percentage of total assets	5.6%	5.3%	3.9%	0.6%

Note: *Net worth calculated on a tangible net worth basis.
Source: National Commission on Financial Institution Reform, Recovery and Enforcement, *Origins and Causes of the S & L Debacle: A Blueprint for Reform* (Washington, D.C.: Government Printing Office, 1993, 30).

and insolvencies in the S & L industry between 1979 and 1982. While a good number of these shutdowns were the result of takeovers, most institutions simply failed as a result of liabilities resulting from high interest deposits in what suddenly became a low inflation economy.[24]

In May 1982, the net worth of U.S. insured Savings and Loan associations witnessed a loss in net worth for the seventeenth consecutive month. Widespread bankruptcy in the thrift industry quickly became a major public concern. Unable to meet their obligations to depositors, S & Ls approached Capitol Hill for relief. Congress, reflecting bipartisan concern for the S & L sector, responded with another revision of law, albeit in quick-fix fashion.[25] The Garn-St. Germain Bill, signed into law by President Ronald Reagan in 1982, further loosened restrictions on the kinds of investments S & Ls could make.

Several measures were introduced to deal with the problem of the thrift industry in a small way in the 100th Congress, but Capitol Hill agreed that a solution would have to await the 101st Congress (1989–1991). Discussion focused more on the urgency of the problem than on the solution.[26] The plan for a commission to address the thrift industry's plight was occasioned by the need to assist committee members' own efforts to wrestle with the thrift puzzle.[27] Repeated hearings were held in both chambers. During the first session of the 100th Congress, the House Banking Committee reported legislation to recapitalize the Federal Savings and Loan Insurance Corporation (FSLIC), which insured deposits held by the nation's thrift institutions. The measure was signed into law as P.L. 100–86, provided the FSLIC with $10. 8 billion to deal with troubled thrifts. The House Banking Committee also reported the failure of, and called for the dissolution of, the Federal Asset Disposition Association (FADA), the agency set up by the Bank Board to assist the FSLIC in the management and disposition of assets acquired from failed thrifts.

The sheer volume of work proved too much for most members of Congress. Resolving the problem entailed swift action by thrifts, thrift regulators, the administration, and Capitol Hill. Lawmakers welcomed the setting up of a single-purpose, independent commission for its capacity to coordinate these varied interests and yield detailed blueprints for the future. "When we face a problem of such magnitude, we cannot afford to work in the dark; we must have a clear idea of what we're up against before there can be any hope of finding a reasonable solution," admonished Representative Stanford E. Parris (R-Va.) during testimony before the House Subcommittee on General Oversight and Investigations.[28] "The Commission will explore feasible options for dealing with the insolvent one-third of the Savings and Loan industry," he declared on a later occasion. "It's a step in the right direction for focusing the attention of a very much needed review of the thrift industry process, and for providing additional support to prior committee efforts." Republican Representative Al McCandless of California said: "I think the direction in which the committee [commission] is going here is certainly a way of focusing the attention of a very much needed review of the entire process."[29]

Concern for time was also a primary motive. The concern became general across jurisdictional committees as adjournment neared and committee members became doubtful of reporting legislation. There was a growing sense that time would inhibit committee consideration, preventing swift and comprehensive policy formulation.[30] Significant legislation would take more than one Congress, prompting the decision to transfer authority to a commission to undertake and coordinate the tasks Congress could not. Delegating to the National Commission on the Thrift Industry laid to rest the concern for time, since the commission relieved the committees' overburdened agendas. Representative Parris voiced concern about the end of the legislative session. "My intention is not to sidestep the jurisdiction of this committee, the responsibilities of the full committee or anything else," he said.[31] "We all know there are just a few legislative days remaining on the legislative calendar year and the ability of Congress to substantively address this issue before the estimated adjournment date is highly problematical at best. We've got to get on with some resolution for this problem."

Representative Chalmers P. Wylie (R-Ohio), the ranking minority member of the House Committee on Banking, Finance and Urban Affairs, who also recommended the Thrift Commission, acknowledged that Congress needed outside assistance:

> While the Banking Committee has held a number of hearings on the stability of the thrift industry and the FSLIC, it is clear that time has run out for the 100th Congress to adequately and substantively address this matter. In this regard, this Commission will be instrumental in maintaining a clear focus on the FSLIC crisis after the 100th Congress adjourns in the weeks ahead. We are particularly pleased that this Commission will report its findings and recommendations early next year so that the 101st Congress and the next Administration will have a solid base from which to attack this problem and, hopefully, provide a number of legislative alternatives or other recommendations for resolving the FSLIC crisis. We feel strongly that it is the responsibility of the Banking Committee to ensure that action on the FSLIC issue continues to move forward in an expeditious manner. The Commission is an important first step in tackling this difficult issue.[32]

Committee members in both chambers urged that the Thrift Commission begin its work before Congress adjourned, in order that the commission's final report could be reported early the next year to the 101st Congress. This way the House and Senate Banking Committees could respond immediately at the commencement of the 101st Congress. "The recommendations of a group of a commission would certainly be useful to the 101st Congress when this matter is expected to be in the forefront early next year," added the then chair of the House Banking Committee, Fernand J. St. Germain (D-R.I.).[33]

ESTABLISHMENT OF THE NATIONAL COMMISSION ON THE THRIFT INDUSTRY

To seek independent advice as well as muster bipartisan support, the National Commission on the Thrift Industry was proposed for the purpose of investigating and making recommendations on the financial problems of the thrift industry at both federal and state levels. Directed to meet at least once a calendar month, the commission would have been responsible for carrying out a multitude of functions. It also would have been charged with examining and reporting on the thrift industry's role in providing mortgage credit, the role of the government-sponsored secondary mortgage market entities in relation to the role of the thrifts' mortgage banks and commercial banks in providing mortgage credit, the need for specialized depository institutions to serve the mortgage market, and the extent to which such institutions affect the availability of low and moderate income housing. It would also have considered options for restructuring the thrift industry regulatory framework, including a separation of the insurance and the regulatory functions of the Federal Home Loan Bank Board, as well as methods for increasing capital in the thrift industry, including permitting bank holding companies to acquire failed as well as healthy Savings and Loans, and investigated whether the capital currently supplied by private investors/acquirers of failed thrifts was adequate.[34]

Similar to the composition of the National Commission on AIDS, the bipartisan composition of the Thrift Commission had the appealing political logic of being broad-based, knowledgeable, and impartial. In each chamber, the banking committees believed that the problem merited a select commission of people who had relevant understanding and background, including thrift industry leaders, academicians, prominent authorities on housing concerns, other individuals with "distinctive qualifications," and members of Congress.[35] Lawmakers did recognize that the ultimate decision on whether or not to implement some of the commission's recommendations might be based on political factors not considered by the commission. But they also thought that the commission should not conduct itself as a political body. Thus, the initial legislative outline creating the commision drawn up by the Senate (S 2653) proposed appointing fourteen members (composed of representatives of the administration, members of Congress, and private citizens), but this number was later expanded to eighteen when the House Banking Committee voted 45 to 2 to approve its own version.[36]

A mixture of individuals was slated for appointment: two citizens, chosen by the president; two senators and two citizens, appointed by the president pro tempore of the Senate upon the recommendation of the majority leader

of the Senate; two senators and one citizen of the United States, selected
by the president pro tempore of the Senate upon the recommendation of
the minority leader of the Senate; two members of the House of Representatives and two citizens, named by the House Speaker upon the recommendation of the majority leader of the House; two members of the House of
Representatives and one citizen, designated by the House Speaker upon the
recommendation of the minority leader of the House; and two citizens, one
Democrat and one Republican, picked by the president-elect.

Congress also worked to keep the commission's non-congressional members independent and professional. "It is the Committee's intent that the
members of the Commission have diverse viewpoints and backgrounds with
strong knowledge of the subject matter," emphasized the House Banking
Committee.[37] Those appointed to the Thrift Commission who were not
members of Congress were individuals who were qualified to serve because
of their education, training, or experience; they included leaders of business
or labor, distinguished academics, and state or local officials. Of these "citizen" commissioners not more than two could be a director, officer, or employee of any federal or state agency or instrumentality with supervisory or
regulatory authority over any thrift institution; or a director, officer, employee, or agent of any trade association which represented any thrift institution. The chairperson of the commission was charged with appointing an
executive director and additional staff deemed advisable to assist the commission.

Operating within a specified budget of one million dollars, the commission could make contracts with state agencies, private firms, institutions,
and individuals for conducting research or surveys. Upon request of the
commission's chair, federal facilities, and the services of personnel and information from federal agencies, on a non-reimbursable basis, were to be
made available to assist the commission. The Thrift Commission was designed without procedural mechanisms designed to obscure the connection
between legislative action and policy result. It did not retain substantial discretion; its authority was advisory. Its final recommendations would go to
the House and Senate Banking Committees, providing members with an opportunity to amend as well as further deliberate on major policy implications.

The politics surrounding the formation of the Thrift Commission was
intense because the stakes were high. Committee Chairman Fernand J. St.
Germain ruled several amendments to the Thrift Commission bill out of order as not germane, including one that would have expanded the measure
to cover all deposit insurance, as in the Senate bill. The most significant
amendment ruled out of order would have expanded the 1987 recapitaliza-
tion of the FSLIC. Representative John J. LaFalce (D-N.Y.) proposed that
the FSLIC be allowed to borrow up to $15 billion to cover its rising costs.[38]
The administration had requested Congress in 1986 to allow the FSLIC to
issue $15 billion in special bonds, but under pressure from industry groups

to reduce the amount—since thrifts would have to pay off the bonds through higher deposit insurance premiums—Congress consented to only $10.8 billion in borrowing.[39]

LaFalce tied his proposal to a $20 billion cap on the promissory notes that the FSLIC was issuing to investors who bought insolvent thrifts. Some in Congress worried that continued use of these notes, when the FSLIC had no cash to cover them, constituted an unauthorized raid on the Treasury, since the federal government presumably would have to honor them if the FSLIC defaulted.[40]

One outspoken objector to the Thrift Commission was Representative Bruce Vento (D-Minn.), who acknowledged that while the goals of the House Banking Committee were commendable, the commission would not advance Congress's efforts. "A National Commission does not add one brick to the foundation that the Committee has laid," he argued. "We do not need a Commission to regurgitate and translate that information for us. . . We do not need a Commission to second guess on the correct course; a National Commission will just be another voice."[41] Other opponents criticized the effort to establish the commission. The commission was criticized by Senator Alfonse M. D'Amato (D-N.Y.), as a "political boondoggle."[42] "I am wondering really what that Commission can accomplish that a number of very distinguished groups would not be able to do—the Federal Reserve and others," he remarked.

Critics also believed that an ad hoc commission would not speed up committee deliberations and was an attempt to draw the administration into the political process. "We know the time constraints that we will be under; the chickens are coming home to roost," charged Representative Vento.[43] "We have had before us most responsible suggestions on the direction that our national policy should take." Those who supported the Thrift Commission refuted this point: "The intention is not to sidestep the jurisdiction of this committee, the responsibilities of the full committee or anything else," said Representative Parris.[44] Stating in his testimony before the House Committee on Banking, Finance and Urban Affairs, Representative St. Germain, who helped shepherd the legislation to establish the Thrift Commission through the House, added: "The creation of a Thrift Commission is not meant to be a final answer or some magical cure-all to the problems of the thrift industry. The Thrift Commission will be available, but it must be regarded as a supplement to the efforts that the Committee has to undertake in a short time frame."[45]

The general sense on Capitol Hill, especially in the banking committees, was that the Thrift Commission would help fix the lingering thrift problem. "The Banking Committee will continue to closely monitor the financial condition of the thrift industry," the House Committee on Banking, Finance and Urban Affairs reported.[46] "At the same time, the Committee recognizes the benefits of an independent Commission to provide additional assistance in estimating the magnitude of the thrift industry crisis, and welcomes all recommendations aimed at solving the thrift problem." Similar sentiments were reported by the Senate Committee on Banking, Housing, and Urban Affairs: "The Committee believes the Commission will provide Congress and the public with hard and fast answers as to the magnitude of the thrift industry's problem."[47]

Another snare came when a few legislators objected that Congress would turn away or avert attention from the Savings and Loan problem. During subcommittee debate, Representative Steve Bartlett (R-Texas) charged that "a Commission to study the problem is not a solution at all."[48] "We know we have to take an orderly disposition. So my question is what would this Commission tell us that we don't already know?" Other opponents heaped scorn on the delegation. Senator James J. Exon (D-Neb.) claimed that the Savings and Loan industry was too important to "sweep it under the rug."[49] "I would hope that we could put through some legislation this year, if we cannot by the scheduled day of adjournment, then I suggest we consider coming back as soon as possible." Commission backers countered this point. Further emphasizing the difficulty of solving the S & L dilemma within the closing days of Congress, witnesses at a House hearing pointed to the benefits of delegating. "I think the time frame that is suggested for the deliberations of the committee would preclude any truly new or innovative solutions coming forth," H. Robert Bartell, second vice-chairman of the National Council of Savings Institutions, said.[50] "It seems to me that the Commission could take an in depth look at the solutions that are proposed and try to coalesce support for one or a few which will deal with the most significant problems that exist, and provide a consensus at least of some well-informed people to the Congress so that the solution to the problem can move forward."

Both chambers passed a bill (S 2653) supporting the National Commission on the Thrift Industry. The House version (HR 2881) was finally approved, 395 to 21. The measure died, however, in the last week of the second session after being ensnared in an eleventh-hour parliamentary maneuver aimed at enacting a broad bank-deregulation bill before Congress adjourned. Senator William Proxmire (D-Wis.), hoping to skirt a jurisdictional dispute in the House that had paralyzed movement on the banking bill, split the Senate version of the banking bill (S 1886) in two, attaching one part to S 2653, the Thrift Commission Bill.[51] But Senator Proxmire finally let the commission bill die along with its banking-regulation rider.

Congress would create the National Commission on Financial Institution Reform, Recovery and Enforcement as a part of the Comprehensive Crime Control Act of 1990 (P.L. 101–647). In its final report the commission made a number of recommendations. Under the heading of "guardians of the public interest" the commission recommended that Congress delegate to the Federal Reserve Board the task of overseeing and commenting on issues relating to federal deposit insurance and regulation. The commission also suggested that congressional oversight was insufficient and ineffective during the collapse of the S & L industry. Increased reliance on the support agency, the Government Accounting Office, the commission noted, improved the situation, but committees would need greater staff expertise and better access to information without relying on regulators.[52] In addition, these committees could enhance their expertise and the perspectives available to them by establishing visiting scholar programs for academic experts.

THE POLITICS OF DISTRIBUTION

Like commissions created for expertise, commissions designed to pare down Congress's workload typically deal with distributive problems, although some can involve self-regulation or redistribution. The mechanics of the S & L subsidy arrangement do differ, however, from the mechanics of AIDS policy, in which numerous laws specified direct beneficiaries. Distributive decisions parcel out the federal pork barrel, giving many people a bite. The process is characterized by distributive decisions, both within a field and between different substantive fields, that are often made individually, without consideration for their overall impact—they are decentralized and uncoordinated.[53] The direct recipients in the thrift industry crisis—savings banks—did not compete directly with each other nor did they pay direct costs. The material nature of the subsidy took the form of a large-scale bailout of the Savings and Loan industry.

The benefits of the bailout tilted heavily toward the affluent. Deposit insurance is an entitlement program without a means test, so everyone with an insured deposit is protected regardless of wealth or income. The affluent received the bulk of benefits because, although most insured accounts at thrifts were relatively small, most of the insured money was in large accounts.[54] Further, more than twenty million depositors held accounts at S & Ls that failed, and all these deposit holders were beneficiaries of the governmental bailout. Many of those who performed services for failed thrifts, obtained loans from them, or sold property to them, Mark Carl Rom observes, also indirectly collected deposit insurance payments.[55] Thus, deposit insurance payments were, like the nation's wealth, "both narrowly concentrated on the wealthy and widely dispersed among the less affluent."

Expertise was not the rationale for creating the Thrift Industry Commission. Unlike AIDS, the issue of national banking involved a task with documented congressional concern and supervision. A web of regulatory machinery had been installed to help maintain the soundness of this industry. Thrift institutions grew and prospered under the regulatory framework that required them to specialize in long-term mortgage lending and retail deposit taking. The system operated smoothly as long as real interest rates held steady. As interest rates increased, however, Congress and the regulatory agencies imposed binding deposit rate-ceilings on all types of accounts.[56] The intention was to limit the cost of liabilities for thrift institutions so they could remain viable housing lenders. The consequence of such distributive forces crafted a cast of characters who were fairly stable over time, and whose interactions were marked with a relatively low degree of publicized conflict and a high degree of mutually rewarding, nonconflictual relationships among the actors. This facilitated a perpetuation of subsidies and continued low visibility until problems worsened and thrifts began suffering net losses totaling tens of billions.

The coalition that formed around this distributive public policy issue was bipartisan and broad. Conflicting viewpoints were cast in political, not ideological, terms; partisan affiliations and geographical regions, campaign contributions, and thrift constituencies affected close to 80 percent of congressional voting on thrift legislation.[57] Generally, the distributive decision mollified the more vocal opponents of delegation. Nor were local interests the sole influence on policy.[58] A principal goal was to avoid the type of financial chaos and loss that had confronted the nation's commercial and thrift banks during the Great Depression, a goal which had little chance of being accomplished in one Congress. The political repercussions of the thrift tragedy were also modest. There was no wholesale rebellion against members of Congress, as few congressional races following the tragedy focused on thrift issues.[59]

CONCLUSION

Besides its traditional lawmaking function, Congress performs other activities: reviewing programs, serving constituents, responding to executive communications, and participating in responsibilities shared with the president. Congress is a resilient organization, however, adapting and acclimating to changes in its internal and external environment. As Joseph Cooper notes, when confronted with stress from outside forces, the institution normally does not radically transform its work.[60] Rather, it pursues alternative strategies. One method is delegating task responsibilities among a variety of distinct units or adding units along existing organizational lines.[61]

Commissions are an expansionary response to a growing workload. These temporary entities represent Congress's ability to modify its workload to manage and reduce the volume and scope of the efforts that must be undertaken in today's legislative environment. They provide an information-gathering stage for policymaking, giving lawmakers the time needed to understand an issue before developing legislation without interfering with other business. In tandem with staff resources, ad hoc commissions enable Congress to cope with its contemporary workload, and develop skills and expertise in specific issues. Institutionalization on Capitol Hill—the fragmented and fractionalized nature of committees—can lead to organizational rigidity which produces paralysis. Certain structures of the congressional establishment are too brittle and can frustrate or delay policymaking, especially in periods of rapid social or political change. These limitations shape occasions for delegation to commissions.

The National Commission on the Thrift Industry helps us understand Congress's habit of setting up a commission to ease its overloaded agenda. To be certain, congressional oversight was inadequate and the process was politicized. Congress appears to have been largely unaware of the severe problems developing in the Savings and Loan industry, and industry lobbying was pervasive and effective. By the time the extent of the problem became clear, Congress found itself unable to consider the S & L problem in the limited period before the scheduled adjournment. According to all accounts of the congressional debate and deliberation, the proposal of a commission was offered largely for managerial purposes: to provide a bridge from one Congress to the next.

Generally, legislative backers mustered widespread support for delegating because the time within one Congress to construct any reasonable resolution of the thrift problem was highly unrealistic. The House Committee on Banking, Finance and Urban Affairs and the Senate Committee on Banking, Housing, and Urban Affairs chose to transfer decision making authority to outsiders to undertake and coordinate tasks the committees could not do. The commission could gather information and develop alternative approaches, and make the choices that would maximize the chances of achieving a rich set of values for government action. Sifting through the huge proportions of work created by the Savings and Loan dilemma was better done by persons outside Congress.

The decision to delegate can be a subjective, political one, which typically occurs because Congress cannot overcome its own shortcomings. Despite the committee system's division of labor or management reform legislation—efforts initiated for the management of the institution's workload—Capitol Hill cannot adequately examine every measure before it, and its lack of technical expertise obstructs speedy and comprehensive policy formulation. Still, other political dynamics occasion yet a third type of commission. When Congress faces controversial issues such as base closures, it delegates to shift the blame. The conditions under which such delegation works are characterized by redistributive policy issues that require legislators to take a clear policy position on something that has greater costs to their districts than benefits or that shifts resources visibly from one group to another. It is this third type of commission that I now examine.

NOTES

1. In this chapter the terms Savings and Loans, *thrifts*, and *associations* are used synonymously.

2. James Ring Adams, *The Big Fix: Inside the S & L Scandal* (New York: John Wiley & Sons, 1989); Kathleen Day, *S & L Hell: The People and the Politics behind the $1 Trillion Savings and Loan Scandal* (New York: W.W. Norton & Company, 1993); Ned Eichler, *The Thrift Debacle* (Berkeley: University of California Press, 1989); Martin Lowy, *High Rollers: Inside the Savings and Loan Debacle* (New York: Praeger, 1991); Martin Mayer, *The Greatest-Ever Bank Robbery: The Collapse of the Savings and Loan Industry* (New York: Charles Scribner's Sons, 1990); Mark Carl Rom, *Public Spirit in the Thrift Tragedy* (Pittsburgh: University of Pittsburgh Press, 1996).

3. This group included five senators who collectively accepted some $1.5 million in political contributions from a Savings and Loan executive named Charles H. Keating, Jr. In return Keating asked the senators to intervene on his behalf with federal regulators who were investigating the failing Lincoln Savings and Loan Bank of California, which was eventually seized by the government. Senator Alan Cranston (D-Calif.) was found to have violated the Senate's general rule against improper behavior; Senators John McCain (R-Ariz.) and John Glenn (D-Ohio) were found guilty only of exercising poor judgment; and Senators Donald W. Riegle, Jr. (D-Mich.), and Dennis DeConcini (D-Ariz.), were reproached in slightly stronger terms by the Senate Ethics Committee.

4. Brooks Jackson, *Honest Graft: Big Money and the American Political Process* (New York: Alfred Knopf, 1988); Brooks Jackson, "As Thrift Industry's Troubles and Losses Mounted, Its PACs' Donations to Key Congressmen Surged," *Wall Street Journal*, February 7, 1989, A26. See also Thomas Romer and Barry R. Weingast, "Political Foundations of the Thrift Debacle," in *Politics and Economics in the Eighties*, ed. Alberto Alesina and Geofrey Carliner (Chicago: University of Chicago Press, 1991).

5. Rom, *Public Spirit in the Thrift Tragedy*, 16.

6. U.S. Congress, Senate, Committee on the Judiciary, *Savings and Loan Crisis*, 101st Cong., 2nd sess., S. Hrg., 101–1195.

7. Rom, *Public Spirit in the Thrift Tragedy*, 211.

8. Ibid.

9. U.S. Congress, House, Committee on Banking, Finance, and Urban Affairs, *National Commission on the Thrift Industry*, 100th Cong., 2nd sess., H. Rept. 100–1042, 1988; Congress, House, Committee on Banking, Finance, and Urban Affairs, Subcommittee on General Oversight and Investigations of the Committee on Banking, Finance and Urban Affairs, *Legislation to Establish the National Thrift Institutions Commission* (H.R. 4894), 100th Cong., 2nd sess., 1988; and U.S. Congress, Senate Committee on Banking, Housing, and Urban Affairs, *National Commission on the Thrift Industry*, 100th Cong., 2nd sess., 1988.

10. Rom, *Public Spirit in the Thrift Tragedy*.

11. National Commission on Financial Institution Reform, Recovery and Enforcement, *Origins and Causes of the S & L Debacle: A Blueprint for Reform* (Washington, D.C.: Government Printing Office, 1993).

12. Edward J. Kane, "The High Cost of Incompletely Funding the FSLIC's Shortgage of Explicit Capital." *Journal of Economic Perspectives* (Fall 1989): 31–48; Edward J. Kane, "The Savings and Loan Insurance Mess, *Society* (March/April 1992): 4–10; and Romer and Weingast, "Political Foundations of the Thrift Debacle."

13. National Commission on Financial Institution Reform, Recovery and Enforcement.

14. Manfred M. Fabritius and William Borges, *Saving and Savings and Loan* (New York: Praeger Publishers, 1989).

15. Quoted in ibid., 52.

16. John R. Cranford, "Savings and Loan Crisis," in *The Encyclopedia of the United States Congress*, ed. Donald C. Bacon, Roger H. Davidson, and Morton Keller vol. 1. (New York: Simon & Schuster, 1995).

17. Michael A. Bernstein, "The Contemporary American Banking Crisis in Historical Perspective," *Journal of American History* 80 (1994): 1387.

18. Cranford, "Savings and Loan Crisis," 1758.

19. "Savings and Loan Controversy," *Congressional Digest* 68 (June–July 1989): 166.

20. Congressional Quarterly, *Guide to Congress*, 4th ed. (Washington, D.C.: Congressional Quarterly Inc., 1991), 289. World oil prices collapsed in 1986–1987, creating economic havoc in the oil-producing American Southwest, and soon afterward the nation's real estate market began to sag.

21. Bernstein, "The Contemporary American Banking Crisis in Historical Perspective."

22. "Savings and Loan Controversy," *Congressional Digest.*

23. Fabritius and Borges, *Saving and Savings and Loan*; and Rom, *Public Spirit in the Thrift Tragedy.*

24. Fabritius and Borges, *Saving and Savings and Loan.*

25. Mayer, *The Greatest-Ever Bank Robbery.*

26. Congressional Quarterly, *Almanac*, vol. 44, 100th Cong., 2nd sess., 1988, 242.

27. U.S. Congress, House, Committee on Banking, Finance, and Urban Affairs, Subcommittee on General Oversight and Investigations of the Committee on Banking, Finance and Urban Affairs, *Legislation to Establish the National Thrift Institutions Commission* (H.R. 4894), 100th Cong., 2nd sess., 1988.

28. Ibid., 13.

29. Ibid., 14.

30. Ibid.; and U.S. Congress, House, Committee on Banking, Finance, and Urban Affairs, *National Commission on the Thrift Industry*, 100th Cong., 2nd sess., H. Rept. 100–1042, 1988.

31. House Committee on Banking, Finance and Urban Affairs 1988, 13.

32. Ibid.

33. Ibid., 2.

34. Andrew S. Carron, *The Plight of the Thrift Institutions* (Washington, D.C.: Brookings Institution, 1982), 4–5.

35. U.S. Congress, Senate Committee on Banking, Housing, and Urban Affairs, *National Commission on the Thrift Industry*, 100th Cong., 2nd sess., 1988, 3.

36. The decision to expand commission membership came after the declaration of the president-elect following the presidential election on November 8, 1988.

37. House Committee on Banking, Housing, and Urban Affairs, *National Commission on the Thrift Industry*, 5.

38. *Congressional Quarterly Almanac*, vol. 44, 100th Congress, 2nd sess., (Washington, D.C.: Congressional Quarterly Inc.) 1988), 245.

39. Ibid.

40. Ibid.

41. House Committee on Banking, Housing, and Urban Affairs, *National Commission on the Thrift Industry*, 4.

42. 100th Cong., 2nd sess., *Congressional Record* October 14, 1988, S31700.

43. House Committee on Banking, Housing, and Urban Affairs, *National Commission on the Thrift Industry*, 15.

44. Ibid.

45. Ibid., 4.

46. Ibid., 5.

47. Senate Committee on Banking, Housing, and Urban Affairs, *National Commission on the Thrift Industry*, 2.

48. Subcommittee on General Oversight and Investigations of the House Committee on Banking, Finance, and Urban Affairs, *Legislation to Establish the National Thrift Institutions Commission*, 32.

49. 100th Cong., 2nd sess., *Congressional Record* September 23, 1988, S25221.

50. Subcommittee on General Oversight and Investigations of the House Committee on Banking, Finance, and Urban Affairs, *Legislation to Establish the National Thrift Institutions Commission*, 32.

51. *Congressional Quarterly Almanac*, vol. 44, 100th Congress, 2nd sess., (Washington, D.C.: Congressional Quarterly, Inc. 1988), 246.

52. National Commission on Financial Institution Reform, Recovery and Enforcement, *Origins and Causes of the S & L Debacle*, 76.

53. Randall B. Ripley and Grace A. Franklin, *Congress, the Bureaucracy, and Public Policy* (Homewood, Ill.: The Dorsey Press, 1984), 18.

54. Rom, *Public Spirit in the Thrift Tragedy*, 214.

55. Ibid.

56. Carron, *The Plight of the Thrift Institutions*.

57. Rom, *Public Spirit in the Thrift Tragedy*.

58. Ibid.

59. Ibid.

60. Joseph Cooper, "Organization and Innovation in the House of Representatives," in *The House at Work*, ed. Joseph Cooper and G. Calvin Mackenzie (Austin: University of Texas Press, 1981), 339.

61. Ibid.

——*Chapter 6*——

A Case of Blame Avoidance: The Base Closure and Realignment Commission

If you have enough concern to create a commission, to solve the problem, then you know what you think the problem is and you ought to be able to come up with a solution for yourself. I don't think commissions are an honest answer. I think that members of Congress recognize that any real solution is such a hot potato and that they don't want to be involved with it.

Chief of staff to a U.S. representative

Congress occasionally uses an ad hoc commission to distance itself from a politically risky decision. Members struggle when local interests collide with larger policy needs. They may want to see things go well for the nation, but they also want to get reelected. Typically, these conflicting preferences are such that no one can reconcile them, because most congressional representatives see themselves as agents of their constituents and are therefore unwilling to sacrifice their districts to the collective good. By enabling lawmakers to turn away or avert their attention from such a dilemma, a commission is supposed to offer protection to individual members, sufficiently obscuring any causal chain. This mechanism paradoxically enables affected legislators to become advocates for their constituents rather than bearers of bad news. They can passionately plead the case for their constituents but also confront a national policy need.

No fights on Capitol Hill are as contested as the ones over whose districts lose defense dollars. Lobbying for military projects comes naturally to members, who are expected to champion local interests.[1] Liberals and conservatives, hawks and doves, Democrats and Republicans all join the fray. As post-Cold War defense cuts made military expansion untenable, the closing of defense facilities lagged behind the cuts in active-duty personnel. Two main roadblocks account for Congress's failure to close unneeded facilities: the parochialism of lawmakers, due to the economic pain of surrendering such prizes; and institutional parochialism, due to rivalry or conflict between the executive and legislative branches.[2]

THE PAROCHIAL DYNAMICS THAT GENERATED THE BLAME AVOIDANCE COMMISSION

At the height of military spending in the early 1980s, nearly 10 percent of the American workforce got all or part of its income from defense.[3] Military installations brought millions of federal dollars to their host communities, employing and housing thousands of civilians while stimulating local economies.[4] Richard Stubbing notes that the defense budget serves local economies as a means of achieving various social and economic goals advanced by the government.[5] Congress required, for instance, that the Department of Defense (DOD) set aside contracts for small businesses and minority firms so that they, too, would receive a share of the defense dollars. Little wonder that Congress so staunchly defended its constitutional authority to raise and support the armed forces, and that some refer to the Committees on Armed Services as "real-estate committees."[6] Military bases are the kind of pork barrel that in the words of Representative Richard K. Armey (R-Texas) "even turns doves into superhawks."[7] Any reduction is dramatically visible, costly, and politically chancy.

Historically, military installations were sought by lawmakers as boons to the local economies.[8] By the late 1970s, however, it became clear that the military base structure bordered on the preposterous. Congress could no longer ignore or excuse this, especially when even the Pentagon—normally reluctant to admit that it can return money to the Treasury—conceded that its installation experts could find close to a billion dollars in excess base capacity.

Despite these signals, under pressure from local economic interests, senators and representatives fought to keep installations open, regardless of need, largely because of the difficulty many states and communities would face in absorbing the economic shifts. Significant changes occurred in the institutional mechanisms that encouraged and institutionalized parochialism in the decisions to close or realign bases.[9] The normal cyclical method of closure announcements made by the secretary of defense gave way to restrictive legislation that virtually paralyzed DOD's efforts to close and consolidate military facilities.

These restrictions were so confining that not one major base closure or realignment was allowed by Congress between 1979 and 1985. Congressional involvement effectively suppressed the ability of the executive branch to close military bases, despite the hundreds of recommended closures and realignments made by the Department of Defense. Some of the more egregious examples of defense facilities protected from budget cuts by federal statutes included Fort Douglas, Utah, which was originally built to guard stagecoach routes; Fort Monroe, Virginia, a moat-encircled army training center, which was built to fend off a British invasion; and the Naval Academy's dairy farm, which was established in 1911 to provide the midshipmen with pure milk following an outbreak of typhoid fever attributed to unprocessed milk.

The elimination of bases as a major policy problem began when President John F. Kennedy proposed closing obsolete and inefficient bases. During this period the closure process was not obstructed with statutory barriers, and the Defense Department could close bases virtually at its discretion. The general pattern was that the secretary of defense would announce a list of intended base closures, Congress would hold hearings (typically at the request of angry legislators whose districts were affected by the closures), and DOD would shut down the installations it wanted to close. Throughout this unencumbered period, large numbers of bases were slated for closure, but remained operational.

Gradually, Congress began initiating a succession of statutory provisions designed to give itself more say over the closure process by enabling it to raise procedural obstacles to shutting down facilities. The first attempt was legislation requiring a 120-day delay period between the secretary's providing Congress with detailed justification for closing bases and the Defense Department's implementing its proposals. Additionally, the administration was prevented from proposing base closures for eight months of each year. President Lyndon Johnson vetoed the bill, claiming that the base closure restriction was repugnant to the Constitution.[10] Congress, however, responded with a watered-down provision cutting the initial 120-day period to a 30-day delay in implementing closures (Military Construction Authorization Act, 1966, Act of September 16, 1965, P.L. 89–188, section 611, 79 Stat. 793 at 818). This alternative bill also mandated that the Pentagon give full justification to the House and Senate Committees on Armed Services concerning any potential closure with more than 250 military and civilian personnel once the 30-day waiting period commenced.

As base closings and realignments continued into the 1970s, Congress became distressed at the perceived economic impacts and convinced that continued closings were being used as punishment by the administration;

upheavals continued in the institutional mechanisms for managing base closures and realignments. The additional statutory mechanisms imposed by Congress for closing bases institutionalized parochialism, and once embedded in the formal mechanism of law and the informal habits of legislators, this parochialism became difficult to erase. Cycles of closure announcements, handled administratively in ways that were anathema to Congress, led to a series of restrictive provisions curtailing DOD's flexibility in implementing major military base closures or realignments.[11]

Congress enacted legislation requiring expensive and time-consuming environmental impact studies before a base could be closed, making it cheaper in the short run to keep an obsolete base open. Without actually prohibiting base closures, these requirements benefited legislators who represented the districts in which bases were located by stating that no base with more than 500 employees could be closed, and no base could have its civilian work force cut by 1,000 people or 50 percent unless the secretary of defense notified the Senate and House Committees on Armed Services; submitted to the Senate and House Committees on Armed Services, as part of the annual budget request, any final decision to carry out the proposed closure or realignment along with detailed justification for such a decision and an evaluation of the fiscal, local economic, budgetary, environmental, strategic, and operational consequences of such an action; and waited sixty days following the submission of the mandatory justification. In addition, the legislation required that the National Environmental Policy Act of 1969 (NEPA) be applied whenever the Pentagon considered consolidating base S.[12]

Congress could effectively veto base closure and realignment proposals, because the legal roadblocks made it unworkable for the Department of Defense to close any military facility. A resourceful legislator now had an array of instruments to undercut proposed base closures in his or her district. Senator Phil Gramm (R-Texas) said: "Since it is always going to be unpopular to close bases . . . the result is that any Congressman or Senator who is the least bit ingenious or hard-working can prevent that from happening."[13] Notable impediments included National Environmental Policy Act court challenges, congressional hearings on the candidate bases and on the detailed justifications DOD submitted, legislation prohibiting certain actions, congressional demands for environmental studies during the authorization and appropriation process even when not otherwise required by law, denial of design funds for base consolidation, disapproval of construction funds to effect closures or realignments, imposition of requirements for alternate-use studies or one-year delays before implementation, and remedial legislation to block entirely DOD's decision to close or realign a military base. The new procedures provided political cover for legislators who might claim that their votes represented good economic sense due to substantial savings and environmental responsibility because of the required adherence to the National Environmental Policy Act.[14] Representative Armey emphasized how these delays sufficiently slowed the base closure process:

> An environmental impact statement (EIS) can take as long as two years and cost over $1 million to complete. Once completed, any congressman or well-organized citizens' group can take the military to court and insist that it be redone to consider some previously unnoticed aspect. After that, the second statement can be found wanting, and a third can be ordered. By this time, several years after the base closing was first announced (a move that by itself has already hurt the local economy), the local citizenry and members of Congress are thoroughly aroused, and the political pressures to cancel the closing order are all but insurmountable.[15]

Congress could further slow the process with military construction authorization and appropriations bills. Members routinely inserted language designed to safeguard individual military bases from closure, despite continued recommendations by the Pentagon that they were obsolete or inefficient. A noteworthy example is the case of Maine's Loring Air Force Base. Although the Air Force followed the procedures by producing an Environmental Impact Statement (EIS) after announcing its intention to close Loring, the Maine delegation overrode these efforts with a line item in an authorization bill. The provision in the fiscal 1980 defense bill prohibited any funds being authorized for the purpose of realigning Loring Air Force Base. Numerous other facilities were spared following the same method, because appropriations and authorization bills were generally noncontroversial and supported by nearly unanimous coalitions.[16]

The unique ability of the political process to concentrate benefits while dispersing costs differentially rewarded legislators who served constituents' parochial ends, which in this case involved maintaining local jobs associated with military bases. By protecting constituent jobs associated with bases, self-interested politicians enhanced their reelection prospects.[17] Forming a closed and autonomous policymaking system,[18] the chairmen of the Armed Services Committees could lobby executive agencies for continued support, and subcommittee decisions could be reached with local needs in mind.[19] One study established that military committee members were better able to safeguard their installations than were rank-and-file members and that key members could influence DOD's decisions concerning military base closures and new base locations.[20] Examining the DOD's army and air force base decisions between 1952 and 1974, the study found that a legislator was concerned with the health of his or her district's economy to the extent that he or she expected to be blamed for its poor performance.

Speaking before the Senate Subcommittee on Military Construction, Senator Gramm said: "Any Member of Congress is going to oppose the closing of a base in that Member's district."[21] "It will be a rare Senator indeed who says: 'We don't really need this base in my State, go ahead and close it. I am against spending more money on defense and I want to prove it.'" As further evidence of congressional resistance, witnesses at a Senate hearing pointed to the problems involved in Congress's closing specific facilities: "If we go through the process of actually having Congress vote on the closings by voting on each specific amount, I think that that would just about put us back into the straightjacket we have been in," said then–Assistant Secretary of Defense Lawrence J. Korb.[22]

Informants on Capitol Hill confirm their distaste for closing defense facilities. "Neither party wants to close bases," a chief of staff commented. "Regardless of what you do or say about it, in the end, members will defer. Everyone backs away from this hot issue." Parochial attention to individual districts rivals efforts for the betterment of the country. "Too often in the past obsolete and unneeded military bases have been kept open far too long by well intentioned yet parochial interests," noted Representative Bruce F. Vento (D-Minn.).[23] In the Senate floor debate, Senator John McCain (R-Ariz.) said: "I think history indicates that we are incapable of acting in any other way because of the enormous political repercussions which result in each of our States as a result of a move to close a base or a military installation."[24] "We are in a situation that we cannot act in an affirmative fashion, and that we abdicate our responsibilities." "What we are doing here is typical of what we do every time we have a tough decision to make," added Senator William S. Cohen (R-Maine).[25] "Congress is taking the cowardly way out by simply shifting this off to a commission," he declared on a later occasion. "When it comes to shutting down a base, for which Congress bears the responsibility of funding, we are saying, 'Don't come to us; we can't afford to bear that kind of responsibility.'"[26] Cohen's views were echoed in the House by Representative Jack Brooks (D-Texas): "The Constitution requires us occasionally to make tough political choices—not to set up Rube Goldberg gimmicks that are purposely crafted to let us avoid making those choices."[27]

With regard to base closures, members wanted insulation. Senator Gramm said the Base Closure Commission would provide it:

> The beauty of this proposal is that, if you have a military base in your district—God forbid one should be closed in Texas, but it could happen—under this proposal, I have 60 days. So I come up here and I say, "God have mercy. Don't close this base in Texas. We can get attacked from the south. The Russians are going to go after our leadership and you know they are going to attack Texas. We need this base." Then I can go out and lie down in the street and the bulldozers are coming and I have a trusty aide there just as it gets there to drag me out of the way. All the people in Muleshoe, or wherever this base is, will say, "You know, Phil Gramm got whipped, but it was like the Alamo. He was with us until the last second."[28]

ESTABLISHMENT OF THE DEFENSE BASE CLOSURE AND REALIGNMENT COMMISSION

In 1988 Congress passed the Defense Authorization Amendments and Base Closure and Realignment Act, intended to insulate decisions on base closures from congressional pressure by establishing a bipartisan commission to draw up a list of military installations targeted for closures. The list would have to be accepted or rejected as a whole, a requirement that made the commission's recommendations difficult to overturn. The first two rounds of base closings, in 1988 and 1991, reduced or eliminated 125 installations, with little or no adverse effect upon lawmakers from the affected areas.[29] The Base Closure Commission gave Congress a way out of its long-lasting problems with regard to closing unneeded facilities, by breaking any chain of traceability to members, because the vote would be predicated on a procedure for accomplishing the base closure process rather than on specific closures or realignments. This took a particularized benefit out of the realm of credit-claiming and into the realm of position-taking,[30] making it possible for members to claim that the decision to close or realign belonged to a bipartisan national commission.[31]

The Defense Base Closure and Realignment Commission (BRAC) was a bipartisan panel whose composition was designed to be politically neutral and geographically representative. Jurisdictional committees, leadership, and rank-and-file members in both chambers wanted an insulated body free from individual parochialism and partisan considerations. BRAC was appointed by the secretary of defense and was to submit its report directly to him; this won support from the chairman and ranking minority member of the House Armed Service Committee, as well as solidifying bipartisan support. If the commission's closure list was satisfactory to the secretary, he transmitted his recommendations to Congress by a set time. The list was accepted or rejected as a whole, a requirement that made the commission's recommendations difficult to overturn. If Congress did not adopt a joint resolution to reject the list within forty-five working days, the secretary proceeded with the closings. No more than half of the commission's staff could be Defense Department personnel, with the remaining half appointed from outside the Pentagon. The commission made its recommendations according to criteria established by the secretary of defense: the military value of the base, the economic and environmental impacts, and cost factors. Additionally, bases could not be considered candidates for closure unless the estimated savings offset the closing costs within six years after closure.

To separate closure funding decisions from logrolling in support of individual bases and facilitate the Defense Department's disposal of excess property, a Base Closure Account would function as an automatic funding mechanism. In the past DOD had to secure congressional approval to implement a closure or realignment. Appropriations targeted at named bases were needed to carry out closure or realignment. Under the new law a revolving fund to finance up-front base closing costs used money earned from military property sales, DOD transfers to the account from funds appropriated by the secretary from unused budget funds, and monies specifically authorized and appropriated each year by Congress for closings.

The timing of the Base Closure Commission's work was designed to minimize political harm. Congress charged the Base Closure Commission with submitting its recommendations to the secretary of defense by December 31, 1988, before the new Congress convened, giving opportunities for extensive planning before the closures took effect, and giving constituents ample time to forget the votes on the initial legislation. After several years, an election, and redistricting, it was nearly impossible for constituents, between rounds of closures, to sort out who had supported what.

The Commission advised the closure, in part or whole, and realignment of 145 bases. BRAC estimated that with these closures $693.6 million a year in base operations could be saved.[32] The secretary of defense approved the list, and Congress did not adopt a joint resolution in opposition. The secretary of defense was then required to close or realign the bases slated for closure and realignment by 1995.

Congress again chose to resuscitate the politically popular commission process in 1991. Unlike the first commission, which terminated shortly after submitting its final report, this second base closing commission had a longer life cycle, to be followed by additional cuts in the nonelection years of 1993 and 1995. The procedures of the 1991 BRAC were also different, with more emphasis placed on open hearings. But in many respects the new commission closely resembled its predecessor.

Eight voting members of the 1991 commission were appointed by the president, with the advice and consent of the Senate. The president was directed to consult with Congress in selecting nominees, with the Speaker of the House designating two appointees, the majority leader of the Senate selecting two appointees, and the minority leaders of the House and Senate choosing one appointee each. Commission members would serve only for the length of a congressional session, the exception being the chairperson (designated by the president) who would remain until a successor was confirmed. No more than one-third of the commission staff came from the Defense Department.

While such provisions of the new statute are similar to those set forth by its predecessor, many others are more complicated. The roles of the defense secretary and the commission were reversed and Congress added a role for the General Accounting Office (GAO). Under the new law DOD would transmit its recommendations to BRAC, which was responsible for holding public hearings and reviewing those recommendations. GAO concurrently audited the secretary's recommendations, determined whether its recommendations rested on proper criteria, and made a report to Congress. During its review the commission had the power to add or delete bases from the

Defense Department's chosen sites if the list deviated from the force structure plan or the eight criteria that the Pentagon used to decide which bases to close: the mission requirements and operational readiness of the total force; the availability and condition of land, facilities, and associated airspace at both existing and potential receiving sites; the ability to accommodate contingency, mobilization, and future total force requirements at both existing and potential receiving sites; the cost and manpower implications; the economic impact on communities; the ability of community infrastructures to support forces, missions, and personnel; the environmental effects; and the costs of closing a base versus keeping it open.[33]

The list of base closures was referred directly to the president who could accept or reject the list in whole or part. By statute, if the president did not accept the recommendations in whole, he had to explain his disapproval to both Congress and the commission, with the commission then submitting to the president a new list of recommended closures. The president approved the commission's final list or the process halted. As before, to reduce parochial proclivities, members cast an all-or-nothing vote on whether to reject the entire base closure package. After concluding its deliberations, the 1991 commission released its final list of eighty-two proposed closures and realignments. After months of deliberation and debate, by a vote of 364 to 60, members of Congress tacitly approved the commission's proposal by rejecting a resolution disapproving the recommendations of the commission.

The base closure commission process had its critics. A coalition of opponents charged that Congress was ceding its power to the Defense Department. Their concern was fueled by the fear of political retaliation. The military long argued that closing bases is an executive function. If the president (with the guidance of the military) were allowed to pick and choose which bases should be closed or realigned, according to his powers as commander-in-chief, he could use this ability to retaliate against any legislator who had defied him on important legislation. Some in Congress remembered ruefully that the Nixon administration chose to close two bases in Massachusetts shortly after it became the only state to support George McGovern. Others recalled the story of President Lyndon Johnson's personal war against the Amarillo Air Force Base. Johnson allegedly told Amarillo city officials that if he did not carry their town in his bid for reelection he might consider closing their air base.[34] For this reason there was an institutional interest in denying the executive branch this political leverage. "What Congress is doing here is handing over exclusively to the Secretary of Defense the right to close whatever bases his commission, using his staff, has determined he wants to do," stated Senator Carl Levin (D-Mich.) during a floor debate.[35] "This is an excessive delegation of power. . . . It is not in keeping with our celebration of the Constitution, which calls for divided power."

Critics charged that the commission process circumvented their own legislative and committee stake in the base closings. Opponents questioned whether Congress would require an affirmative or automatic act to approve the closure of the bases. "We are taking away all congressional power, giving up our involvement in the process, ceding it to the Secretary of Defense who picks the people who close the domestic bases without any involvement of the Congress," declared Senator Alan J. Dixon (D-Ill.).[36] Senator Dixon's view was echoed by Representative Brooks: "No matter how laudable the abstract goal of closing unneeded military installations might be, it should be recognized that the 'base closure commission' concept, in any form, constitutes a significant transfer of power from elected representatives of the legislative branch to unelected officials in the executive," he said.[37] "I believe that it would be a serious mistake and a dangerous precedent for the Congress to hand over constitutionally based authority in a mechanism that provides nothing more than window dressing for our branch of government." Proponents of the process refuted this point: "The Congress has probably abdicated its responsibilities," said Senator McCain.[38] "However, I would like to point out that it is very clear that we are at a condition of gridlock as far as base closings are concerned." During a floor debate, then-Representative Jon Kyl (R-Ariz.) stated:

> I do not think we are fooling anyone when we say we are all for closing obsolete bases, but then we attach so many preconditions to it that we know we are never going to end up closing the bases. One of these is the difference between automatic closure and the provision that would require Congress to affirmatively act. Who among us believes that we will actually close bases if we have to affirmatively act?[39]

Representative Vento shared Kyl's view: "Congress should send a clear message on this," he noted.[40] "Let us charge the Commission to do the task that we are unfortunately unable to do ourselves in this institution."

Supporters of the commission process cited the need to create an insulated body free from individual parochialism and partisan considerations. "I think there is a legitimate case that has been made that we need a procedure, a mechanism by which sound and rational judgments may be made on the alignment and operation of military facilities throughout the United States," declared Representative Herbert H. Bateman (R-Va.).[41] Others gave high marks to delegation. Senator Strom Thurmond (R-S.C.) claimed that the commission was an effective method to get able people familiar with DOD's list of base closures. "You have got on this Commission people who can approach this from a viewpoint that I believe no Member of Congress can hardly do, because most of us feel we have a duty to our States to try to help our States," he said.[42] "Whereas this Commission will view this in a different light and can approach it in a way that will be best for our Nation."

Another obstacle during debate presented itself when protesting members objected that Congress would ignore the environmental clean-up costs associated with base closings. Then-Representative Barbara Boxer (D-Calif.) contested that the savings estimated by the Base Closure Commission did not account for the cost of removing the toxic waste and contamination that had accumulated over the years from many sources: artillery shells, jet fuels, paint, radiation, and other hazardous chemicals. "The Armey bill, as proposed, by waiving all the environmental requirements could really be devastating to communities," said Boxer.[43] The concern was that the military would leave behind land that was unsafe for residential purposes, and that surrounding communities, eager to obtain the land quickly, would be unwilling to pay for the time-consuming decontamination process. Serious conflict could occur between the interests of economic development and the interests of environmental restoration.

THE POLITICS OF REDISTRIBUTION

The tendency for lawmakers to give primary consideration to constituent's interests when faced with losing a military installation in their district is typical of the delicate problems of redistribution. Delegating to BRAC was also a way to avoid the pain of breaking a decades-old bipartisan tradition: funneling Defense Department dollars to constituents and businesses back home. When Congress could no longer ignore the problem of keeping so many bases open, it avoided confronting the issue, which required a clear policy position on something with greater costs than benefits to districts by shifting responsibility to an ad hoc commission. This broke the chain of traceability and avoided possible electoral repercussions for those members who faced an imminent base closure in their district.

Any congressional action which reduces and relocates functions and civilian personnel positions involves the most conspicuous long-run allocations of resources. Because it necessarily means clear winners and losers, the policymaking process is marked by a high degree of visibility, conflict, and compromise among a broad spectrum of political actors. Congress responds to this sort of redistributive dilemma by masking legislators' individual contributions and delegating responsibility for making unpleasant decisions to a commission. In this case delegating is a technique devised to transfer responsibility but still make it possible for beneficial outcomes to be attributed to individual legislators. Members avoid blame by saying the decision is out of their hands; they protect themselves from going on record in favor of something negative to their district. "Handing over federal authority to the Base Closure and Realignment Commission to downsize the military infrastructure was clearly a way to take the politics out of the issue," a Hill staffer commented. "Base closing is a political hot potato, and the last thing somebody wants to do is to vote to have a base closed in their district. By letting Congress deny the commission's recommendations, rather than support it, members can cover their backsides."

Shifting the blame for any negative side effects disguises the pain to constituents. This method enables lawmakers to vote for the general benefit of the country without ever having to support specific costs to their constituents. In the strong words of Representative Don Young (R-Alaska), "Placing the national interest ahead of the wishes of a particular congressional district is socialism."[44]

The base-closing process camouflaged the causal chain in several ways. Congress's role was limited to accepting or rejecting the entire list of bases. All base-closing rounds featured a "fast track" authority that went with the commission's findings. There were fixed deadlines for each action in the base closure process; every base closure action, from commission appointment to final closure, took place according to a legislatively mandated schedule. Congress retained no effective means of stopping the commission from shutting down bases; it could not amend the list or refuse to fund base closings because of the revolving closure fund. Individual legislators took no direct action to close any particular base, so constituent's wrath was directed at a bureaucratic entity that was dissolved after each round. By short-circuiting the committee process and denying any opportunity to amend, Congress made its role merely one of ratifying the final decision, and it was a simple ratification, since in the absence of any action, the commission's recommendations silently and automatically become law. Even though the extensive delegation of power to the commission is legitimate in the realm of public law, motive and the nature of the policy issue are frequently of greater relevance in assessing whether legislative or administrative action is within the affirmative reach of government's power.[45] The automatic closure mechanism of base closings provided Congress with a backdoor escape from a problem it had had a large hand in creating—one it recognized but avoided fixing despite its ability to do so, because the shifting of allocations meant clear winners and losers.

The coalitions that form over any redistributive issue may change in composition depending on the issue, but they generally consist of a proponent group and an opponent group. Liberals and conservatives, hawks and doves, Democrats and Republicans all entered the controversy. The commission was a rational way of picking the bases to be closed. Congress designed the base-closing procedure to limit its own opportunity to interfere, which left members with few options beyond their own skill in lobbying the commission. Votes for the resolution rejecting the Base Closure and Realignment Acts of 1988 and 1991 routinely came from members whose districts contained a base on the closure list.

CONCLUSION

Cutting spending is not easy for members of Congress, especially when the cuts affect their districts. For years, determining which facilities to close has been a painful process. Political wrangling dates back to the waning days of the Federalist administration of John Adams when the newly elected president, Thomas Jefferson, attempted to cut already appropriated spending on six naval shipyards. Aside from the large, visible bases, the military is the proprietor of thousands of smaller tracts of land, which legislators from areas containing these facilities covet because of their contributions to local economies. The politically unpalatable decision to reduce rather than expand military installations is, therefore, no easy matter, as voters tend to be more sensitive to the real or potential losses. Thousands of jobs are at stake. Communities long dependent on bases have to build a new economic base. The incentive to shift responsibility is high, which leads to buck-passing. This permits officeholders simultaneously to claim credit and minimize blame. Senator Arlen Specter (R-Penn.), for instance, could challenge the legality of the base-closing process after the 1991 round targeted the Philadelphia Naval Shipyard. Although his efforts failed, by arguing the case himself before the Supreme Court, he obtained credit with constituents.

The timing of the Base Closure Commissions was intentionally designed to minimize political harm. In the 1988 round Congress charged the commission with submitting its recommendations to the secretary of defense by December 31, 1988, before the new Congress convened, giving opportunities for extensive planning before the closures took effect, and giving constituents ample time to forget the votes on the initial legislation. After several years, an election, and redistricting, it was hard for constituents to tell who had supported what.

By contrast, the National Commissions on AIDS and the Thrift Industry lacked any "fast track" mechanism. Neither functioned according to a mandated schedule as did the Base Closure Commission; except for the dates when their interim and final reports were due, as well as their termination date, there were no fixed deadlines for every action of the commission.

In an effort to overcome its parochial proclivities associated with closing unneeded defense facilities, Congress set up a commission to make recommendations. This approach circumvented the problems normally associated with policies that cause the dual characteristics of the institution to come into direct conflict. The Base Closure Commission was an organization through which Congress could surmount political obstacles to base closings as well as manage a policy problem in which local interests collide with larger policy needs in irreconcilable fashion. The panel was designed to insulate Congress and remove visibility and political uncertainty.

NOTES

1. Roger H. Davidson and Walter J. Oleszek, *Congress and Its Members*, 5th ed. (Washington, D.C.: CQ Press, 1996), 394.

2. Charlotte Twight, "Institutional Underpinnings of Parochialism: The Case of Military Base Closures," *Cato Journal* 9 (1989): 73–105.

3. Ronald J. Fox, *The Defense Management Challenge* (Boston: Harvard Business School Press, 1988), 5.

4. Christopher J. Deering, "Congress, the President, and Automatic Government: The Case of Military Base Closures," in *Divided Democracy: Cooperation and Conflict Between the President and Congress*, 2nd ed., edited by James A. Thurber (Washington, D.C.: CQ Press, 1996), 5.

5. Richard A. Stubbing, *The Defense Game: An Insider Explores the Astonishing Realities of America's Defense Establishment* (New York: Harper & Row, 1986), 163.

6. Lewis Anthony Dexter, "Congressmen and the Making of Military Policy," in *New Perspectives on the House of Representatives*, ed. Robert L. Peabody and Nelson W. Polsby (Chicago: Rand McNally, 1969), 182.

7. Richard K. Armey, "Base Maneuvers: The Games Congress Plays with the Military Pork Barrel," *Policy Review* 43 (1988): 71–75.

8. Davidson and Oleszek, *Congress and Its Members*, 5th ed., 395.

9. Twight, "Institutional Underpinnings of Parochialism: The Case of Military Base Closures."

10. Andrew Taylor, "Base Closures Get Big Boost in Military Spending," *Congressional Quarterly Weekly Report*, June 20, 1992, 1821.

11. Twight, "Institutional Underpinnings of Parochialism: The Case of Military Base Closures," 75.

12. USC, Title 10, Chapter 159, Section 2687.

13. U.S. Congress, Senate Committee on Armed Services, Subcommittee on Military Construction, *Base Closures*, 99th Cong., 1st sess., 1985, Committee Print, 11.

14. Deering, "Congress, the President, and Automatic Government: The Case of Military Base Closures," 9.

15. Armey, "Base Maneuvers: The Games Congress Plays with the Military Pork Barrel," 72.

16. David Soherr-Hadwigger, "Balancing National Interest and Constituency Demands: Congressional Voting on Military Base Closures," typescript, 1995, 13.

17. David R. Mayhew, *Congress: The Electoral Connection* (New Haven, Conn.: Yale University Press, 1974); John P. Ferejohn, *Pork Barrel Politics: Rivers and Harbors Legislation, 1947–1968* (Stanford, Calif.: Stanford University Press, 1974); and Morris P. Fiorina, *Congress: Keystone to the Washington Establishment* (New Haven, Conn.: Yale University Press, 1977).

18. Leiper J. Freeman, *The Political Process* (New York: Random House, 1955); Douglass Cater, *Power in Washington* (New York: Random House, 1964); Dorothy B. James, *The Contemporary President* (Indianapolis: Bobbs-Merrill, 1974); Hugh Heclo, *A Government of Strangers: Executive Politics in Washington* (Washington, D.C.: Brookings Institution, 1977); Gordon Adams, *The Politics of Defense Contracting: The Iron Triangle* (New York: Council on Economic Priorities, 1981); and James A. Thurber, "Dynamics of Policy Subsystems in American Politics," in *Interest Group Politics*, 3rd ed., edited by Allan J. Cigler and Burdett A. Loomis (Washington, D.C.: CQ Press, 1991).

19. Samuel P. Huntington, *The Common Defense* (New York: Columbia University Press, 1961), 135.

20. R. Douglas Arnold, *Congress and the Bureaucracy* (New Haven, Conn.: Yale University Press, 1979).

21. Senate Committee on Armed Services, Subcommittee on Military Construction, *Base Closures*, 16.

22. Ibid., 20.

23. Congress, 100th Cong., 2nd sess., *Congressional Record* July 7, 1988, H17073.

24. Congress, 100th Cong., 2nd sess., *Congressional Record* May 10, 1988, S10225.

25. Congress, 100th Cong., 2nd sess., *Congressional Record* May 10, 1988, S10223.

26. Ibid.

27. Congress, 100th Cong., 2nd sess., *Congressional Record* July 7, 1988, H17063.

28. Senate Committee on Armed Services, Subcommittee on Military Construction, *Base Closures*, 17.

29. Tim Curran and Craig Winneker, "Base Closing List Could Be Political Boon, Not Wane," *Roll Call*, March 18, 1993.

30. Mayhew, *Congress: The Electoral Connection*.

31. R. Douglas Arnold, *The Logic of Collective Action* (New Haven, Conn.: Yale University Press, 1990).

32. U.S. Department of Defense, Defense Secretary's Commission, *Base Realignments and Closures: Report of the Defense Secretary's Commission* (Washington, D.C.: Government Printing Office, 1988).

33. U.S. Congress, House, Committee on Armed Services, Military Installations and Facilities Subcommittee, *Base Closures and Realignments*, 99th Cong., 1st sess, June 12, 1985.

34. Andrew C. Mayer and David E. Lockwood, *Military Base Closures: Issues for the 103rd Congress*, Congressional Research Issue Brief, no. IB92113 (Washington, D.C.: Congressional Research Service, 1994).

35. Congress, 100th Cong., 2nd sess., *Congressional Record* May 10, 1988, S10197.

36. Congress, 100th Cong., 2nd sess., *Congressional Record* May 10, 1988, S10196.

37. Congress, 100th Cong., 2nd sess., *Congressional Record* July 7, 1988, H17080.

38. Congress, 100th Cong., 2nd sess., *Congressional Record* May 10, 1988, S10224.

39. Congress, 100th Cong., 2nd sess., *Congressional Record* July 7, 1988, H17064.

40. Congress, 100th Cong., 2nd sess., *Congressional Record* July 7, 1988, H17073.

41. Congress, 100th Cong., 2nd sess., *Congressional Record* July 7, 1988, H17059.

42. Congress, 100th Cong., 2nd sess., *Congressional Record* May 10, 1988, S10209.

43. Quoted in Mike Mills, "Members Go on the Offensive to Defend Bases," *Congressional Weekly Report*, July 2, 1988, 1816.

44. Quoted in Benjamin Sheffner, "Young: GOP's Old Bull," *Roll Call*, February 27, 1995.

45. Laurence H. Tribe, *American Constitutional Law*, 2nd ed. (Mineola, N.Y.: The Foundation Press, Inc., 1988), 303.

—————Chapter 7—————

The Significance of Commissions in Understanding Legislative Behavior

Ad hoc commissions as instruments of government have a long history. They are used by almost all units and levels of government for almost every conceivable task. Ironically, the use which Congress makes of commissions—preparing the groundwork for legislation, bringing public issues into the spotlight, whipping legislation into shape, and giving priority to the consideration of complex, technical, and critical developments—receives relatively little attention from political scientists. As noted in earlier chapters, following the logic of rational choice theory, individual decisions to delegate are occasioned by imperfect information; legislators who want to develop effective policies, but who lack the necessary expertise, often delegate fact-finding and policy development. Others contend that some commissions are set up to shift blame in order to maximize benefits and minimize losses.

Rational choice theory and principal-agent modeling are not without merit or place. Yet anyone who spends a reasonable amount of time and energy talking to and listening to legislators and their staffs comes away with a different perspective on congressional delegation as it applies to commission formation. It is not always possible to construct a purely rational decision making process for any but the simplest, lowest-level decisions.

The legislative way of life is full of problems such as the impossibility of distinguishing facts from values and ends from means, the impossibility of reaching consensus among lawmakers on predominant goals, the changing and ambiguous nature of many policy goals on Capitol Hill, the pressures of time to make a decision when it is needed, and the inability of lawmakers to handle a vast amount of information at any one time. Other reasons why normal legislative channels may fail to address important issues are the inability of members to give their undivided attention to a single problem or decision, the cost of information acquisition, the failure to acquire all possible data because of time constraints, and the inability to foresee all the consequences of a given decision.

No definitive or complete answer to the question of why commissions are formed is possible. Individual careerism is not always the chief determinant of the structure and operations of Congress. Intricate, colorful, steeped in tradition, rich in controversy, the institution is very much a collection of the individuals who serve in it at any given time and whose personal motives, goals, and talents are quite unevenly distributed.[1] "Government is not physics," noted Democratic Senator Bob Graham of Florida. "A physics exercise, if done correctly, will yield similar results every time. But government involves people, with different ideas, which means inconsistencies and unpredictability." Therefore, one is not always able to establish why different individuals and clusters of individuals want commissions. Still, identifying these three dominant motives for delegating is of value to congressional scholars for the development of a general theory of commission formation and behavior, as other research has looked at only single case studies and no one has grappled with the complete question.

Practitioners of politics will use nearly any apparatus or process to achieve their ends. Over the years Congress has been a remarkably adaptive institution, finding different means to address and formulate public policy. In the past two decades substantial changes have occurred in congressional policymaking. Barbara Sinclair uses the term "unorthodox lawmaking" to distinguish the change in the contemporary legislative process.[2] Where the route to enactment used to be linear and predictable, now it is "flexible and varied." Today, crafting legislation is comparable to climbing a tree with many branches: "if one route is blocked there is always another one can try."[3] The ad hoc commission is a creative tool (or a tree limb) that has been fashioned in response to different problems, goals, and opportunities. It illustrates the adaptability of Congress to the dynamics of national politics. As Charles O. Jones observes, "This adaptability should not surprise us."[4] When challenged by outside forces the institution will maneuver itself to discover alternative procedures.[5] In some cases, commissions grow out of inadequacies in Congress; in other instances they develop more because of the unusual nature and complexity of a given policy problem. All convey a valuable insight about Congress: procedurally, the institution is very inventive.

Ad hoc commissions seem destined to coexist with the traditional legislative process, and we may conclude with reasonable certainty that these entities will be increasingly common. They remain far too tempting a device to abandon,[6] in part, because they are relatively cheap to authorize. "You're not creating additional bureaucracy with a commission," a congressional aide asserted as she explained her boss's marketing scheme for a commission. "The commission is temporary. When it's finished, that's it, Congress hasn't created any long-term headache." And as a former lawmaker commented, "My own anecdotal feeling is that the several commissions that I have been a member of have been worthwhile. If you didn't have some commissions, there would be people who would think you should have one."

The increased use and development of ad hoc commissions by Congress reveals a growing pattern: the use of alternative mechanisms in formulating policy. For the most part, commissions have been set up in response to the extraordinary growth in the complexity and size of the federal government's responsibility since the New Deal, and especially during the "Great Society" years of the 1960s.[7] When the first Congress convened, the United States had a tiny population, mostly rural and uneducated; its social and industrial structure was simple. Changes occurred slowly, and the government's tasks were few.[8] The contemporary situation is radically different. "Today," reflected former Senator Nancy Landon Kassebaum (R-Kan.), "there's an almost information overload, a bombardment by news, by faxes. Everything is instantaneous with too little time for thoughtful reflection."[9] In the Capitol, elevator operators still greet members and visitors, and paintings of powder-wigged Founding Fathers still gaze down from their gilded frames. But now they share the corridors of power with fiber-optic cable links, PCs, cell phones, and wireless modems. Staffers can even order lunch from the House food system over the Internet at www.specialordersdeli.com.

A longtime watcher of Congress summed up the hectic, new-age legislative life:

> Legislators have very little time for reflection. There are demands upon their attention literally every minute of the day—and these demands would be made every minute of the night too if not for unlisted telephone numbers. They are utterly dependent upon typed cards which they receive from their press secretaries the moment they arrive in the office. These cards, broken down almost minute by minute, list every engagement of the day and every committee and subcommittee meeting, with a brief addendum of the agenda.
>
> They are dependent upon hasty briefings from aides who scurry alongside as they dash about the Capitol. Too often, their only time for studying a complex legislative problem is when they are driven to and from their offices by aides, wives, or chauffeurs.[10]

If Congress did not delegate certain tasks to commissions, it would cede a good portion of its responsibilities to other decision makers. The ad hoc commission enables Congress to maintain its autonomy. It shows some of Congress's aggressiveness in seeking out new areas of endeavor. In certain areas of policymaking Congress has, in the past two decades, usually been peripheral or reluctant to assert itself. Delegating to a temporary commission may prove to be a source of influence in negotiations with other decision makers. Most commission recommendations, in fact, are eventually accepted and implemented.[11]

Political scientists contend that Congress runs in harmony with members' desires, but the members know otherwise. In a 1987 survey of 114 House and Senate members, "inefficiency" was what most surprised them about Congress (forty-five gave this response).[12] Members report that their duties allow them little time for personal or family matters. Nearly half of the respondents in the 1987 survey, for example, indicated that they had "no personal time after work"; a third said they did not have "time for family."[13] Ad hoc commissions are frequently set up to divide the volume of Congress's work into manageable amounts, to temporarily free the institution and its members from the grind of Capitol Hill life.

Lawmaking is a learned activity. James Madison and his colleagues recognized this. "A few of the members," wrote Madison in No. 53 of the *Federalist*, "as happens in all assemblies, will possess superior talents; will, by frequent reelections, become members of long standing; will be thoroughly masters of the public business, and perhaps not willing to avail themselves of those advantages. The greater the proportion of new members, and the less the information of the bulk of the proportion of new members, the more apt will they be to fall into the snares that may be laid for them."[14] Whatever their skills and enthusiasms, newly elected officeholders are rarely "masters of the public business." It takes two or three terms for attentive members to accumulate the necessary specialization, experience, organizational skill, and ability and inclination to compromise. Even after they have mastered the workings of Congress, they still need the specialized expertise and relief of ad hoc commissions.

"As the world is changing," wrote former House Speaker Newt Gingrich, "we need to be flexible and find ways to get people with competence in a room together to solve problems."[15] When used astutely, ad hoc commissions foster bargaining, consensus, and compromise in relation to policy proposals, mitigating conflict within Congress that might incapacitate the institution. Such commissions help elected officials make necessary but unpopular decisions and deal with complex social crises, policy issues, and studies. This is largely because commissions are usually in a better position to perform in a visibly fair and politically neutral manner that increases the perceived caliber and efficacy of their eventual product. People on Capitol Hill acknowledge that Congress lacks the time to legislate every detail of every issue, and that some actions necessary in the public interest are so sensitive that they can be taken only if they are not subjected to an up-or-down roll-call vote. At their most productive, commissions provide Congress with a flexible option for policymaking. They are especially valuable tools when controversial and elaborate legislation is at stake. When Congress faces a huge problem such as health care, rather than looking at the entire solution, it acts sequentially, approaching the solution in small steps, building policy and agreement from the bottom up. Commissions work well for this process because they are an incremental step toward a policy end. Through commissions, Congress acquires an informed and timely baseline for decision making that may otherwise be subject to uncoordinated or political criteria. Appointing a commission can shift responsibility from lawmakers for a year or so while the commision deliberates. Further, commissions avoid the rigidities of institutionalization and the loss of an originally intended purpose, both of which frequently plague other institutions in government. This is because their operation is limited to a defined purview: they collect and analyze data, arrive at conclusions, submit their recommendations, and terminate shortly thereafter—an attractive feature to a Congress that is increasingly made up of relatively conservative members who express skepticism about many federal agencies.[16] Finally, commissions fit a pluralistic decision making process that conforms to the public's ideal of how decisions should be made by government—from the bottom up. A plebiscitary quality has seeped into legislative life.[17] And the ad hoc commission can be a more direct avenue of communication between constituents and lawmakers than the committee rooms and chamber floors of Capitol Hill, for commissions enable all the major political interests affected by a given situation to be represented by appointment.

Congressional commissions have reached the point where they can take over various fact-finding functions formerly performed by Congress itself. Once the facts have been found by a commission, it is possible for Congress to subject those facts to the scrutiny of cross-examination and debate. And if the findings stand up under such scrutiny, there remains for Congress the major task of determining the policy to be adopted with reference to the known factual situation. Once it was clear, for example, that the acquired immune deficiency syndrome (AIDS) yielded an extraordinary range of newfound political and practical difficulties, the need for legislative action was readily apparent. The question that remained was one of policy: how to prevent the spread of AIDS. Should it be by accelerated research? By public education? By facilitating housing support for people living with AIDS? Or by implementing a program of AIDS counseling and testing? The AIDS Commission could help Congress answer such questions.

As the use of ad hoc commissions increases, so too does the criticism of them, principally on the ground that elected officials shirk unwanted responsibilities, but also on the ground that decisions take place behind closed doors. Politicians, pressed to make decisions that could prove unpopular, have taken the easy way out by appointing a commission.[18] Alternatively their creation may be a deliberate dilatory tactic intended to mollify one or more interests by demonstrating that a matter is receiving its rightful quota of consideration while a concrete response is discreetly deferred.[19] Some of the most vocal critics are found in the corridors and committee rooms of Capitol Hill.

"Congress has all the expertise it needs," argued the chief of staff to a Republican representative in debunking his fellow practitioners' claims that there was a shortage of in-house experts. "And if Congress doesn't have enough resident experts it can go get them." But as noted in chapter 2, most people on Capitol Hill regard this allegation as short-sighted and as a philosophical vision of what Congress ought to be, not a practical possibility. Still, there is some basis for these critiques and concerns and for the challenges commissions pose to traditional forms of representative government.

The creation of an ad hoc commission should be the outcome of a well-considered decision that is better suited to resolving the policy problems in the field of its assignment than is the normal legislative process. In choosing to delegate, Congress should closely examine the advantages and disadvantages of using ad hoc commissions and check that the applicability of using a commission has been established with reasonable confidence.[20] Many in Congress look to the Base Closure and Realignment Commission as a template. But the base-closing process cannot be replicated across all issues. Government by commission is not a panacea. It is important to distinguish between those commissions set up to recommend solutions to specific problems and those whose mandates are so broad that they can succeed only if lawmakers have already begun to form a consensus.[21]

Sharply divided reports do little to resolve problems. The National Economic Commission (1988–1989), modeled on the National Commission on Social Security Reform (1981–1983), was expected to produce bipartisan recommendations on how to reduce the federal budget deficit. Its members divided along partisan lines and issued a majority report accompanied by a sharp dissent from the minority. The result was a continuation of previous conflict.[22] The Pepper Commission (named after Representative Claude Pepper [D-Fla.], an advocate for the elderly) was intended to produce a consensus on reform of the American health care system. Its members could not reach a consensus and issued a divided report, which did nothing to promote either consensus or action in Congress.[23]

Finally, care should be taken to avoid overusing the ad hoc commission. Only a few commissions can compete for congressional attention at a time, and lawmakers can act upon only so many reports in an effective manner. Too many commissions will feed current skepticism, make it more difficult to retain congressional support, cause problems of financing, enlarge the already hard task of finding qualified commissioners and thereby injure their credibility, which is so important to the success of most ad hoc commissions.[24] Despite successful legislative outcomes from commission recommendations, when the traditional channels of lawmaking are manipulated or bypassed, deliberation and the quality of legislation suffer.

Should we cast this delegation process aside? The answer depends on our perception and idea of the legislative process. As Austin Ranney noted in an article about commissions,[25] what was perhaps America's first commission was composed of fifty-five men who met in Philadelphia in the summer of 1787 to draft the Constitution. Given this auspicious example, it is difficult to ignore the value of the ad hoc commission in formulating public policy.

NOTES

1. Randall B. Ripley, "The Impact of Congress on Public Policy: Goal-Oriented Performance," in *Legislative Politics U.S.A.*, 3rd ed., edited by Theodore J. Lowi and Randall B. Ripley (Boston: Little, Brown and Company, 1973), 378.

2. Barbara Sinclair, *Unorthodox Lawmaking: New Legislative Processes in the U.S. Congress* (Washington, D.C.: CQ Press, 1997), xii.

3. Ibid., 31.

4. Charles O. Jones, *The United States Congress: People, Place, and Policy* (Homewood, Ill.: The Dorsey Press, 1982), 3.

5. Joseph Cooper, "Organization and Innovation in the House of Representatives," in *The House at Work*, ed. Joseph Cooper and G. Calvin Mackenzie (Austin: University of Texas Press, 1981).

6. Hugh Davis Graham, "The Ambiguous Legacy of American Presidential Commissions," *The Public Historian* 7 (1985): 5–25.

7. John R. Johannes, *To Serve the People: Congress and Constituency Service* (Lincoln: The University of Nebraska Press, 1984); Allan Schick, *The Federal Budget: Politics, Policy, Process* (Washington, D.C.: Brookings Institution, 1995); and Burdett A. Loomis, *The Contemporary Congress*, 2nd ed. (New York: St. Martin's Press, 1998).

8. Roger H. Davidson and Walter J. Oleszek, *Congress and Its Members*, 6th ed. (Washington, D.C.: CQ Press, 1998), 411.

9. Quoted in Francis X. Clines, "Weary Political Noise, a Senator Sees a Peaceful Farm in Her Future," *New York Times*, December 3, 1995, 30.

10. Samuel Shaffer, *On and Off the Floor: Thirty Years as a Correspondent on Capitol Hill* (New York: Newsweek Books, 1980), 14.

11. John B. Gilmour, "Blue Ribbon Commissions," in *The Encyclopedia of the United States Congress*, ed. Donald C. Bacon, Roger H. Davidson, and Morton Keller (New York: Simon & Schuster, 1995).

12. Center for Responsive Politics, *Congressional Operations: Congress Speaks— Survey of the 100th Congress* (Washington, D.C.: Center for Responsive Politics, 1988).

13. Ibid.

14. Federalist No. 53 in Garry Wills, The Federalist Papers by Alexander Hamilton, James Madison, and John Jay (New York: Bantam Books, 1982).

15. Newt Gingrich, "Leadership Tasks Forces: The 'Third Wave' Way to Consider Legislation," *Roll Call*, November 16, 1995, 5.

16. Loomis, *The Contemporary Congress*, 2nd ed., 13.

17. Davidson and Oleszek, *Congress and Its Members*, 6th ed., 412.

18. Gilmour, "Blue Ribbon Commissions."

19. Jerrold Zwirn, *Congressional Publications and Proceedings: Research on Legislation, Budgets, and Treaties*, 2nd ed. (Englewood, Colo.: Libraries Unlimited, Inc., 1988)

20. Alan L. Dean, "Ad Hoc Commissions for Policy Formulations?" in *Presidential Advisory Systems*, ed. Thomas E. Cronin and Sanford D. Greenberg (New York: Harper and Row, 1969).

21. Susan F. Rasky, "Congress Says: A Commission Made Us," *New York Times*, January 29, 1989, E4.

22. Gilmour, "Blue Ribbon Commissions."

23. Ibid.

24. Dean, "Ad Hoc Commissions for Policy Formulations?" 115.

25. Quoted in Rasky, "Congress Says: A Commission Made Us," E4.

—*Appendix 1*—

Method and Scope of Research

Because I have not been able to observe the decisions to delegate in action, I rely on the data from approximately fifty-five interviews: fifty face-to-face interviews and five telephone interviews. A search of the workload for the 93rd (1973–1975) through 105th (1997–1999) Congresses suggests that an average of seventy-one bipartisan congressional commissions are proposed each Congress (see chapter 3). One might be tempted to think the interview sample is too small but the relevant comparison is between the total number of interviews and the total number of proposed commissions in each Congress.

Throughout the book, I include non-interview data—descriptive and analytical summaries of the steps in the legislative and political history of each commission examined in the study—to confirm the descriptions derived from the interviews. But the interviews provide the leading edge of the description. This methodological approach proved to be illuminating because of the varied nature of the issues surrounding commission formation and the available evidence. As other congressional scholars who use what Richard F. Fenno, Jr., calls the "soaking and poking" approach will attest, in exploratory research, the importance is on discovering relationships or motives and on generating ideas about them rather than using rational choice or formal models which assume answers to the very questions I investigate: the motivations and reasoning of members of Congress. A problem with structured interview schedules is that the academic's instruments might strike the elite respondent as overly simplistic or awkward, the result being that the instruments are not always taken seriously.

Throughout the interviews, respondents were guaranteed anonymity. All interviews were semi-structured, and the contents were largely reproduced immediately following the interview. When interviewing a member of the political elite, the interviewer must establish rapport with the respondent. In a few cases, a tape recorder was used during the interview and notes were transcribed verbatim. Certain key questions, all open-ended, were asked of all respondents holding similar positions. These questions focused on the factors that influence members of Congress to delegate. For example, each interview began by briefly noting my research and outlining what could not be uncovered from the records—generally, the institutional and individual motivation for creating commissions—and hence what needed to be known that could only be obtained from the respondent. My initial inquiry to respondents was: *Please explain the reason for this commission.* This was typically followed by clarification. For instance, if the respondent indicated that expertise was the primary motive for creating a commission, the respondent would then be asked to explain how the subject matter was beyond the expertise of the representative/senator or the congressional office: *How is this issue beyond your [representative/senator or staffer's] expertise?* The respondent would then be asked to compare the case in question with a similar circumstance from the past in which no commission was proposed, and to then explain the difference(s) between the two situations: *Based on your experience, can you think of a case that was similar in that you also lacked expertise, but in which you did not propose a commission, and what differentiates this case from that case?* Interviews with staff members were concluded by asking them to compare their responses to those of their bosses: *Would your boss answer these questions any differently and, if so, how?* After the initial interviews, additional questions were crafted that sought to clarify both the respondent's descriptions and the previous questions. The interviews tended to be short—thirty to forty minutes on average, through they ranged from ten minutes to two hours.

Most interviews took place in Washington, D.C., during the 103rd Congress (1993–1995) and the early part of the 104th Congress (1995–1997), with a few telephone interviews taking place during the 105th Congress (1997–1999) and 106th Congress (1999–2001). House and Senate staff (both personal and committee) associated with House and Senate offices that proposed legislation to establish ad hoc commissions were interviewed for the study. These people had the primary responsibility for preparing and shepherding the bills that proposed creating commissions. In the House, there was a response rate of 48 percent. In the Senate, there was a response rate of 69 percent. The overall success rate was 54 percent. Initial contact was made with each congressional office by a letter describing my research and expressing my desire to interview the member about the particular commission in question. The letters were followed by at least six attempts (if needed) to contact the office in person, over the phone, or by electronic mail. Some members of Congress refuse academic interviews as a matter of office policy. Additional interviews were conducted with respondents who were not a part of Congress during this study but who, at some point, were a part of the commission process. For example, two former committee and personal staff members, who had worked on the legislation that led to the creation of the Base Closure and Realignment Commission, and a former member of Congress who was active in several congressional commissions were interviewed. These respondents were typically recommended by other respondents.

A range of public records was also examined. Transcripts of committee and subcommittee hearings as well as the *Congressional Record* of the debates behind each case study commission were studied to assess the positions taken by the key legislators in the formation of each case study commission. The language of the legislative bills creating the commissions was analyzed. Other information came from the *Congressional Directory, Congressional Yellow Book, U.S. Code: Congressional and Administrative News, U.S. Statutes at Large,* the *Encyclopedia of Governmental Advisory Organizations,* the Library of Congress computer search systems (SCORPIO and THOMAS), the Library of Congress Information Service (LOCIS), the relevant commission or board, and the media (NEXIS-LEXIS). Major Congressional Quarterly publications were consulted. *Congressional Quarterly Almanac,* an annual compendium of biographical and organizational data, summaries of action taken in each session of Congress, roll-call votes, and analyses of congressional voting; *Congress and the Nation,* which includes a summary of all major legislation, biographical information on members of Congress, and key roll-call votes; and the *Congressional Quarterly Weekly Report,* a weekly summary of important congressional news, roll calls, and analyses of congressional voting. It is not possible to track systematically the creation of all congressional commissions, because many mandates are attached as riders to omnibus measures.

—Appendix 2—

Congressional Language to Propose a Commission

H.R.376, Department of Energy Elimination and National Security Protection Act of 2001 (Introduced in the House)

SEC. 201. ENERGY LABORATORY FACILITIES COMMISSION.

(a) ESTABLISHMENT—There is established an independent commission to be known as the "Energy Laboratory Facilities Commission," for the purpose of reducing the number of energy laboratories and programs at those laboratories, through reconfiguration, privatization, and closure, while preserving the traditional role the energy laboratories have contributed to the national defense.

(b) DUTIES—The Commission shall carry out the duties specified for the Commission in this title.

(c) APPOINTMENT—

(1) IN GENERAL—The Commission shall be composed of 7 members appointed by the President, by and with the advice and consent of the Senate. The President shall transmit to the Senate the nominations for appointment to the Commission not later than 3 months after the date of the enactment of this Act.

(2) CONSULTATION—In selecting individuals for nominations for appointments to the Commission, the President should consult with—

(A) the Speaker of the House of Representatives concerning the appointment of 2 members; and

(B) the majority leader of the Senate concerning the appointment of 2 members.

(3) CHAIRPERSON—At the time the President nominates individuals for appointment to the Commission, the President shall designate one such individual who shall serve as Chairperson of the Commission.

(d) TERMS—The term of each member of the Commission shall expire on the termination of the Commission under subsection (1).

(e) MEETINGS—Each meeting of the Commission, other than meetings in which classified information is to be discussed, shall be open to the public.

(f) VACANCIES—A vacancy in the Commission shall be filled in the same manner as the original appointment.

(g) PAY AND TRAVEL EXPENSES-

(1) BASIC PAY—

(A) PAY OF MEMBERS—Each member, other than the Chairperson, shall be paid at a rate equal to the daily equivalent of the minimum annual rate of basic pay payable for level IV of the Executive Schedule under section 5315 of title 5, United States Code, for each day (including travel time) during which the member is engaged in the actual performance of duties vested in the Commission.

(B) PAY OF CHAIRPERSON—The Chairperson shall be paid for each day referred to in subparagraph (A) at a rate equal to the daily equivalent of the minimum annual rate of basic pay payable for level III of the Executive Schedule under section 5314 of title 5, United States Code.

(2) TRAVEL EXPENSES—Members shall receive travel expenses, including per diem in lieu of subsistence, in accordance with sections 5702 and 5703 of title 5, United States Code.

(h) DIRECTOR—

(1) IN GENERAL—The Commission shall appoint a Director who—

(A) has not served as a civilian employee of the Department of Energy during the 4-year period preceding the date of such appointment;

(B) has not been an employee of an energy laboratory during the 5-year period preceding the date of such appointment; and

(C) has not been an employee of a contractor operating an energy laboratory during the 5-year period preceding the date of such appointment.

(2) PAY—The Director shall be paid at the rate of basic pay payable for level IV of the Executive Schedule under section 5315 of title 5, United States Code.

(i) STAFF—

(1) APPOINTMENT BY DIRECTOR—Subject to paragraphs (2) and (3), the Director, with the approval of the Commission, may appoint and fix the pay of additional personnel.

(2) APPLICABILITY OF CERTAIN CIVIL SERVICE LAWS—The Director may make such appointments without regard to the provisions of title 5,

United States Code, governing appointments in the competitive service, and any personnel so appointed may be paid without regard to the provisions of chapter 51 and subchapter III of chapter 53 of that title relating to classification and General Schedule pay rates, except that an individual so appointed may not receive pay in excess of the annual rate of basic pay payable for level IV of the Executive Schedule under section 5315 of title 5, United States Code.

(3) LIMITATIONS—Not more than one-third of the personnel employed by or detailed to the Commission shall be individuals employed by the Department of Energy on the day before the date of the enactment of this Act. No employee of an energy laboratory, or of a contractor who operates an energy laboratory, may be detailed to the Commission.

(4) SUPPORT FROM OTHER AGENCIES—Upon request of the Director, the head of a Federal agency may detail any of the personnel of that agency to the Commission to assist the Commission in carrying out its duties under this title.

(5) SUPPORT FROM COMPTROLLER GENERAL—The Comptroller General of the United States shall provide assistance, including the detailing of employees, to the Commission in accordance with an agreement entered into with the Commission.

(j) OTHER AUTHORITY—

(1) TEMPORARY AND INTERMITTENT SERVICES—The Commission may procure by contract, to the extent funds are available, the temporary or intermittent services of experts or consultants pursuant to section 3109 of title 5, United States Code.

(2) AUTHORITY TO LEASE SPACE AND ACQUIRE CERTAIN PROPERTY—The Commission may lease space and acquire personal property to the extent funds are available.

(k) FUNDING—There are authorized to be appropriated to the Commission such funds as are necessary to carry out its duties under this title. Such funds shall remain available until expended.

(l) TERMINATION—The Commission shall terminate not later than 30 days after the date on which it transmits its final recommendations under section 202(f)(4).

SEC. 202. PROCEDURE FOR MAKING RECOMMENDATIONS FOR LABORATORY FACILITIES.

(a) SELECTION CRITERIA—In making recommendations for the reconfiguration, privatization, and closure of energy laboratories and termination of programs at such laboratories under this section, the Secretary or the Administrator, as appropriate, and the Commission shall—

(1) emphasize the importance of establishing the security of defense research and activities;

(2) give strong consideration to closure or privatization of activities performed by the private sector;

(3) give strong emphasis in transferring or selling non-defense research laboratories to universities and private organizations that currently manage and operate such laboratories;

(4) give strong consideration to the closure or reconfiguration of energy laboratories;

(5) eliminate duplication of effort by energy laboratories and reduce overhead costs as a proportion of program benefits distributed through an energy laboratory;

(6) seek to achieve cost savings for the overall budget for such laboratories;

(7) define appropriate missions for each energy laboratory, and ensure that the activities of each such laboratory are focused on its mission or missions;

(8) consider the number of participants in programs conducted through an energy laboratory and staff resources involved;

(9) estimate the cost savings and increases that would accrue through the reconfiguration of energy laboratories;

(10) consider the potential of each energy laboratory to generate revenues or to offset costs;

(11) consider the transfer of energy laboratories to other Federal agencies;

(12) consider the privatization of the energy laboratories as an alternative to closure or reconfiguration; and

(13) be subject to the requirements of section 601 of this Act.

(b) RECOMMENDATIONS—

(1) PUBLICATION AND TRANSMITTAL—Not later than 3 months after the date of the enactment of this Act, the Secretary or the Administrator, as appropriate, shall publish in the Federal Register and transmit to the congressional energy committees and to the Commission a list of the energy laboratories that the Secretary or the Administrator, as appropriate, recommends for reconfiguration, privatization, and closure.

(2) SUMMARY OF SELECTION PROCESS—The Secretary or the Administrator, as appropriate, shall include, with the list of recommendations published and transmitted pursuant to paragraph (1), a summary of the selection process that resulted in the recommendation for each energy laboratory, including a justification for each recommendation.

(c) EQUAL CONSIDERATION OF LABORATORIES—In considering energy laboratories for reconfiguration, privatization, and closure, the Secretary or the Administrator, as appropriate, shall consider all such laboratories equally without regard to whether a laboratory has been previously considered or proposed for reconfiguration, privatization, or closure by the Secretary of Energy.

(d) AVAILABILITY OF INFORMATION—The Secretary or the Administrator, as appropriate, shall make available to the Commission and the Comptroller General of the United States all information used by the Secretary or the Administrator, as appropriate, in making recommendations under this section.

(e) INDEPENDENT AUDIT—

(1) Within 30 days after the date of the enactment of this Act, the Director of the Office of Management and Budget shall issue a request for proposals for the performance of an audit under paragraph (3). (2) Within 60 days after the date of the enactment of this Act, proposals shall be due in response to the request under paragraph (1). (3) Within 90 days after the date of the enactment of this Act, the Director of the Office of Management and Budget shall enter into a contract with an independent financial consulting firm for an audit of the energy laboratories and their programs, facilities, and assets. Such audit shall assess the commercial potential of the energy labs and their programs and make recommendations on how the Government could best realize such potential. The audit shall be completed and transmitted to the Commission, the Secretary or the Administrator, as appropriate, and the congressional energy committees within 6 months after the contract is entered into under this subsection.

(f) REVIEW AND RECOMMENDATIONS BY THE COMMISSION—

(1) PUBLIC HEARINGS—After receiving the recommendations from the Secretary or the Administrator, as appropriate, pursuant to subsection (b), the Commission shall provide an opportunity for public comment on the recommendations for a 30-day period.

(2) INITIAL REPORT—Not later than 1 year after the date of the enactment of this Act, the Commission shall publish in the Federal Register an initial report containing the Commission's findings and conclusions based on a review and analysis of the recommendations made by the Secretary or the Administrator, as appropriate, and the audit conducted pursuant to subsection (e), together with the Commission's recommendations for reconfiguration, privatization, and closure of energy laboratories. In conducting such review and analysis, the Commission shall consider all energy laboratories.

(3) DEVIATION FROM RECOMMENDATIONS—In making its recommendations, the Commission may make changes in any of the recommendations made by the Secretary or the Administrator, as appropriate, if the Commission determines that the Secretary or the Administrator, as appropriate, deviated substantially from the criteria described in subsection (a) in making recommendations. The Commission shall explain and justify in the report any recommendation made by the Commission that is different from the recommendations made by the Secretary or the Administrator, as appropriate.

(4) FINAL REPORT—After providing a 30-day period for public comment following publication of the initial report under paragraph (2), and after full consideration of such public comments, the Commission shall, within 15 months after the date of the enactment of this Act, transmit to the Secretary or the Administrator, as appropriate, and the congressional energy committees a final report containing the recommendations of the Commission.

(5) PROVISION OF CERTAIN INFORMATION—After transmitting the final report under paragraph (4), the Commission shall promptly provide, upon request, to any Member of Congress information used by the Commission in making its recommendations.

(g) ASSISTANCE FROM COMPTROLLER GENERAL—The Comptroller General of the United States shall—

(1) assist the Commission, to the extent requested, in the Commission's review and analysis of the recommendations made by the Secretary or the Administrator, as appropriate, pursuant to subsection (b); and

(2) not later than 6 months after the date of the enactment of this Act, transmit to the congressional energy committees and to the Commission a report containing a detailed analysis of the recommendations of the Secretary or the Administrator, as appropriate, and the selection process.

SEC. 203. RECONFIGURATION, PRIVATIZATION, AND CLOSURE OF ENERGY LABORATORIES.

(a) IN GENERAL—Subject to subsection (b), the Secretary or the Administrator, as appropriate, shall—

(1) reconfigure, within 1 year after the date of the transmittal of the final report under section 202(f)(4), all energy laboratories recommended for reconfiguration by the Commission in such report;

(2) provide for and complete the privatization, within 18 months after the date of the transmittal of the final report under section 202(f)(4), of all energy laboratories recommended for privatization by the Commission in such report; and

(3) except as necessary to achieve the privatization of an energy laboratory under paragraph (2), close, within 1 year after the date of the transmittal of the final report under section 202(f)(4), all energy laboratories recommended for closure by the Commission in such report.

(b) CONGRESSIONAL DISAPPROVAL—

(1) IN GENERAL—The Secretary or the Administrator, as appropriate, may not carry out any reconfiguration, privatization, or closure of an energy laboratory recommended by the Commission in the report transmitted pursuant to section 202(f)(4) if a joint resolution is enacted, in accordance with the provisions of section 207, disapproving the recommendations of the Commission before the earlier of—

(A) the end of the 45-day period beginning on the date on which the Commission transmits the report; or

(B) the adjournment of Congress sine die for the session during which the report is transmitted.

(2) EXCLUDED DAYS—For purposes of paragraph (1) of this subsection and subsections (a) and (c) of section 207, the days on which either House of Congress is not in session because of an adjournment of more than three days to a day certain shall be excluded in the computation of a period.

SEC. 204. IMPLEMENTATION OF RECONFIGURATION, PRIVATIZATION, AND CLOSURE ACTIONS.

(a) IMPLEMENTATION—In reconfiguring, privatizing, or closing an energy laboratory under this title, the Secretary or the Administrator, as appropriate, shall—

(1) take such actions as may be necessary to reconfigure, privatize, or close the energy laboratory;

(2) take such steps as may be necessary to ensure the safe keeping of all records stored at the energy laboratory; and

(3) reimburse other Federal agencies for actions performed at the request of the Secretary or the Administrator, as appropriate, with respect to any such reconfiguration, privatization, or closure, and may use for such purpose funds in the Account or funds appropriated to the Department of Energy and available for such purpose.

(b) MANAGEMENT AND DISPOSAL OF PROPERTY—

(1) IN GENERAL—The Administrator of General Services shall delegate to the Secretary or the Administrator, as appropriate, with respect to excess and surplus real property and facilities located at an energy laboratory reconfigured, privatized, or closed under this title—

(A) the authority of the Secretary or the Administrator, as appropriate, to utilize excess property under section 202 of the Federal Property and Administrative Services Act of 1949 (40 U.S.C. 483);

(B) the authority of the Secretary or the Administrator, as appropriate, to dispose of surplus property under section 203 of that Act (40 U.S.C. 484);

(C) the authority of the Secretary or the Administrator, as appropriate, to grant approvals and make determinations under section 13(g) of the Surplus Property Act of 1944 (50 U.S.C. App. 1622[g]); and

(D) the authority of the Secretary or the Administrator, as appropriate, to determine the availability of excess or surplus real property for wildlife conservation purposes in accordance with the Act of May 19, 1948 (16 U.S.C. 667b).

(2) EXERCISE OF AUTHORITY—

(A) IN GENERAL—Subject to subparagraph (C), the Secretary or the Administrator, as appropriate, shall exercise the authority delegated to the Secretary or the Administrator, as appropriate, pursuant to paragraph (1) in accordance with—

(i) all regulations in effect on the date of the enactment of this Act governing the utilization of excess property and the disposal of surplus property under the Federal Property and Administrative Services Act of 1949; and

(ii) all regulations in effect on the date of the enactment of this Act governing the conveyance and disposal of property under section 13(g) of the Surplus Property Act of 1944 (50 U.S.C. App. 1622[g]).

(B) REGULATIONS—The Secretary or the Administrator, as appropriate, after consulting with the Administrator of General Services, may issue regulations that are necessary to carry out the delegation of authority required by paragraph (1).

(C) LIMITATION—The authority required to be delegated by paragraph (1) to the Secretary or the Administrator, as appropriate, by the Administrator of General Services shall not include the authority to prescribe general policies and methods for utilizing excess property and disposing of surplus property.

(c) WAIVER—The Secretary or the Administrator, as appropriate, may reconfigure, privatize, or close energy laboratories under this title without regard to any provision of law restricting the use of funds for reconfiguring, privatizing, or closing such energy laboratories included in any appropriations or authorization Act.

SEC. 205. ACCOUNT.

(a) ESTABLISHMENT—There is hereby established on the books of the Treasury an account to be known as the "Energy Laboratory Facility Closure Account" which shall be administered by the Secretary or the Administrator, as appropriate, as a single account.

Source: Thomas, www.congress.gov.

—Appendix 3—

Proposed Commissions: 93rd–107th Congresses

93rd CONGRESS (1973–1975)

Advisory Commission on Federal Tax Forms

Advisory Commission on Freight Rates for Farm Products

Advisory Commission on Intergovernmental Relations

Advisory Commission on the Reconstruction and Redevelopment of Southeast Asia

Airport Noise Curfew Commission

American Railroad Consolidation Commission

Auto Rates Reduction Commission

Bicentennial Constitutional Commission

Commission for Improvement of Government Management and Organization

Commission on an Independent Permanent Prosecutor

Commission on Citizens' Suggestions, Inventions, and Proposals

Commission on Economic and Natural Resources Planning

Commission on Economic Efficiency

Commission on Electronic Fund Transfers

Commission on Federal Paperwork

Commission on Federal Taxation

Commission on Fertilizer Availability

Commission on Foreign Procurement Practices

Commission on Highway Beautification

Commission on Medical Technology and Dignity of Dying

Commission on Mental Health and Illness of the Elderly

Commission on Penal Reform

Commission on Philippine Guerilla Recognition

Commission on Revision of Antitrust Laws

Commission on the Bankruptcy Laws of the United States

Commission on the Executive Office of the President

Commission on the Reform of the Federal Income Tax Laws

Commission on the United States Participation in the United Nations

Commission to Investigate Alleged Criminal, Irregular, or Wrongful Conduct in the Presidential Election Campaign of 1972

Commission to Investigate the Increase in Law Violations

Countryside Development Commission

Defense Manpower Commission

Federal Pay Commission

Federal Scholastic and Amateur Sports Commission

Freedom of Information Commission

Interdisciplinary Clearcutting Practice Study Commission

Military Installation Closing Commission

National Advisory Commission on Correctional Standards

National Advisory Commission on Education

National Capital Planning Commission

National Commission for Full Employment Policy Studies

National Commission for the Preservation of Foreign Language Resources

National Commission for the Protection of Human Subjects of Biomedical and Behavioral Research

National Commission for the Review of Federal and State Laws on Wiretapping and Electronic Surveillance

National Commission on Alien Labor

National Commission on Arthritis and Related Musculoskeletal Diseases

National Commission on Crime and Drugs

National Commission on Diabetes

National Commission on Epilepsy and Its Consequences

National Commission on Executive Security

National Commission on Fuels and Energy

National Commission on Health Science and Society

National Commission on Individual Rights and Personal Security

National Commission on Inflation

National Commission on International Trade and the Environment

National Commission on Productivity and Work Quality

National Commission on Regulatory Reform

National Commission on Social Security

National Commission on Supplies and Shortages

National Commission on Veterans' Benefits

National Commission on the Compensation of Authors for Library Uses of Their Works

National Commission on the Economy

National Commission on the Olympic Games

National Commission on the Prevention of Raw Material Shortages

National Commission to Study and Report on the Impact of the Independent Regulatory Agencies upon Commerce

National Commission to Study the Relationship between Drug Addiction and Crime

National Flag Commission

National Forest Reservation Commission

National Geothermal Energy Commission

National Landlord and Tenant Commission

National Lottery Commission

National Medical Devices Standards Commission

National Public Employee Relations Commission

National Studies Commission on Federal Records and Documents of Federal Offices

Nonpartisan Commission on Campaign Reform

Nonpartisan Commission on Federal Election Reform

Relocation Benefits Commission

Special Commission on Guadalupe-Hidalgo Land Rights

Special Historic Commission on Watergate and Related Activities

Watergate Investigation Commission

94th CONGRESS (1975–1977)

Advisory Commission on Future Civilian Manpower Requirements at United States Military Installations

Advisory Commission on Intergovernmental Relations

Airport Noise Curfew Commission

Antitrust Revision Commission

Bicentennial Commission on Presidential Nominations

Bicentennial Constitutional Commission

Commission for Re-establishing Constitutional Principles

Commission of Lifelong Adult Education

Commission on Federal Aid Reform

Commission on Fertilizer Availability

Commission on Mental Health and Illness of the Elderly

Commission on School Integration

Commission on Tax Revision

Commission on the Adequacy of the Annual Federal Payment to the District of Columbia

Commission on the Federal Judicial System

Commission on the Humane Treatment of Animals

Commission on the Operation of the Senate

Commission on the Organization of the Executive Office of the President

Commission on the Political Status of Guam

Commission on the Security and Cooperation in Europe

Commission on the United States Participation in the United Nations

Commission to Examine the Effect of Northwest Indian Off-Reservation Fishing Rights

Commission to Investigate the Increase in Law Violation and to Fix Responsibility for the Breakdown in Law Enforcement

Commission to Study the Quality of Instruction at the Service Academies

Competition Review Commission

Employment Statistics Commission

Government Executive Analysis and Reform Commission

National Advisory Commission on Education

National Commission for the Preservation of Language Resources

National Commission for the Review of Federal and State Laws Relating to Wiretapping and Electronic Surveillance

National Commission on Alternatives to Busing

National Commission on Diabetes

National Commission on Economic Growth and Stability

National Commission on Epilepsy and Its Consequences

National Commission on Food Production, Processing, Marketing, and Pricing

National Commission on Health Science and Society

National Commission on Housing for the Elderly

National Commission on Individual Rights

National Commission on Neighborhoods

National Commission on New Technological Uses of Copyright Works

National Commission on Regulatory Reform

National Commission on School Busing

National Commission on Small Business in America

National Commission on Supplies and Shortages

National Commission on Victimless Crimes

National Commission on the Economy

National Commission on the Observance of International Women's Year, 1975

National Commission on the Olympic Games

National Commission on the Social Security Program

National Forest Reservation Commission

National Health Research and Development Advisory Commission

National Landlord and Tenant Commission

National Presidential Elections Commission

National Study Commission on Records and Documents of Federal Officials

National Transportation Study Commission

Privacy Protection Study Commission

Select Commission on Nationality and Naturalization

Select Commission on Territorial Immigration Policy

Special Commission on Quality Assurance and Utilization Control in Home Health Care

Special Commission on Rural Poverty and Guadalupe-Hidalgo Land Rights

Special Investigative Commission on Postal Service Operations

95th CONGRESS (1977–1979)

Advisory Commission on Intergovernmental Relations

Airport Noise Commission on American Government

Bicentennial Commission on American Government

Bill of Rights Commemoration Commission

Citizens' Commission on Economic Regulatory Oversight

Commission for the Preservation of American Heritage Abroad

Commission on a Balanced Budget

Commission on American Government

Commission on Defensive Weapons

Commission on Domestic and International Hunger and Malnutrition

Commission on Genetic Research and Engineering

Commission on Legislative-Judicial Relations

Commission on National Primary Health Care Costs

Commission on Natural Gas Resources

Commission on Proposals for a National Academy of Peace and Conflict Resolution

Commission on South Korean Influence

Commission on the Adequacy of the Annual Federal Payment to the District of Columbia

Commission on the Feasibility of Nationalizing the Nation's Railroads

Commission on the Humane Treatment of Animals

Commission on the Operation of the Senate

Commission on the Reorganization of the Executive Branch of the Government

Commission on the Social Security Program

Commission on the Victims of the Holocaust

Commission to Study the Effect of Northwest Indian Off-Reservation Fishing Rights

Competition Review Commission

Cultural Park Advisory Commission

District of Columbia Boundary Commission

Employment Statistics Commission

Federal Judicial Nominating Commission

National Advisory Commission on Education

National Alcohol Fuels Commission

National Commission for the Study of Recombinant DNA Research and Technology

National Commission on Air Quality

National Commission on Basic Education

National Commission on Diabetes

National Commission on Energy Policy

National Commission on Hospital Costs

National Commission on Housing for the Elderly

National Commission on Immigration Policy

National Commission on Interfuel Competition

National Commission on Neighborhoods

National Commission on New Technological Uses of Copyrighted Works

National Commission on Parity Farm Income

National Commission on Preventive Health

National Commission on Regulatory Reform

National Commission on the Use of Computers in Education

National Commission on Victimless Crimes

National Landlord and Tenant Commission

National Science Policy Commission

Puerto Rico Statehood Commission

Select Commission Immigration and Refugee Policy

Special Commission on Quality Assurance and Utilization Control in Home Health Care

Temporary Federal Intergovernmental Planning Commission

96th CONGRESS (1979–1981)

Advisory Commission on Intergovernmental Relations

Advisory Commission on Public Diplomacy

Advisory Commission on Regulations Concerning Trapping and Capturing of Mammals and Birds

Advisory Panel on the Removal of Administrative Restrictions Not Required by Federal Law or Court Order

Airport Noise Curfew Commission

Bipartisan Task Force on Federal Regulatory Practices

Citizens' Commission for the Federal Government Bicentenary Era

Citizens' Commission on Economic Regulatory Oversight

Citizens' Commission on the Efficiency of Federal Programs

Citizens' Commission on the Organization and Operation of Government

Commission for the Commemoration of the Bicentennial of the U.S. Constitution

Commission on Alternative Mortgage Instruments

Commission on a North American Economic Alliance

Commission on Domestic and International Hunger and Malnutrition

Commission on Federal Laws

Commission on Federal Paperwork

Commission on Governmental Organization and Regulation

Commission on Legislative-Judicial Relations

Commission on More Effective Government

Commission on National Service

Commission on Presidential Nominations

Commission on Security and Cooperation in China

Commission on Tax Revision

Commission on the Future of Nuclear Power in the United States

Commission on the International Application of the United States Antitrust Laws

Commission on the Nationalization of the Oil Industry

Commission on Wartime Relocation and Internment of Citizens

Commission to Recommend an Appropriate Memorial to Former U.S. Representative Allard K. Lowenstein

Commission to Study and Evaluate the Multiple Protective Structure System and the Air Mobil/Transportation Local System for Protecting the Land Based Intercontinental Ballistic Missiles of the United States

Commission to Study U.S. Policy Concerning the Role of Gold in the Domestic and International Monetary Systems

Competition Review Commission

Congressional Redistricting Commission

Delegation to Organize a Convention of Delegations from Parliamentary Democracies

Federal Jurisdictional Review and Revision Commission

Government Executive Analysis and Reform Commission

Hawaiian Native Claims Settlement Study Commission

Independent Investigating Commission on Ethics

Kalaupapa National Historical Preserve Advisory Commission

Lake Tahoe National Scenic Area Advisory Commission

National Commission on Alcoholism and Alcohol-Related Problems

National Commission on Compulsive Gambling

National Commission on Diabetes

National Commission on Digestive Diseases

National Commission on Food Production, Marketing, and Pricing

National Commission on Hospital Cost Containment

National Commission on Hospital Costs

National Commission on Libraries

National Commission on Literacy

National Commission on Military Manpower Needs

National Commission on Regulatory Reform

National Commission on Spectrum Management

National Commission on the Scientific and Technological Implications of Information Technology in Education

National Commission on Unemployment Compensation

National Consumer Usury Commission

National Economic Commission

National Energy Council

National Geothermal Energy Commission

National Hostel System Study Commission

National Workers' Compensation Advisory Commission

Native Hawaiians Study Commission

San Joaquin del Canon del Rio de Chama Grant Commission

Special Commission for the Investigation and Review of Nuclear Power

Special Commission on Quality Assurance and Utilization Control in Home Health Care

Special Investigatory Commission on Americans Listed as Missing in Southeast Asia

Study Committee of National Trails

Temporary Commission on Financial Oversight of the District of Columbia

Temporary Commission to Evaluate the Damage Caused by the Oilspill in the Bay of Campeche, Mexico

Trails West National Historical Park Advisory Commission

United States Constitution Bicentennial Commission

Veterans Advisory Task Force

Washington Metropolitian Region Study Commission

Women's Rights National Historical Park Advisory Commission

97th CONGRESS (1981–1983)

Advisory Commission on Federal Wildlife and Federal Lands Trappings

Advisory Commission on Intergovernmental Relations

Airport Noise Curfew Commission

Commission for the Commemoration of the Bicentennial of the United States Constitution

Commission for the Protection of Animals in Research

Commission on Capital Markets

Commission on Educational Problems of America's Linguistic Minority Children

Commission on Monetary Policy

Commission on More Effective Government

Commission on Neurofibromatosis

Commission on Presidential Nominations

Commission on Strategic and Critical Materials Stock Piling Needs

Commission on Tax Revision

Commission on the Bicentennial of the United States Constitution

Commission on the Budget Process

Commission on the International Application of the United States Antitrust Laws

Commission to Determine What Is the Budget of the United States

Commission to Recommend an Appropriate Memorial to Former Representative Allard K. Lowenstein

Commission to Study the Feasibility of Providing Rapid Rail Transit Service between Mississippi and Louisiana

Congressional Pay and Benefits Commission

Federal Courts Study Commission

Federal-State Radioactive Waste Management Commission

Gold Commission

Government Executive Analysis and Reform Commission

Guillain-Barre Syndrome Compensation Commission

Historical Publications and Records Commission

National Advisory Council on Asylum and Refugee Policy

National Commission for Expansion of Language Resources

National Commission for the Commemoration of the Federal Government between 1776 and 1800

National Commission on Compulsive Gambling

National Commission on Down Syndrome

National Commission on Interest Rates

National Commission on Science, Engineering, and Technology Education

National Commission on the Rebuilding of America

National Commission on the Regulation of Nursing Homes

National Commission on Training and Employment

National Export Policy Commission

National Hostel System Study Commission

National Land Resources Protection Commission

North American Commission for Cooperation

North American Economic Alliance Commission

Presidential Protection Commission

President's Commission on Ethical Problems in Medicine

Prime Ridgelands National Study Area Commission

San Joaquin del Canon del Rio de Chama Grant Commission

Select Commission on Voluntary Service Opportunities

Special Commission on Quality Assurance and Utilization Control in Home Health Care

United States Constitution Bicentennial Commission

Youth Employment Commission

98th CONGRESS (1983–1985)

Commission for the Advancement of Educational Computer Software

Commission for the Study of Suicide

Commission of Independent Experts

Commission on an Alternative to the Legislative Veto

Commission on Capital Markets

Commission on Deficit Reduction

Commission on Employment Discrimination in the Legislative Branch

Commission on Federal Retirement Reform

Commission on High Technology and Employment Potential

Commission on Merchant Marine and Defense

Commission on Modern Farm Animal Practices

Commission on More Effective Government

Commission on Pay Equity

Commission on Poverty Definition Reform

Commission on Tax Revision

Commission on Teacher Education

Commission on the Bicentennial of the United States Constitution

Commission on the Centennial Review of the Civil Service

Commission on the Extraterritorial Application of the United States Laws

Commission on the Transition of Industry in Our Future Economy

Commission on the Ukraine Famine

Commission on the Wartime Occupation of Guam

Commission to Recommend an Appropriate Memorial to Former Representative Allard K. Lowenstein

Commission to Reform Federal Campaign Finance

Congressional Advisory Commission on Amateur Boxing

Congressional Advisory Commission on Boxing

Congressional Commission on Defense Planning

Congressional Commission on National Defense Planning

Congressional Compensation Commission

Decentralization Study Commission

Federal Courts Study Commission on the Future of the Federal Judiciary

Government Executive Analysis and Reform Commission

International Trade and Export Policy Study Commission

Martin Luther King, Jr., Federal Holiday Commission

Medicare Financing and Benefit Review Commission

National Advisory Commission on Child Care

National Bipartisan Commission on a Balanced Budget

National Bipartisan Commission on Latin America

National Commission for a Responsible Budget

National Commission on Agricultural Trade and Export Policy

National Commission on Deficit Reduction

National Commission on Educational Excellence

National Commission on Entitlement Reform

National Commission on Environmental Monitoring

National Commission on Federal Spending Reform

National Commission on Immigration

National Commission on Improved Child Support Enforcement

National Commission on Industrial Competitiveness

National Commission on Industrial Policy

National Commission on Missing Children

National Commission on Monetary Policy

National Commission on Natural Gas Policy/Pricing

National Commission on Neurofibromatosis

National Commission on Orphan Diseases

National Commission on Science, Engineering, and Technology Education

National Commission on Technological Innovation and Industrial Modernization

National Commission on the Improvement of America's Infrastructure

National Commission on the Public Lending of Books

National Commission on the Rebuilding of America

National Commission on Women's Small Business Ownership

National Commission to Study Rising Health Care Costs

National Groundwater Commission

National Heroes Day Commission

National Lottery Commission

National Oceans Policy Commission

National Offshore Operators Safety Advisory Committee

National Outdoor Recreation Resources Review Commission

National Summit Conference on Education

National Task Force on Organ Procurement and Transplant Reimbursement

National Trucking Industry Commission

National Youth Land Use Commission

Peace Corps Strategy Commission

Presidential Advisory Panel for Coordination of Government Debt Collection and Delinquency Prevention Activities

Privacy Protection Commission

Select Commission on Climate and Agriculture

Select Commission on Drug Interdiction and Enforcement

Select Commission on Voluntary Service Opportunities

Superfund Commission

Task Force on Agricultural Credit

Task Force on the Taxation of Real Property by State and Local Governments

99th CONGRESS (1985–1987)

Advisory Commission on Tactical Nuclear Forces

Advisory Panel on Governmental Debt Collection

Aviation Safety Commission

Bipartisan Commission on Congressional Campaign Financing

Bipartisan Commission on the Budget Deficit

Bipartisan Commission to Study the U.S. Trade Deficit

Commission for the Amelioration of Parkinsonism Disease

Commission for the Bicentennial of the Congress

Commission for the Study of Youth Suicide

Commission on a Constitutional Amendment Regarding Impeachment

Commission on Back Injuries

Commission on Budget Process Review

Commission on Elections in the Philippines

Commission on Employment Discrimination in the Legislative Branch

Commission on Equitable Pay Practices

Commission on Federal Retirement Reform

Commission on Improving Defense Procurement

Commission on More Effective Government

Commission on Poverty Definition Reform

Commission on Tax Revision

Commission on the Centennial Review of the Civil Service

Commission on the Deficit

Commission on the Liability Insurance Crisis

Commission on the United States House of Representatives Bicentenary

Commission to Investigate Federal Involvement with the Immigration of Nazi Collaborators

Commission to Recommend an Appropriate Memorial to Former U.S. Representative Allard K. Lowenstein

Commission to Review the Precedents of the House of Representatives Relating to Contested Elections

Commission to Study the Electoral College

Congressional Advisory Commission on Amateur Boxing

Congressional Advisory Commission on Intercollegiate Athletics

Disability Advisory Council

Domestic Industries Priorities Commission

Dwight David Eisenhower Centennial Commission

Federal Accounting Practices Review Commission

Federal Coal Export Commission

Federal Courts Study Commission

Gulf Islands National Seashore Advisory Commission

Information Age Commission

Insurance Availability Crisis Commission

International Trade and Export Policy Study Commission

Medicare Financing and Benefit Review Commission

National Commission for the Utilization and Expansion of Language Resources

National Commission on Agricultural Policy

National Commission on Amusement Ride Safety

National Commission on Bioethics

National Commission on Classified Information and Security Clearance Procedures

National Commission on Dairy Policy

National Commission on Federal Budget Deficit Reductions

National Commission on Health Care Reform

National Commission on Illiteracy

National Commission on Lending of Authors' Works

National Commission on Neurofibromatosis

National Commission on POWs and MIAs

National Commission on the Farm Credit System

National Commission on Women's Business Ownership

National Commission to Prevent Infant Mortality

National Council on Access to Health Care

National Drug Enforcement Policy Board

National Lottery Commission

National Marine Policy Development Commission

National Nuclear Reactor Safety Study Commission

National Planning for Peace Commission

National Task Force on the Problem of Functional Illiteracy

Perot Commission on Americans Missing in Southeast Asia

Professional Football Fan Protection Commission

Select Commission on National Service Opportunities

Task Force on Elder Abuse

Task Force to Address Long-Range Concerns of the U.S. Agricultural Industry

Temporary National Commission on Economic Concentration

United States Commission on Improving the Effectiveness of the United Nations

100th CONGRESS (1987–1989)

Advisory Panel for Coordination of Government Debt Collection

Battle of Lake Erie One Hundred and Seventy-fifth Anniversary Celebration Commission

Bipartisan Commission on the Budget Deficit

Bipartisan Commission on the Consolidation of Military Bases

Bipartisan Commission to Review the Medicare Catastrophic Coverage Act

Commission for the Amelioration of Parkinsonism Disease

Commission on Compensation Equity

Commission on Economic Set-Asides

Commission on Employment Discrimination in the Legislative Branch

Commission on Equitable Pay Practices

Commission on Federal Voluntary Service Opportunities for Young People

Commission on Intercollegiate Athletics

Commission on International Security and Satellite Monitoring

Commission on More Effective Government

Commission on National Debt Reduction, Savings, and Economic Reform

Commission on National Fiscal Priorities

Commission on National Service Opportunities

Commission on Racially Motivated Violence

Commission on the American Family and Employment

Commission on the Budget Process

Commission on the Effects of Deregulation on Air Travel

Commission on the Freedom of the Department of Defense Press

Commission on the Importation of Japanese Semiconductors and Integrated Circuits

Commission on the Review of House Ethics

Commission on the United States House of Representatives Bicentenary

Commission on the United States Trade in the 1990s

Commission on the Veterans' Administration Home Loan Guaranty Program

Commission on Values Education

Commission to Recommend an Appropriate Memorial to Former U.S. Representative Allard K. Lowenstein

Commission to Study the Causes of the Current Decline in the Industrial Base of the United States

Congressional Advisory Commission on Amateur Boxing

Congressional Task Force on Concurrent Jurisdiction over Lorton

Deficit Reduction Commission

Delinquency Prevention Activities Allied Commission on Out-of-Area Issues

Federal Accounting Practices Review Commission

Federal Council on Women

Federal Courts Study Commission on Judicial Administration

Federal Courts Study Commission on the Future of the Federal Judiciary

Federal Task Force on Food and Shelter for the Homeless

Financial Intermediaries Review Commission

Interagency Commission on Methanol

Medicare Home Health Care Benefits Commission

National Advisory Committee on Rural Health

National Advisory Commission on the Future of Rural America

National Bipartisan Commission on Central America

National Bipartisan Commission on the International Debt

National Commission on Acquired Immune Deficiency Syndrome

National Commission on Children

National Commission on Commercial and National Defense Application of Superconductors

National Commission on Deficit Reduction

National Commission on Economic Challenges

National Commission on Executive Organization and Management

National Commission on Health Care Reform

National Commission on Human Resources

National Commission on International Competitiveness

National Commission on Natural Resources Disasters

National Commission on Rural Development

National Commission on Superconductivity
National Commission on the 1987 Natural Resources Disaster
National Economic Commission
National Film Preservation Commission
National Insurance Crop Commission
National Lottery Commission
National Marine Policy Development Commission
National Mars Commission
National Oceans Policy Commission
National Thrift Institutions Commission
Nuclear Waste Policy Review Commission
Special Commission on Civil Service Policy
Special Commission on Travel and Tourism
Task Force on Clandestine Drug Laboratories
Task Force on the Incorporation of the Commonwealth of Puerto Rico
Task Force to Reduce the Emission of Ozone-Depleting Chlorofluorocarbons and Halons
Temporary National Commission on Economic Concentration
Territorial Sea Commission
United States Bipartisan Commission on Comprehensive Health Care
United States Commission on Improving the Effectiveness of the United Nations

101st CONGRESS (1989–1991)

Advisory Committee on Native-American Veterans
Advisory Committee on Telecommunications Policy
Advisory Committee on the Development and Maintenance of Nursing Resources
Advisory Committee on the Records of the Congress
Anti-Drug Task Force
Anti-Money Laundering Advisory Commission
Asbestos Abatement Scientific Commission
Bipartisan Commission on Comprehensive Health Care
Bipartisan Commission to Review the Medicare Catastrophic Coverage Act
Bipartisan Task Force on Export Development and Promotion
Blue Ribbon Commission to Address the National Agenda for Foreign Language Instruction in Elementary Schools
Civil War Sites Advisory Commission
Commission on Aviation Security and Terrorism
Commission on Base Realignment and Closure

Commission on Department of Energy Environmental Remediation Activities

Commission on Employment Discrimination in the Legislative Branch

Commission on Energy Independence

Commission on Federal Taxation of Savings and Investment

Commission on International Security and Satellite Monitoring

Commission on Leave

Commission on National Fiscal Priorities

Commission on Obesity

Commission on Racially Motivated Violence

Commission on Realignment and Major Mission Change

Commission on the United States Representatives Bicentenary

Commission on Values Education

Commission to Study the Use of Former Military Installations for Drug Rehabilitation Centers

Committee on Earth Sciences

Congressional Advisory Commission on Amateur Boxing

Economic and Budgeting Commission

Environmental Sciences Review Panel

Farm Safety Task Force

Federal Council on Women

Gulf of Mexico Marine and Coastal Resources Commission

Health Care Crisis Policy Commission

Joint Commission on the Applicability of Federal Law

Joint Federal-State Commission on Policies and Programs Affecting Alaska Natives

Judicial Nomination Commission

Medicare Financing and Benefit Review Commission

Mississippi River Corridor Study Commission

National Advisory Committee for Review of the Organ Procurement Process

National Advisory Committee for the Review of Federal Excess and Surplus Personal Property

National Advisory Committee on Child Care Standards

National Advisory Committee on Rural Health

National Advisory Council on the Public Service

National Advisory Medical Policy Council

National Bipartisan Commission on Central America

National Bipartisan Commission on International Debt

National Commission on Choices in Health Care Reform

National Commission on Defense and National Security

National Commission on Drug Abuse Treatment Effectiveness

National Commission on Entrepreneurial Education

National Commission on Financial Institution Reform

National Commission on Human Resources Development

National Commission on Judicial Impeachment

National Commission on Medicare Reform

National Commission on Research Needs

National Commission on Savings and Loans

National Commission on Severely Distressed Public Housing

National Commission on Wildlife Disasters

National Commission to Aid Homeless Mentally Ill Individuals

National Commission to Study the Causes of the Demand for Drugs in the United States

National Commission to Support Law Enforcement

National Committee on Education

National Environmental Institute Commission

National Infrastructure Council

National Literacy Commission

National Lottery Commission

National Mars Commission

National Workplace Safety Commission

Niobrara Scenic River Advisory Council

Presidential Commission for Evaluating United States International Broadcasting Services

President's Advisory Commission on National Commemorative Events

Select Review Commission on Legal Immigration Reform

Statehood of New Columbia Transition Commission

Temporary National Commission on Economic Concentration

Thomas Cole Advisory Commission

200-Day School Year Study Commission

United States Flag Commission

Wayport Development Commission

102nd CONGRESS (1991–1993)

Advisory Committee on Emerging Telecommunications Technologies

Advisory Committee on Recycling of Automotive Materials

Advisory Council on Social Security

AIDS Disability Advisory Panel

American Samoa Study Commission

Bankruptcy Review Commission

Bipartisan Commission on Total Quality Government

Blue Ribbon Commission on Foreign Language Instruction

Commission on Broadcasting to the People's Republic of China

Commission on Closure and Relocation of the Lorton Correctional Complex

Commission on Employment Discrimination in the Legislative Branch

Commission on Energy Independence

Commission on Environment and Development

Commission on Executive Organization

Commission on Information Technology and Paperwork Reduction

Commission on Leave

Commission on National Fiscal Priorities

Commission on Obesity

Commission on Peace and Prosperity

Commission on Retirement Income Policy

Commission on United States Relations with the People's Republic of China

Commission on the Advancement of Women in Science and Engineering Work Forces

Commission on the Airplane Crash at Gander, Newfoundland

Commission on the Bicentennial of the United States' Democratic Party

Commission on the Conservation of Biological Resources

Commission on Values Education

Commission to Determine Appropriate Measures of Homelessness

Commission to Study Reparation Proposals for African Americans

Congressional Advisory Commission on Amateur Boxing

Council on Interjurisdictional Rivers Fisheries

Critical Technology Commission

District of Columbia Judicial Nomination Commission

Education Emergency Task Force

Ethical Advisory Board

Federal Council on Women

Federal Interagency Task Force

Federal Open Market Advisory Committee

Federal Senior Citizen Personnel Support Council

Glass Ceiling Commission

Health Care Policy Commission

Home and Community-Based Care Advisory Council

House Bipartisan Legal Advisory Group

House Commission on Congressional Reform

House Commission on Legislative Process Reform

Intergovernmental Health Care Fraud and Abuse Commission

Interstate Taxation Commission

Joint Commission on the Applicability of Federal Law

Mineral Policy Review Commission

National Advisory Body on the National Writing Project

National Advisory Medical Policy Council

National Commission on American Labor Law

National Commission on Arms Control

National Commission on Board and Care Facility Quality

National Commission on Civil Justice Reform

National Commission on Drug Abuse Treatment Effectiveness

National Commission on Entrepreneurial Education

National Commission on Intercollegiate Athletics

National Commission on Intergovernmental Mandate Reform

National Commission on Private Pension Plans

National Commission on Research Needs

National Commission on the Environment and National Security

National Commission on Time and Learning

National Commission to Study the Causes of the Demand for Drugs in the United States

National Commission to Support Law Enforcement

National Council on Education Standards and Testing

National Education Commission on Time and Learning

National Financial Services Oversight Committee

National Workplace Safety Commission

Panel to Recommend an Appropriate Process to the House for Its Selection of the President Whenever the Right Choice Devolves upon the House under the 12th and 20th Amendments to the Constitution

Reorganization for Efficient Field Office Reduction and Management Commission

Sierra Nevada Forests Scientific Committee

Social Security Notch Fairness Investigatory Commission

Statehood Transition Commission

Thomas Jefferson Commemoration Commission

United States Census Commission

United States Commission on Quality and Equality of American Life

Working Committee on Biological Diversity

103rd CONGRESS (1993–1995)

Advisory Committee on Telecommunications Policy

Advisory Council on Health Claim Processing Standardization

American Samoa Study Commission

Bankruptcy Review Commission

Bipartisan Health Care Reform Commission

Cabinet-Level Interagency Task Force on Welfare Reform

Capitol Budget Commission

Civilian Facilities Closure and Realignment Commission

Commission on Child Support Guidelines

Commission on Closure and Relocation of the Lorton Correctional Complex

Commission on Employment Discrimination in the Legislative Branch

Commission on Environment and Development

Commission on Executive Organization

Commission on Information Technology and Paperwork Reduction

Commission on Integration of Workers' Compensation Medical Benefits

Commission on International Coordination of Financial Regulation

Commission on Leave

Commission on National Drug Policy

Commission on Protecting and Reducing Government Secrecy

Commission on Retirement Income Policy

Commission on the Advancement of Women in the Science and Engineering Work Forces

Commission on the Airplane Crash at Gander, Newfoundland

Commission on the Dual-Use Applications of Facilities and Resources at White Sands Missile Range

Commission on the Presentation of the Budget of the United States

Commission on the Review of National Policies toward Gambling

Commission on the Roles and Capabilities of the United States Intelligence Community

Commission on United States Participation in a Permanent United Nations Peacekeeping Force

Commission to Develop Recommendations for a Standardized Honor Code for the Use at the Military Service Academies and Officer Candidate Schools

Commission to Eliminate Welfare

Commission to Reduce Federal Spending

Commission to Study Reparation Proposals for African Americans

Congressional Advisory Commission on Amateur Boxing

Currency Design Commission

Department of Energy Laboratory Facilities Commission

Environmental Financial Advisory Board

Ethical Advisory Board

Federal Derivatives Commission

Federal Interagency Task Force to Identify Means to Facilitate Interagency Collaboration at Federal, State, and Local Levels to Improve Services for At-Risk Students

Federal Open Market Advisory Committee

Federal Reserve Accountability Commission

Federal Workforce Reduction and Realignment Commission

Gambling Impact Study Commission

Geno Baroni Commission on Neighborhoods

Hardrock Mining Royalty Review Commission

Health Care Crisis Policy Commission

Industry and Academia Advisory Council

Interactive Entertainment Rating Commission

Interagency Task Force on Depressed Smaller Cities

Interagency Working Committee on Biological Diversity

Joint Commission on the Applicability of Federal Law

Managed Care Advisory Committee

Markets and Trading Commission

Motor Vehicle Industry Competitiveness Commission

National Advisory Board on Workforce Preparation and Development

National Advisory Council on Adoption

National Commission on AIDS

National Commission on Crime and Violence in America

National Commission on Early Childhood Assessment

National Commission on Educational Readiness

National Commission on Executive Organization Reform

National Commission on Fairness in Military Compensation

National Commission on Financial Services

National Commission on Gay and Lesbian Youth Suicide Prevention

National Commission on School Finance to Meet the National Education Goals

National Commission on the Environment and National Security

National Commission on the Future of Disability

National Commission to Ensure a Strong and Competitive United States Maritime Industry

National Commission to Ensure Small Aircraft Safety

National Commission to Study the Delivery and Funding of Poison Control Services

National Commission to Support Law Enforcement

National Firearms Policy Commission

National Health Care Reform Commission

National Park System Strategic Planning Commission

National Physician Work Force Commission

National Sports Heritage Commission

National Task Force on Violence against Women

Northern Great Plains Rural Development Commission

Ohio Corridor Study Commission

President's Advisory Council on Recreational Camps

Privacy Protection Commission

Reinventing Government Commission

Second Blue Ribbon Commission to Eliminate Waste in Government

Statehood Transition Commission

Ted Weiss Memorial Commission on Health Care Fraud and Abuse

United States-Japan Joint Antitrust Consultative Commission

Voter Turnout Enhancement Study Commission

104th CONGRESS (1995–1997)

Advisory Commission on Intergovernmental Relations

Advisory Commission on Revitalization of National Security

Advisory Committee for Religious Liberty Abroad

Advisory Committee on Telecommunications Policy

American Samoa Study Commission

Bipartisan Campaign Practices Commission

Bipartisan Commission on the Future of Medicare

Bipartisan Commission to Oversee the Protection of Surplus Funds to Protect and Preserve the Social Security System

Camino Real Corridor Commission

Campaign Finance Reform Commission

Capitol Budget Commission

Commission for Environmental Mitigation of Electric Utility Restructuring

Commission on Chemical and Biological Warfare Agent Exposure

Commission on Closure of the Lorton Correctional Complex

Commission on Concentration in the Livestock Industry

Commission on Employment Discrimination in the Legislative Branch

Commission on Programs and Policies for Combatting the Proliferation of Weapons of Mass Destruction

Commission on Reducing the Burden of Regulations and Paperwork on Small Rural Hospitals

Commission on Retirement Income Policy

Commission on Service Members and Veterans Transitions Assistance

Commission on the Advancement of Women in the Science and Engineering Work Forces

Commission on the Economic Future of the Virgin Islands

Commission on the Future for America's Veterans

Commission on the Minimum Wage

Commission on the Review of National Policies toward Gambling

Commission on the Year 2000 Computer Problem

Commission on Women's Art in the United States Capitol

Commission on Women Suffrage Statute

Commission on Structural Alternatives for the Federal Courts of Appeals

Commission on 21st Century Production Agriculture

Commission to Study Reparation Proposals for African Americans

Commission to Study the Federal Statistical System

Commission to Study Ways to Improve the Accuracy of the Consumer Price Indexes in Stating the Rate of Inflation

Congress 2000 Commission

Corporate and Farm Independence Commission

Creative Revenues Commission

Department of Energy Laboratory Facilities Commission

Emergency Commission to End the Trade Deficit

Fair Elections Commission

Federal Derivatives Commission

Federal Election Law Reform Commission

Harold Hughes Commission on Alcoholism

Housing Trust Fund Advisory Committee

Independent Commission on Medicare

Individual Privacy Protection Board

Interagency Banking and Financial Services Advisory Committee

Joint Commission on the Applicability of Federal Law

Joint Federal-State Outer Continental Shelf Task Force

Joint United States-Canada Commission on Cattle and Beef

Law Enforcement and Industrial Security Cooperation Commission

National Advisory Board on Adoption

National Advisory Medical Policy Council

National Child Support Guidelines Commission

National Commission on Fairness in Military Compensation

National Commission on Gay and Lesbian Youth Suicide Prevention

National Commission on Medicare Reform

National Commission on Telemedicine

National Commission on the Future of Disability

National Commission on the Long-Term Solvency of the Medicare Program

National Financial Services Oversight Committee

National Firearms Policy Commission

National Gambling Impact Study Commission

National Land and Resources Management Commission

National Park System Review Commission

National Task Force on Violence against Women

Ohio River Corridor Study Commission

Presidential Debate Commission

Second National Blue Ribbon Commission to Eliminate Waste in Government

Statehood Transition Commission

Thrift Charter Merger Commission

Total Realignment of Amtrak Commission

Voter Turnout Enhancement Study Commission

White Sands Fair Compensation Commission

105th CONGRESS (1997–1999)

Berlin and the Androscoggin River Valley Heritage Commission

Bipartisan Panel to Design Long-Range Social Security Reform

Campaign Finance Reform Commission

Centennial of Flight Commission

Citizens' Commission on Congressional Ethics

Commission for American Mathematics Leadership

Commission on Chemical and Biological Warfare Agent Exposure

Commission on Electronic Commerce

Commission on Internet Taxation and Regulation

Commission on Military Justice and Fairness

Commission on Military Training and Gender-Related Issues

Commission on National Drug Policy

Commission on Ocean Policy

Commission on Probabilistic Methods

Commission on Structural Alternatives for the Federal Courts of Appeal

Commission on the Advancement of Women in Science, Engineering, and Technology Development

Commission on the Future for America's Veterans

Commission on the Year 2000 Computer Problem

Commission to Promote a National Dialogue on Bioethics

Commission to Study Reparation Proposals for African Americans

Commission to Study the Federal Statistical System

Congress 2000 Commission

Emergency Commission to End the Trade Deficit

Fairness in the Workplace Commission

Federal Agency Sunset Commission

Government 2000 Commission

Harold Hughes-Bill Emerson Commission on Alcoholism

High Level Commission on International Narcotics Control

Information Technology Worker Shortage Commission

International Financial Institutions Advisory Commission

Joint Commission on the Applicability of Federal Law

Joint United States-Canada Commission on Cattle and Beef

Legal Reform Commission

National Commission for the New National Goal: The Advancement of Global Health Act

National Commission on Catastrophe Risk and Insurance Loss Costs

National Commission on the Cost of Higher Education

National Commission on the Long-Term Solvency of the Medicare Program

National Drought Policy Commission

National Women's Business Council

Retirement Savings Commission

Second National Blue Ribbon Commission to Eliminate Waste in Government

Task Force to Assess Activities in Previous Base Closure Rounds

Total Realignment of Amtrak Commission

Trade Deficit Review Commission

TVA 2000 Regional Commission

Voter Turnout Enhancement Study Commission

Web-Based Education Commission

WTO Dispute Settlement Review Commission

106th CONGRESS (1999–2001)

Abraham Lincoln Bicentennial Commission

Advisory Commission on Electronic Commerce

Advisory Commission on Holocaust Assets in the United States

Advisory Commission on Public Diplomacy

Airline Deregulation Study Commission

Centennial of Flight Commission

Commission for American Mathematics Leadership

Commission for Assessment of the Reliability, Safety, and Security of the United States

Nuclear Deterrent

Commission for the Comprehensive Study of Privacy Protection

Commission on Military Training and Gender-Related Issues

Commission on Ocean Policy

Commission on Service members and Veterans Transition Assistance

Commission on Structural Alternatives for Federal Courts of Appeals

Commission on the Advancement of Women in Science, Engineering, and Technology Development

Commission on the Economic Future of the Virgin Islands

Commission on Veterans and Smoking

Commission to Assess the Performance of the Civil Works Functions of the Secretary of the Army

Commission to Study the Culture and Glorification of Violence in America Act

Coordinated Oceanographic Program Advisory Panel

Drug and Device Review Advisory Commission

Earthquake Hazards Reduction Advisory Body

Health Care Access, Affordability, and Quality Advisory Commission

Legal Reform Commission

Medical Education Advisory Commission

Medicare Payment Advisory Committee

Methane Hydrate Research Advisory Panel

National Child Support Guidelines Commission

National Commission for the New National Goal: The Advancement of Global Health Act

National Commission on Cybersecurity

National Commission on Marginal Tax Rates for the Working Poor

National Commission on Public Education Facilities Construction and Rehabilitation

National Commission on Tax Reform and Simplification

National Commission on Terrorism

National Commission on the Death Penalty

National Drought Policy Commission

National Police Training Commission

National Recourse Governance Commission

National Youth Violence Commission

Presidential and Senatorial Commission on Nuclear Testing Treating

Second National Blue Ribbon Commission to Eliminate Waste in Government

Trade Deficit Review Commission

United States Commission on International Religious Freedom

Utilization of Electronic Commerce Advisory Panel

Voter Turnout Enhancement Study Commission

107th CONGRESS (2001–2003), 1ST SESS.

Advisory Committee on Cargo Theft

Bipartisan Commission on Social Security Reform

Commission on Election Law Reform

Commission on Elections Procedures

Commission to Study Reparation Proposals for African Americans

Congress 2004 Commission

Dairy Farms Viability Commission

Election Administration Commission

Energy Laboratory Facilities Commission

Mental Health Advisory Committee

National Advisory Commission on Tax Reform and Simplification

National Commission on the Modernization of Federal Elections

National Commission on Youth Crime and School Violence

National Commission to Eliminate Waste in Government
National Energy Self-Sufficiency Commission
White House Quadrennial Commission on Small Business

Note: Those "presidential" commissions that are included in the list of congressionally created ad hoc commissions had language in their proposals instructing them to deliver final recommendations to both Congress and the president.

Selected Bibliography

Altman, Dennis. 1987. "The Politics of AIDS." In *AIDS: Public Policy Dimensions*, ed. John Griggs. New York: United Hospital Fund of New York.

Aranson, Peter H., Ernest Gellhorn, and Glen O. Robinson. 1982. "A Theory of Legislative Delegation." *Cornell Law Review* 68: 1–67.

Armey, Richard K. 1988. "Base Maneuvers: The Games Congress Plays with the Military Pork Barrel." *Policy Review* 43: 70–75.

Bell, Daniel. 1966. "Government by Commission." *The Public Interest* 3: 3–9.

Carr, Cecil T. 1921. *Delegated Legislation*. London: Cambridge University Press.

Collie, Melissa. 1988. "The Legislature and Distributive Policy Making in Formal Perspective." *Legislative Studies Quarterly* 13: 427–58.

Cox, Gary W., and Mathew D. McCubbins. 1993. *Legislative Leviathan: Party Government in the House*. Berkeley: University of California Press.

Day, Kathleen. 1993. *S & L Hell: The People and the Politics behind the $1 Trillion Savings and Loan Scandal*. New York: W.W. Norton & Company.

Dean, Alan L. 1969. "Ad Hoc Commissions for Policy Formulations?" In *Presidential Advisory Systems*, ed. Thomas E. Cronin and Sanford D. Greenberg. New York: Harper & Row.

Epstein, David, and Sharyn O'Halloran. 1999. *Delegating Powers: A Transaction Cost Politics Approach to Policy Making under Separate Powers*. New York: Cambridge University Press.

Fenno, Richard F., Jr. 1990. *Watching Politicians: Essays on Participant Observation*. Berkeley, Calif.: IGS Press.

Ferejohn, John P. 1983. "Congress and Redistribution." In *Making Economic Policy in Congress*, ed. Allen Schick. Washington, D.C.: American Enterprise Institute.

Fiorina, Morris P. 1981. "Universalism, Reciprocity, and Distributive Policy Making in Majority Rule Institutions." In *Research in Public Policy Analysis and Management*, ed. John Crecine. Greenwich, Conn.: JAI Press, Inc.

————. 1986. "Legislator Uncertainty, Legislative Control, and the Delegation of Legislative Authority." In *Regulatory Policy and the Social Sciences*, ed. Roger G. Noll. Berkeley: University of California Press.

Gilmour, John B. 1993. "Summits and Stalemates: Bipartisanship Negotiations in the Postreform Era." In *The Postreform Congress*, ed. Roger H. Davidson. New York: St. Martin's Press.

Hall, L. Richard. 1996. *Participation in Congress*. New Haven, Conn.: Yale University Press.

Hanlon, Natalie. 1991. "Military Base Closures: A Study of Government by Commission." *Colorado Law Review* 62: 331–64.

Kiewiet, D. Roderick, and Mathew D. McCubbins. 1991. *The Logic of Delegation: Congressional Parties and the Appropriations Process*. Chicago: University of Chicago Press.

Kingdon, John W. 1989. *Congressmen's Voting Decisions*. 3rd ed. Ann Arbor: The University of Michigan Press.

Lindblom, Charles E. 1959. "The Science of Muddling Through." *Public Administration Review* 19: 79–88.

Lowy, Martin. 1991. *High Rollers: Inside the Savings and Loan Debacle*. New York: Praeger.

Lupia, Arthur, and Mathew D. McCubbins. 1994. "Who Controls? Information and the Structure of Legislative Decision Making." *Legislative Studies Quarterly* 19: 361–84.

Mayer, Kenneth R. 1995. "Closing Military Bases (Finally): Solving Collective Dilemmas through Delegation." *Legislative Studies Quarterly* 20: 393–413.

Mayer, Martin. 1990. *The Greatest-Ever Bank Robbery: The Collapse of the Savings and Loan Industry*. New York: Charles Scribner's Sons.

Mayhew, David R. 1974. *Congress: The Electoral Connection*. New Haven, Conn.: Yale University Press.

McCubbins, Mathew D., Roger G. Noll, and Barry R. Weingast. 1987. "Administrative Procedures as Instruments of Political Control." *Journal of Law, Economics, and Organization* 3: 243–277.

Moe, Terry M. 1984. "The New Economics of Organization." *American Journal of Political Science* 28: 739–77.

Price, David E. 2000. *The Congressional Experience: A View from the Hill*. 2nd ed. Boulder, Colo.: Westview Press.

Rom, Mark Carl. 1996. *Public Spirit in the Thrift Tragedy*. Pittsburgh: University of Pittsburgh Press.

Romer, Thomas, and Barry R. Weingast. 1991. "Political Foundations of the Thrift Debacle." In *Politics and Economics in the Eighties*, ed. Alberto Alesina and Geoffrey Carliner. Chicago: University of Chicago Press.

Schepsle, Kenneth A., and Barry R. Weingast. 1994. "Positive Theories of Congressional Institutions." *Legislative Studies Quarterly* 19: 149–180.

Schoenbrod, David. 1993. *Power without Responsibility: How Congress Abuses the People through Delegation*. New Haven, Conn.: Yale University Press.

Twight, Charlotte. 1989. "Institutional Underpinnings of Parochialism: The Case of Military Base Closures." *Cato Journal* 9: 73–105.

Weaver, R. Kent. 1987. "The Politics of Blame Avoidance." *Journal of Public Policy* 6: 371–98.

Weingast, Barry R. 1984. "The Congressional Bureaucratic System: A Principle-Agent Perspective." *Public Choice* 41: 147–91.

Wolanin, Thomas R. 1975. *Presidential Advisory Commissions: Truman to Nixon.* Madison, WI: The University of Wisconsin Press.

Index

About the Author

COLTON C. CAMPBELL is Assistant Professor of Political Science, Florida International University. He has co-edited five earlier books on Congressional politics and practices.